JURIES ON TRIAL

JURIES ON TRIAL

Faces of American Justice

by Paula DiPerna

DEMBNER BOOKS
NEW YORK

Dembner Books
Published by Red Dembner Enterprises Corp., 1841 Broadway, New York, N.Y. 10023
Distributed by W. W. Norton & Company, Inc., 500 Fifth Avenue, New York, N.Y. 10110

Library of Congress Cataloging in Publication Data

DiPerna, Paula.
    Juries on trial.

    Includes index.
    1. Jury—United States.   I. Title.
KF8972.D56   1984   347.73'752   84-9406
ISBN 0-934878-43-9   347.307752

This book is dedicated to the
justice within us all.

Contents

ACKNOWLEDGMENTS

I am indebted to many people for the completion of the project, among them the Fund for Investigative Journalism and the National Center for State Courts in Williamsburg, Virginia, particularly Tom Musterman and Judith Hawes, who let me make myself at home in their library. There are many other judges, clerks, librarians, and lawyers, of course, around the country, who helped me ferret out information and who shared their views. Finally, I owe a great vote of thanks to the jurors—the called and the chosen—who were willing to share their private and potentially troubling jury experiences with me. Without the willingness of many people to talk about juries, I could not have written this book.

P. D.

New York, New York
January 1, 1984

Introduction

The concept of the jury system is as close as any society has ever come to true democracy. Yet in today's complicated and precarious world, where competent social decisions require more, not less, citizen involvement, the jury system seems a burden. It draws criticism that is often unrelated to its actual performance and blame for poorly executed justice.

However, a scratch of the surface of so-called bad decisions will often expose underlying factors for which no jury can be blamed. This is not to say that the jury system functions without flaw, or that there aren't ways to help it function better. But in an age when it is increasingly difficult for individuals to feel they can have an impact on events, the jury remains a refuge where each individual's reasoning affects a collective result.

This is not a propitious moment to erode the jury's role, and yet one senses—in the public's indifference to being summoned, in official pronouncements about changing, even eliminating the jury system for certain kinds of cases—a whittling away. Criticism of the jury has peaked and ebbed before, but one wonders if today's jury system can withstand the widespread public fear of crime, compounded by general public cynicism regarding official institutions, and a lack of public information on the actual workings of a trial jury. Surely any jury system weakened by these factors cannot help but produce long-term, negative social, economic, and political consequences. As surely, a jury system held to be of benefit only to the parties in a trial and not to the society at large cannot easily survive.

The fact that the jury system tends to be idiosyncratic—even rambunctious—makes it a convenient target. Yet, its unpredictability is its inherent strength. The jury system brings a pot-au-feu approach to justice, and for all its potential chaos, it works at least as well as a great thick soup does when one is hungry. How, why, from what traditions, for what gain? Because of a jury summons, I was plunked into the jury system and thus began this odyssey.

The concept of community justice is almost as old as dispute between human beings, but still no other human institution but the jury has evolved which introduces previously unaffiliated people, shuts them in a room with their individual opinions afire, and expects them to make a very serious decision together, most often unanimously, with no training in how to do so. As Erwin Griswold, dean of Harvard Law School, wrote in 1962, "It is the apotheosis of the amateur."

According to the Center for Jury Studies of the National Center for State Courts, approximately 3 million United States citizens are called for jury duty each year, on local, state, and federal levels, paid an average of $10 a day for their services, at a total annual cost of $200 million. Approximately 300,000 cases—civil involving monetary damage matters and criminal involving crimes and victims—come to trial in the United States annually before juries, which only 5 percent of the time cannot reach a verdict and end up "hung." However, less than 10 percent of all cases filed in the United States reach the jury trial stage, the rest either being settled, plea-bargained, or otherwise "disposed of."

"Ladies and gentlemen, you are the final determiners of the facts," nearly every judge tells nearly every jury, adding that jurors play an essential role, for justice cannot be done without them. Yet despite what the judges say, one senses that the professionals of the legal system—judges, attorneys, clerks—resent this bond with the common man. They seem to think of themselves as hovering somewhere above the jury system.

Juries come in different sizes, and they are selected in different ways, but they share one universal task: to make decisions in the name of all of us. Perhaps there is no more active, hands-on civic duty, no more direct way of having a say in the proceedings of society. Certainly it is a closer touch than voting, for the juror learns more about a case than he or she will ever learn about a candidate or the average political issue. When one is on jury duty, there seem to be palpable causes, direct effects. Something happened; the jury considers the case, decides, and gets sent home. Guilty/not guilty, for/against—days, weeks, months of testimony and deliberations are boiled down to the few words the jury speaks when it has completed its job. Thus, even the most complex maze of transactions is concluded.

Along with pressures to speed up trials, process more cases, and reduce court costs, have come pressures on the jury system as well. The Chief Justice of the U.S. Supreme Court, Warren E. Burger, has predicted that under the weight of its caseload, the American system of justice "may literally break down before the end of this century." He recommended that the United States adopt England's speedier jury selection system, where voir dire and challenges are all but eliminated and where, he asserts, cases that take "three, four, or five days in our courts are regularly completed in one day or less." He regards the increasing use of six-person, rather than twelve-person, juries as progress in the battle against delay and rising judicial costs. He has written that juries in civil cases in the United States could perhaps be eliminated altogether.

In states where attorneys question prospective jurors, some legislatures wish to turn the process over to the judge, in order to save voir dire time. In 1983, New York Governor Mario Cuomo supported the idea, as did New York Mayor Edward I. Koch. But when both suggested an experiment be conducted, the chief judge of the state's Court of Appeals said, "I don't think it is necessary to do experiments. . . . I don't think we can afford that luxury today. In the court system, time's a-wasting and we've got so much to do."

Long, complicated, technical cases—involving antitrust, or scientific issues, for example—which are increasing in this technological age, may be decided more and more by judges alone, because it is felt that juries aren't up to understanding the complexities involved, and because of the time expended in trying to make those complexities clear to them. Judge Richard D. Dunn, chief administrative judge of Wayne County, Michigan, hopes for jury system reform, at least in civil cases. He told me, "The jury system is engrained in our legal system, but today I am not sure if it is really working. I am not sure today's jury is sophisticated enough to deal with the complex issues they have to deal with. We could speed up dispositions of cases by 50 percent if we did away with the jury system."

While some critics feel that the jury system should be changed because of administrative considerations, a different kind of change is emanating from within the legal profession. A growing number of professional jury researchers are spending thousands of dollars and hours inquiring into the backgrounds of prospective jurors—essentially derandomizing what is supposed to be a random selection process—in order to select the most favorable, rather than the most capable, jurors. Utilizing all the tools of the social scientist and public relations specialist, they work hard to improve an attorney's ability to "sell" the jury his case.

While the jury system is not exactly under siege, it is clearly in a period of transition, not necessarily from an internal need to change but from external needs that work to change it. In my amateur's apotheosis, I wanted to try to understand what these changes mean for the future of the jury and for the quality of justice juries are expected to dispense.

I had hoped to write a definitive general account of how the jury system works today, including grand juries—those bodies which decide whether or not an indictment shall be brought in criminal matters. Very soon, however, I realized that grand juries were a matter unto themselves, and so this book is concerned only with petit or trial juries. The grand jury's role is every bit as important as that of a trial jury, and clearly a "bad" case can begin bad at grand jury level. However, since grand juries serve an investigatory purpose, and since the rules governing their behavior are quite different from those for the petit jury, it seemed wiser to leave them for a separate discussion.

I realized too that to be definitive about juries, one will have to wait for the invention of a device that a writer can dispatch to each ongoing jury trial in the country, which will send back images and sound enabling the writer to be present, in a sense, at all trials at once. No one book could begin to encompass all the variations in cases and juries that take place around the nation.

So, I have tried instead to take a slice, and not the loaf, and I have tried to select cases which not only demonstrated points about juries but which also were of interest in and of themselves (certain names have been changed in the interests of privacy). I have dwelled more heavily on criminal than on civil matters and have tended to concentrate on nearby geographical areas, due to practical limitations. So this book is really only a view—my view—of how the justice within us all is tapped through the jury system.

[1]
An Amateur's Apotheosis

I couldn't speak to them; I couldn't know who they were. While they had lunch together congenially everyday, everyday I ate alone, in silence, wondering what they might be talking about, what they might be thinking. For they were jurors in the midst of hearing a case, and I was not. That made them pure. It made me taint.

I had almost been among them. I had been called too, but in the end, only they were chosen.

Jury duty in Manhattan, New York City, can almost be said to begin in the subway, for that is how most people called to serve reach the southern tip of the island where the courts are located. The subway too randomizes people: there are executives, male and female, in crisp well-tailored suits, carrying stream-lined leather briefcases; there are also mechanics and truckdrivers, street cleaners and building cleaners and all-night grocery-shop salespeople.

The jury room can be as dirty as the subway at times, its windows streaked with the grease of a thousand hands, like the doors of public telephone booths. The buildings of the court system even smell like the subway—that same "we used Lysol but it didn't help" smell. In the elevators, defendants meet jurors who meet lawyers. Often you cannot tell the players apart; a man on trial for murder may hold an elevator door for someone who may well decide his fate.

A herd of peers, we all followed the instructions briskly given as the jury controllers snapped the stubs off our summonses and sent us to the first holding area. Room 452 of the Supreme Court of the State of New York is a fabulous hall with bright Art Deco murals of New York harbor. These murals offer the first bit of color, and maybe the last, that a juror in this court system will see. We were instructed to sit on the long wooden benches, as close together as possible. I felt like an immigrant at my citizenship hearing or a hymn singer in a cavernous creaking church.

No sooner had we settled into our pews, than a voice—no face—informed us that we'd have to move to Room 775, which also turned out to be subwaylike. Once settled there, we got the call to move again, en masse, to be considered for a jury. A rumor swept through our group that the case involved child pornography. Reality—the subway of life—in the form of the criminal court, had scooped us up.

We potential jurors milled around outside the courtroom, waiting. Many in the group dreaded the experience to come; veterans of previous jury duty shared their knowledge with those who asked and those who didn't. Then we were called into the courtroom, a room too large for the average human voice to carry. We spread out along the long oak benches, eyeing the sixteen seats of the jury box at the front of the room and the cast of characters before us.

The judge was gray-haired, very ruddy, and Irish. He laid out the essentials of the moment. It would take, he expected, a week to pick a jury to hear this case, then two weeks to try it. Jurors who could not make that time commitment would be excused. About one quarter of our group of about a hundred left. What made the rest stay? I wondered, for here was an excuse being handed to them. Then the judge outlined the nature of the case. The defendants were charged with, among other things, the promotion of pornographic films, depicting children under sixteen engaging in obscene sexual acts. As the judge matter-of-factly read the indictment, the jury pool fell into hushed awkward silence.

Being a juror in this case might, the judge said, require the viewing of films depicting sexual acts, therefore, those jurors who preferred not to be involved in this case would also be summarily excused. About another twenty-five people left. The first cuts of the deck had been made. We slid along the benches to close up ranks. The questioning would now begin.

Many have written that this is the most important phase of trial work, the voir dire, an expression from Old French meaning roughly "to see [them] talk." It describes the part of the proceedings where the attorneys and the judge (sometimes just the judge) question potential jurors. Not only is this the first chance the attorneys have to test parts of their case against perfect strangers, but done in depth, voir dire acquires the quality of a theatrical preview.

From their seats facing the front of the court, the attorneys and their clients turned awkwardly around to look us over. We were nothing more than the lot they had drawn. Still, they stared intently, as if seated behind one-way glass. But we stared too.

The defendants were both white—one a thin, frail, blond male who wore a pair of beige corduroy trousers and a beige shetland sweater. As it turned out, he would wear this outfit almost every day during the trial. His name, we learned eventually, was Rod Wyman. He looked vulnerable. His codefendant, Jeb D'Arazzio, was a stocky man with black hair combed back in a slick, 1950s style. His skin was pockmarked; he let a white T-shirt show under the *V* of his outer shirt. He looked gruff, as though he would, and had, willingly put his squared jaw into many fights. A large gold crucifix dangled outside his shirt, and later the jurors would tell me they found both the dangling cross and the defendants' casual dress very ill-advised.

The attorney for the younger defendant, Wyman, was also the younger defense attorney. He wore a dark suit and looked concerned but confident. The attorney for D'Arazzio had reddish hair and was balding and a touch overweight. He seemed to condescend to everyone in the room just in the disinterested way he sat.

The prosecution team consisted of two female assistant district attorneys, both also white. The lead, clearly the more experienced, had dark hair and did not smile much. Her assistant had a fashionable, almost flighty look, but seemed smart. It felt a bit like the pitting of maternal females, protecting society's children, against more cynical males. Indeed, once the trial got under way, the women had to wheel their evidence in and out of the courtroom in what looked like a grocery cart.

The attorneys turned to face the empty jury box. The court clerk called the roll from the summons stubs he had collected.

The procedure reminded me of elementary-school roll call—people said, "Present!" The clerk seemed to hate his job. When three people told him their names had not been called, he reprimanded them, though he had lost their stubs. He sent them back to the main jury room to rectify the problem themselves, as if they and not he had made the error.

Once the voir dire began, the one-way glass lifted, and there was interaction. Attention focused on the sixteen people who filled the box—their names, addresses, faces, clothing, comportment, occupations. The first round included two Chinese, several Hispanics, a good mix of black and white. The clerk even spelled out their names as they took their places so the attorneys could pronounce them correctly.

The light in the courtroom was dim and flickering. The acoustics were terrible, and everyone had to shout so the entire sixteen—as well as those of us still outside the rail—could hear the transaction. Too many things were going on in the courtroom at once. Some attorneys from another case came in to discuss a matter with the judge. We were given a recess. In a space of time too short to make a phone call, we were called in again, and the voir dire that had not really started resumed. Most of us tried to listen as the first sixteen people were questioned. One man behind me slept, snoring too quietly for the judge to hear. (This juror, I later learned, was retired, and I saw him every day for four weeks, shuffling from courtroom to courtroom trying to get on a case.) The court reporter also seemed to be asleep, literally under the judge's nose.

The attorneys' questions began to sound the same. Though the DA was polite to everyone, she was no pushover. She asked about all possible biases the jurors in the box might have that pertained to the case—attitudes toward First Amendment protections, tapes, hidden microphones, undercover agents—shedding a sliver of light on what had supposedly happened to warrant this trial. She was greatly interested in jurors' attitudes toward the police and honed in on that. She was extremely competent and clear, though I was surprised that she did not ask if there was anyone who condoned sex between adults and consenting children. It might not have occurred to her that some adults do, and a juror under oath would be expected to admit it, though it seemed unlikely anyone would.

The defense attorneys were looking for the cynics, especially those who would give full benefit of the doubt. One defense attorney took a lot of time breaking down a former military policeman to get him to admit that he would, because of his prior experience, be sympathetic to the police.

The idea of the questions is, in principle, to strip away a potential juror's protective covering and reveal hidden biases. Once sworn in, jurors are supposed to drop down a force field between themselves and their prejudices. On the other hand, in the adversary system, the attorneys prey on juror prejudice, calling forth every stereotypic idea they harbor to stack a group in their client's favor.

At the end of the first round, all but three of the sixteen were dismissed, including both Chinese and all the Hispanics. One Chinese man had not understood the words the prosecutor used for the sex acts, as he left the jury box, he looked dazed, as if newly returned from a trip to Mars.

We were all sent outside while the attorneys made this first selection. In the hallway, we speculated on who would get "it," as if "it" were a prize, a job, a disease. The three who were chosen first had not said much, but I have since had many attorneys tell me they "avoid the ones who can do damage." In other words, they avoid the actives.

As the selection wore on, the wall between attorneys and jurors began to drop; we all felt permitted to laugh or smile; the tension was relieved. Then a new group of sixteen was questioned. The three chosen from the first round were made to sit far away from the rest of us.

The lead prosecutor was asking jurors about hearing problems—her case evidently would require the jury to listen to tape recordings. A woman who worked as a cleaner in a hospital volunteered that she had no problem except when her daughters phoned her. "What is the problem?" the DA wanted to know. "I can't tell which daughter it is who is calling me from the voice. I always think it is another one than it is," the woman replied somewhat sheepishly. She was not chosen.

The judge then posed the general question of whether anyone

in this new panel had had any experience with crime. Many
people raised their hands, and one man asked to speak to the
judge privately at the bench. All four attorneys followed, leaning
in close, each keeping one hand behind, up so as not to take space.
Arranged around the judge and the juror, they looked like a
singing group arranged around a microphone. Then the huddle
broke, the man returned to his seat in the box. He too was not
chosen.

The defense attorneys had made much of the apparent fact
that probably neither defendant would testify on his own behalf.
Every juror questioned except one said he or she would not
expect a defendant to prove innocence—that is, that he or she
understood that the burden of proving guilt rested on the
prosecution, "the People." It seemed like a big leap over expecta-
tions to me, but the attorneys seemed to accept what the jurors
said.

The attorneys did select a tall, long-haired man who said he
worked for "one of our public utilities." He looked ill-kempt and
strange to me and, at about forty, too old to be living harmonious-
ly with his mother, as he claimed to be. When pressed about his
ability to be fair and impartial, he said in a too loud clear voice, "I
find that kind of sex disgusting," meaning sex with children, but
he added, "I could be fair and impartial."

They did not accept a very articulate former actress, now
cashier, who had paid dues to the American Civil Liberties Union
for twenty years or so. She was the only person among fifty who
admitted to belonging to an organization. We had no PTA
members, as far as the jurors would admit, no members of
professional organizations, museums, or cultural groups, few
union members. It was hard to believe. This juror later told me
she assumed she was rejected for her ACLU membership and was
sorry she had mentioned it; she felt she could have been a fair
juror. But attorneys rarely take risks. They tell me they avoid the
blatant. With a case apparently resting on tapes and undercover
cops, the prosecution would not risk even an inactive ACLU type.

It just wasn't coming clear whom they wanted. They rejected a
counselor for retarded adults who had a Ph.D., and a Cambridge-
educated investment counselor who, unbeknownst to the attorneys, had been wooing another juror with flowers and love notes

as the voir dire went into its second day. The attorneys rejected a woman who said she knew doctors just well enough to say "good morning" to on her job at the clinic. They also rejected a European airline manager—he never said which airline—who looked like Prince Rainier. He had a retarded daughter who once, but no longer, saw psychiatrists. They rejected a black bus driver, a woman mosaic designer, a male editor for a trade publication, a woman who taught at John Jay College of Criminal Justice, a man who confessed to a history of mental illness, a woman who said she might have a nervous breakdown if she was chosen, and a retired man who had the honesty to say he had nothing better to do than serve on the jury.

In the end, after one week, they picked twelve jurors and two alternates: seven women, seven men; eleven whites, three blacks. They had picked a man who said he was unemployed and that gambling was his hobby, a magazine circulation director, a bond saleswoman, a college admissions officer, a bank teller, a landscape designer, a part-time bartender who had once been arrested in Texas for vagrancy, an owner of a travel agency, a few retired people, a railroad conductor, a director of a foundation for the blind, the public utility man, and a graphics designer who became forewoman because she had been first chosen.

It was a well-mixed jury—"what I wanted," one defense attorney later told me, as if picking the jury had been exclusively up to him. To my mind, they had picked the people about whom they knew the least, the people who had said the least. One defense attorney told me he didn't think jury selection was ever worth the time and trouble that some attorneys devoted to it and certainly not worth the expense of hiring expert psychologists to help in the choice. There are those, he had said, who think that just picking the first twelve is the best way to go. We would see.

Today's average juror probably enters the courtroom with the idea that the law is a stable, solid structure upon which the order of society rests. The juror soon finds, however, that the law is instead a series of moving plates, sliding around each other, trying to fit where they may not have fit before, trying to avoid collision. A friend of mine calls it the tectonics theory of law. Attorneys and judges slide these pieces around to come up with something called the case.

The case, from the jury's point of view, is distinct from the trial. The trial is essentially an artificial screen placed over human events to put them in order so they can be discussed. But however artificial, the trial is the form on which the jury must rely to re-create events long past; its order and rules make the jury system possible.

Every trial has a judge. Almost every trial has attorneys for each side, though sometimes parties to a case represent themselves. The judge is most often compared to a referee, an objective arbiter who has not yet heard the evidence presented. What can be used as evidence is governed by strict legal rules—hearsay, for example, is usually inadmissible as legal evidence, except for rare and special occasions; opinions are inadmissible as evidence unless the witness is certified as an expert in his subject (a fingerprint man, a psychiatrist, a documents specialist). The rules govern how evidence may be presented, how questions may be posed, how far into a subject is too far.

A trial has a standard form. The judge arbitrates and administers the rules. Attorneys make opening statements; these are not considered evidence, simply attorney opinions. Witnesses testify. Attorneys examine, cross-examine, reexamine, and recross-examine their own and each other's witnesses. They may introduce physical evidence—fingerprints, documents, charts. When the adversaries have fully presented their side, the attorneys usually deliver a summation statement to the jury, which draws for the jurors a plausible picture of the evidence according to each attorney's view of the matter.

When both sides have rested, the judge "charges" or instructs the jury on the rules of law that apply to the case. The jury then deliberates. When the jury has a question, it communicates with the judge in the form of a note handwritten, often on whatever scraps of paper are handy in the deliberation room. The judge reads the note to the attorneys, an answer is formulated or not, and the deliberations continue. Against the infinite human variety that composes juries, the trial format remains infinitely the same.

The child pornography case took about forty minutes for the prosecutor to summarize in her opening statement. After the jury had been picked, I decided to follow the case to its verdict, and so I secured a release from my remaining jury duty obligation by prevailing on the good graces of the summons clerk, telling him I doubted I would ever be picked anyway. Puffing on a big cigar, standing before a gallery of photographs of famous and unfamous jurors—"people send me their pictures after they serve sometimes"—the summons clerk said I was probably right, and let me go. When I reappeared in the courtroom, the court clerk scowled. The judge stopped the proceedings and sent him to ask me what I was doing. I simply said I wanted to sit in. The clerk scowled again, but there was nothing he could do; the courts are open to the public.

The lead assistant district attorney, I would later learn, was Hispanic, one of the few in the Manhattan prosecutor's office at the time. A Princeton University and Yale Law School graduate, she had grown up in the slums and public housing of the South Bronx, the daughter of parents who came from Puerto Rico. She was fair and looked more Middle European than anything else. The jurors later told me they would not have guessed her origin.

She looked comfortable in front of the uninitiated jury, confident of what she was saying—a fact not lost on the jury.

The DA presented her case with little rhetoric. She apologized for any inconvenience the jurors may have suffered, and thanked them for the time they were about to give. This kind of attention to the jurors' personal reactions and needs was noticed and appreciated. The jurors missed it at other points during the trial.

The DA told the jury, as many attorneys do, that the case would be a collection of pieces that may not make sense in the order presented. The opening statements are intended to give jurors the "big picture." This is the first big contradiction a jury has to face: On the one hand, the judge has reminded them that nothing in the opening statement is evidence, that the jury may disregard it all, if it chooses. On the other hand, the lawyers use the opening statement to convince the jury that this overview is the one true view of the case.

The indictment in the child pornography case had forty-three counts in total. The gist of the indictment was that the two defendants had conspired to obtain money by selling, retail and wholesale, films of sexual conduct between children under sixteen years of age. They had, unfortunately for them, agreed to sell the films to an undercover policeman, who had taped his conversations with Wyman, the middleman, as well as one key conversation between Wyman and D'Arazzio. The policeman, however, never actually met D'Arazzio, alleged to have been the wholesaler.

The DA had her dates, times of day, amounts of money, and numbers of films down pat. She had been meticulous in her recitation of what the indictment alleged—a fact not lost on the jury, which later during deliberations used the dates as handles. But one point stood out—the wholesale transaction on which the case rested had never been consummated. The seized films were evidence of retail transactions only; neither the undercover policeman nor his backup team had seen money change hands for films.

The prosecutor intended, it seemed, to show these films to the jury. The obvious question was, Why were the police unable to meet the wholesaler face to face? The prosecutor's answer was that the child pornography business is so secretive that sellers don't make public contact with buyers. Her implication was that the big fish stay clean. Even though she described the acts—intercourse, anal penetration, and oral sex between prepubescent children—she told the jury that no one could imagine the impact or true intent of these films without seeing them. Although the DA in her opening talked as if the showing was definite, the defense continued to object to the showing of the films and was seeking to have the judge reconsider his ruling allowing them to be shown. I wondered what the jury would think if they were to be told later that, after all, the films would not be shown. Would they think the films were less or more heinous because they were not shown? What would become of the DA's point about secrecy in the business?

The question was shelved for the time being, except that during the prosecutor's opening, the defense asked for a conference at the judge's bench. The attorneys talked with the judge in low, almost whispered voices. The defendants laughed and joked with the guards; the jurors even laughed a bit and talked among themselves. For a few minutes the seriousness of the events was waived. (During this station break, I almost expected a commercial.) Then all four attorneys were back on their spots, and the proceedings resumed. The jury snapped back to attention.

There seemed to be a few holes in the prosecutor's case. Why, for example, did the police wait six months after the events occurred to arrest D'Arazzio? Why were they unable to complete the final wholesale deal? The prosecutor had simply said that, by the time the police had all the details together, the wholesaler had grown impatient and would not wait. It became patently clear why there had been so much questioning about attitudes toward police during jury selection—police credibility was going to be a major factor in this case. The case against D'Arazzio came down to a matter of his voice being identified on tape.

It was hard to imagine how, after this narrative, the jury could keep an open mind, although the DA had asked that the jury wait until all the facts were presented to them before coming to a conclusion. To me, it all sounded quite incriminating. Wyman, the middleman, sounded as though he had made very foolish moves; if I were the wholesaler I would not have been joking with him as though he were my partner in a good story and not the man who set me up to get caught. Then I wondered if their friendly behavior was all a pose to appear cool, in control, before the jury. As awful as the films sounded, I felt caught up in a whodunit and not uncomfortable about being in the same room with these defendants. Cloaked in the presumption of innocence, they did not seem at all threatening. In fact, I chatted with them casually from time to time. When D'Arazzio learned I was a writer, he rubbed his hands together and commented, "Boy I'll write a book wicha. I can tell ya a lot about these cops." Courtroom procedures make reality seem less real, imposing a niceness on the reconstructed events of the wild world of the streets. Jurors react to this unreality too.

Next up was the redheaded attorney for D'Arazzio, the wholesaler, who neither apologized to nor thanked the jury, but continued, in a rather confident way, to attempt to set himself and his defendant above the proceedings, an attitude which the jurors would ultimately resent.

He referred at the outset to the DA's opening, paying a somewhat mock compliment to the story the "seasoned prosecutor" had put together. His defense consisted of several elements:

There was confusion as to the true identity of the wholesaler with whom the middleman worked, and—invoking the principle on which many criminal defenses depend—there was "reasonable doubt" about who was guilty. "See if this evidence has any weight," the attorney cautioned the jury. "See if it is not, in the end, just padding." Talking in a tantalizing, stay-tuned tone of voice, he said he would explain his client's movements on the dates in question. He told the jury another DA had once handled the case and asked rhetorically why it took six months for the police to arrest his client.

He also suggested that the jury put yet another partition into their minds—one between the defendants. "Weigh the evidence," he said, "then divide it and see to whom it applies." Very little, he added, would apply to his client; what did apply, he concluded, could be easily explained.

The second defense attorney took a different approach altogether. He began by alluding to the venerable tradition of the jury system, and noted that the forelady—to whom he referred by name—was forelady by virtue of the fact that she had been selected first. There was no change of expression on her face as he talked about her.

This attorney had, he said, no dispute with anything the prosecutor had presented. He and his client did not dispute that the tape recordings the jury would hear would show that conversations had taken place about the sale of the films, nor did they dispute that the films depicted sexual acts between children under sixteen, or that the films were obscene. In fact, he quipped to the jury, "You might well say to yourselves, 'Why is this guy standing up there?'"

He then flattered the jury, reminding them that they had been selected because they had each said they could follow the instructions and consider "each and every element of the crime." To be a good juror, worthy of having been selected, you must believe my interpretation of events—that appeared to be his drift. "One thing you will learn," he predicted, "is that the defendant must be aware and intend the consequences." Here, the DA made her first objection, which was sustained. She then apologized for objecting during an opening statement, which is generally regarded as bad form among lawyers. The judge reminded the jury that he alone could instruct on the elements of the crime. The jurors looked at the judge and then back to the defense attorney. In the match for the jury's fidelity, the defense had lost one round.

The attorney then introduced yet another player that the prosecutor had not mentioned at all, a bigger fish, a gentleman named . . . But then the attorney stopped and said he ought not call him a "gentleman." This man, named Lewis, according to the attorney, brought his defendant into this case in the first place. This man, he said, was sexually involved with children, molested children, and had been convicted of taking children across state lines for illicit purposes. The attorney then mentioned the name of a drugstore from which this man distributed . . . Again, the DA, this time on her feet, objected. Another bench conference. It was clear the attorney had embarked on touchy ground when mentioning this ungentleman. The attorneys went back to their places. The defense attorney's point had been reworded, he continued.

The man in question had been owner and operator of a drugstore and engaged in various legal and illegal activities, as a result of which the defendant Wyman came in to fill prescriptions for Quaaludes, depressant drugs. This clarified why there had been a lot of questions during jury selection about Quaaludes and drug use.

This attorney's view was that his defendant depended on this bigger fish for a supply of Quaaludes, of which he was taking as many as ten a day, when half a pill a day is a normally prescribed dose. The defendant, in the attorney's words, was "zonked" on drugs, addicted, and under the control of his supplier who eventually asked him to obtain some "kiddie porn" films. It was this drug supplier who would eventually introduce the undercover policeman to the defendant Wyman as a "friend," telling Wyman to "take care of him" by procuring the films. The attorney recommended to the jury that they listen carefully to Wyman's voice on tape to determine if he really knew what he was doing, if his train of thought was on track. Finally, Wyman's attorney told the jury he would not ask them to decide whether Wyman sold films to a police officer, but he asked, even begged the jury to consider why the defendant did, and whether he was, in fact, competent at the time.

The attorney thanked the jurors for their time and sat quickly in his seat. It had been a very emotional opening statement.

The court adjourned with the judge's admonition to the jurors not to discuss this case among themselves or with others, or to read about it or visit any of the locations mentioned. The jury now had to let all these apparently contradictory interpretations go to work inside them without being publicly discussed. Juries are pressure-forced into events and then denied the relief of talking about them.

I was bursting to talk about what I had just heard, and I realized that all I needed to do to pollute this jury was to catch one juror in the hall and murmur, "I think they did it." But since that could cause a mistrial and win a jury-tampering charge for me, I kept mum. Besides, like the jurors I later questioned, I was not sure at this point what I truly did believe.

We left the courtroom quickly after the jurors had filed out first. "Jury coming through," the court clerk announced, and the attorneys ceased even their small talk until the jury had gotten past. I made no eye contact with any of the jurors.

A case seems like a block of situations or facts set before the jury, then hacked, shaped, framed, caressed, finessed, and managed by each attorney. The judge in effect rules what blows at the block each side may take, and then finally an image, subject to interpretation, is left.

As in sculpture, a finger—a point—hacked away cannot easily be put back. A finger not sculpted precisely enough is not a finger simply because the attorney sees it so. The jury has to recognize the finger, too. But jurors theoretically can make no alterations to the image they receive—it is a finished work about which they may not speak for the duration of the time they have been watching it being formed.

When the charge from the judge is completed, the jury is "given" the case—the sculpture—to take into their room and evaluate. It has fallen to them to say what the ultimate image is.

Opening statements are the opening round in the creation of the image, and after the openings in Wyman–D'Arazzio, the case had surely become the central matter in the jurors' lives. But they had to avoid discussing it.

As they walked down the hall, I heard their silence longing to burst into conversation. Yet against the wholly understandable human urge to say what they thought after days of being questioned and a full day of listening to very convincing but opposing interpretations of the same events, the jurors now were sealed like Mason jars.

[2]
Absolvo ... Condemno ... Non Liquet: A Brief History of the Jury

The purpose of a jury system—in whatever form it has been found at whatever point in history—has been to buttress or buffer official power. The buttressing jury simply confirmed the view of the holder of power—the King, for example. (In medieval England, the King had only to accuse in order to have a jury convened.) The buffering jury evolved when accusations—criminal or civil—needed to be proved to a collection of people who represented, if not the entire community, at least the community of the parties to the trial. The jury represented the community's view, the community's wisdom.

When that wisdom opposed the ruling power, the jury became a political institution, and when it acquired the freedom to disagree with the ruling power without fear of retribution, it became a political force. Today, parties to a case count on the jury to protect them from the potential arbitrariness of a judge; defendants in a criminal proceeding hope the jury will spare them from conviction on an unwarranted prosecution. The rest of us count on the jury to administer justice in our name—jurors become our deputies. Directly involved in the case or not, we see the jury as a repository of fairness. Theoretically, if one party to a trial is trying to perpetrate an affront on the other, the jury—in the name of the larger society—will not permit it. Nor, theoretically, will the jury permit the state to abuse its authority and railroad its opponents.

In a sense, the jury achieves symbolically what cannot be achieved practically—the presence of the entire populace at every trial. This has almost always been an essential part of the jury's role. Even nomadic Siberian tribes have had the concept that the community—represented either by elders or those who are thought to be wise—must have a say in justice. It is not so novel an idea that any one culture can lay original claim to it.

However, most historians place the origin of the Western jury system in classical Athens, and indeed the jury plays a major role in at least one major Greek dramatic tragedy.

In the trilogy *Agamemnon* by Aeschylus, the family of Atreus is racked by a series of infidelities and murders, including matricide. Orestes kills his mother, Clytemnestra, to avenge his father, Agamemnon, whom she has betrayed. Orestes is thus pursued by the Furies until the matter of his judgment comes to rest before Athena—a goddess so important, she reminds us, that she is the only other one, besides Zeus, who knows where the thunderbolts are kept. But even she will not take on the deciding of Orestes' fate alone, although the facts are clear—he had pleaded guilty to crime. Athena remarks to Orestes in the third play of the trilogy, *The Eumenides*, "the matter is too big for any mortal man who thinks he can judge it. Even I have not the right to analyze cases of murder where wrath's edge is sharp and all the more since you have come and clung, a clean and innocent supplicant, against my doors." She decides not to decide and, to set a precedent, perhaps to relieve the gods of the burden of exclusive justice, adds: "I shall elect judges of manslaughter and swear them in, establish a court into all time to come. . . . I will pick the finest of my citizens and come back."

She returns with twelve men, whom she has advised to listen to the testimony and vote. But before they do, she admits to them that her vote, should it be necessary for her to cast a vote to break a tie, would be in favor of mercy for Orestes. It was perhaps the original of what is now known as a "directed verdict." However, Orestes' jury does not blindly follow Athena's direction. Only six vote with her, and so the tiebreaker is needed to free Orestes.

Despite the outrage of the Furies at what has happened, Orestes suffers no punishment, and Athena establishes on the Hill of Ares in Athens a locale for trials "forevermore." In discharging the jury, she proclaims, "In all goodwill toward these citizens I establish in power spirits who are large, difficult to soften. To them is given the handling entire of men's lives."

The Greeks grew fond of jury trials, and Athens was so

renowned for them that in Aristophanes' comedy *The Clouds*, a character refuses to believe that a point on a map is Athens because he sees "no courts are sitting" there.

Until the midfifth century, the Athenian legal system was operated entirely by amateurs—there were no paid attorneys, no public prosecutors; anyone could bring a charge, and defendants conducted their own cases. Professionalism, first in the form of speech writers, presented itself in the Athenian courts when oratory became an academic subject and courtroom speeches became important persuasive tools.

The Greek jury, called a dicastery, little resembled a present jury. The jurors, or dicasts, had to be male, over thirty years of age, free and full citizens, and free of debt. Normally there were 501 dicasts for a public, or criminal, case—as in the jury that convicted Socrates of atheism in 399 B.C.—and 201 dicasts for a private, or civil, case. There could be, however, as many as 1,500 to 6,000 dicasts. Verdict was by majority vote, and the ballots—black and white stones—were put in urns for secrecy. Jurors' names were drawn by lot by the magistrates, also amateurs, from the larger universe of people who volunteered to do dicast service. Sometimes, though, it was necessary to draft dicasts, and recruits were told to come prepared with rations for three days. Pericles, in the midfifth century, is credited with instituting pay, about ten cents a day, to gain favor with the voters. (Plutarch, in his biography of Pericles, calls the institution of pay for jury service an attempt by Pericles to "caress the people.")

Once fees were available, jurors tended to congregate around the courthouse hill, hoping to be called for a trial, so as to, as the Greek orator Isocrates described it, "secure the means of subsistence." During this period, too, there was a shortage of dicasts from time to time, because of increasing litigation. The fees induced Athenians to give of their time—especially the poor, who with the elderly apparently comprised a high percentage of the dicasts. (This kind of class and economic skew exists today and is a major problem of the jury system.) Dicasts could serve over and over again once they were chosen, and indeed Aristophanes, in *The Wasps*, satirizes the overzealous dicast. The play is about Philocleon, who so loves to be a juror that his son locks him up under slave guard to keep him from running off to court each day. Finally, to placate his father who is pining to sit again in the dicastery, the son establishes a court at home, with household dogs as both prosecutors and defendants, "heard" by barking to the one-man, housebound jury.

One doesn't want to romanticize Athenian democracy, but it is nevertheless impressive that the dicastery was highly prized as a democratic institution. While the magistrates were subject to annual review of their performance, the dicasts were immune to any inquiry into their actions. If a prosecutor did not convince at least one fifth of the dicasts of the validity of the charges, he himself could be fined or later tried for perjury. But while the jury enjoyed respect in Athens, it was not above reproach. Bribery was not unknown; in 409 B.C., one of Socrates' prosecutors was acquitted of treason and is said to have successfully bribed his jury.

The Athenian courtroom was no model of decorum. Jurors might be chosen, or volunteer, for a specific case precisely because they had knowledge or information about it. Preformed opinions were common, and these were widely and roundly discussed among the dicasts as evidence unfolded. The dicasts were also free to ask questions of the parties to a case, which contributed to a general brouhaha. The jury convened behind ropes, outdoors, and was not prevented from yelling, hissing, or booing to express opinions. During Socrates' trial in 399 B.C., Plato, acting as attorney, often had to call for silence. On other occasions, Plato compared jury behavior to that of a theater audience. Apollodorus, the second century B.C. grammarian, wrote that the dicasts, for one case he tried, simply would not listen to him, having been so impressed by the speech of the other attorney. The dicast's attention, like that of today's juror, faded in and out, and one cannot be surprised at that if cases were held in the blazing Greek sun. Demosthenes once caught a dicastery off guard by interrupting his oratory in a criminal case with a joke about the shadow of a jackass. He stopped the story midway. When the jury protested, insisting he tell the end, he admonished them for paying more attention to the life of a jackass than to his client.

Still, attorneys then, as today, understood quite well that arousing jury sentiment can often be what trial practice is all about. The dicastery, like today's jury, was a combustible unit of prejudices, attitudes, and fears. No shred of available evidence was kept from a dicastery, and no detail of a defendant's life was off-limits. Relatives and friends of the parties could address the jury, once the basic testimony had been given; children of victims were often presented to the jury to arouse sympathy. (Today, they are allowed to sit behind the rail but the intent is the same.) Socrates, tried for creating his own gods and corrupting young men, refused to cater to the jury in this way. About overtures to dicastery emotion, he said, "I say these things ought not to be done," and told the jury it ought not to permit them. But the fact is that Socrates, aloof, even scornful of the jury, may have been a leading cause of his conviction, as there was little evidence.

In ancient Greece, the magistrates kept the trial proceedings from becoming entirely chaotic, but did not play the role of judge. The Greek dicasts decided both fact and law and often passed sentence too. But the juror's multipurpose role changed as it moved west and through history.

The Romans studied the Greek system of law and adopted a system of judices, who heard criminal trials once a year. These were, for the most part, members of the Senatorial class, who voted on tablets by writing *C*, *A*, or *NL* for *condemno* ("I condemn"), *absolvo* ("I acquit"), or *non liquet* ("it is not clear"). When the Romans conquered Britain, they brought the jury system with them. However, historians agree that it was not a Roman seed from which the English jury system grew but a Norman one, planted when the Normans invaded England in 1066 A.D.. Ironically, while the jury was born in continental Europe, it died away there but remained alive in England, where it flourished vigorously enough to travel and take root in colonial America.

Jury scholars like to debate the exact origins and evolution of the jury. Suffice it to say here that the jury, as we know it, unquestionably came from England, although the idea itself has ancient ancestry.

Between the Roman and Norman invasions, there were interesting forms and precursors to the jury. Charlemagne, King of the Franks, established the "inquisition" in 780 A.D. This court was called into session only at the command of the King, and usually for his benefit. The jury was chosen from among free men who had knowledge of the dispute; jury size appears to have ranged from thirteen to two hundred. Typical cases included disputes over property boundaries and fishing rights. The jurors were also the witnesses, giving as well as evaluating evidence. This dual job continued until the end of the fourteenth century.

There were several precursors to trial by jury. King Alfred in ninth century England divided the country into tithings, about ten neighboring households. When there was a dispute, every member of the tithing came together to debate it. Trial by oath meant a defendant had to retell his side of the story repeatedly, each time swearing to it, never wavering from the original version in each retelling. A slip of detail meant the defendant lost his case.

Compurgation was another mode of trial. In this system, the defendant had to find and present people to the court who would swear to his side of the matter under question. All compurgators had to agree. For very serious crimes, the defendant had to produce eleven compurgators and add his own vote to make twelve.

Trial by ordeal was a grim alternative, which had Biblical origins. It was the means to justice when a defendant had committed perjury, been caught in the act, or could not find enough compurgators. Nonfreemen were almost always tried by ordeal. Ordeals included such painful rituals as forcing the accused to walk barefoot on hot iron plowshares or carry hot iron weights barehanded, or reach into a pot of boiling water. If the defendant's skin remained unblemished or uninjured, he was declared innocent. Cold water ordeal had the defendant tied up and thrown into a body of water. An innocent man sank, presumably to be retrieved in time to enjoy his acquittal. At the time of the Norman conquest in England, trial by ordeal was the most common form of judgment. During most of these rituals, priests and other clergy were present; consequently, after Pope Innocent III, in the early thirteenth century, forbade churchmen to participate in them, trial by ordeal increasingly gave way to trial by jury.

Up until about 1200 A.D., the jury system, such as it was, was restricted mostly to civil matters such as property questions. Henry II, who reigned from 1154 to 1189, established the Grand Assize, a court of four knights and twelve neighbors, who ruled on challenged claims to land. There were also lesser courts and lesser juries. Jurors were not supposed to argue with the judge on the law, but they were considered to have knowledge of the matter at hand, and even went on tours of the disputed land parcel before the trial began. But the foreknowledge held jurors responsible for reaching a "correct" verdict, and in civil cases an incorrect verdict could result in a jury itself charged with "attaint." This accusation meant that the jury was suspected of perjury, and a second jury was called to retry the case. If the second jury's findings were deemed correct, the first jury was considered guilty of attaint. Attainted jurors could lose their property, be imprisoned, or both. In cases where the King was a party, an attaint finding was possible only if the verdict went against the King.

To bring the King under the rule of law, English nobility demanded the King sign the Magna Carta in 1215 A.D. Though there is considerable debate on this point, the contemporary idea that jury trial by one's peers is a right of all citizens derives from both Article 36 of the Magna Carta (which guarantees the right of "inquisition" or trial), and Article 39 (which sets out that "no free man shall be taken or imprisoned . . . nor will we send upon him unless by the lawful judgment of his peers, or by the law of the land.") These newly guaranteed rights, reinforced by Pope Innocent's condemnation of trial by ordeal, placed jury trials in prominence.

They became so prominent that defendants who did not consent to them were either pronounced guilty outright or tortured until they consented to meet the jury. This practice, called *peine forte et dure,* persisted until the mideighteenth century. Jurors too were kept without food or drink until they reached a verdict. In fact, jurors caught with food in the deliberating room were fined.

Jurors were subjected to other indignities that make today's courtroom inconveniences seem mild. If the jury did not reach a verdict by the time a circuit judge had to move on to the next jurisdiction, the jurors were simply packed into a cart and taken along with the judge until they reached their decision.

The jury was never intended to determine the rules of law or flout the judge's instructions about how to apply the law. But until about 1700, the jury had the power, if not the right, to disagree with the law—and act accordingly, what today is called jury nullification. In 1685, a woman named Alice Lisle went on trial for hiding a fugitive named Hicks, who had been active in Monmouth's rebellion against King James II. The jury was not convinced that Lisle had known of the man's involvement when she hid him, but when they told the judge of their doubt, he said that the evidence had indeed been sufficient to show him that the defendant had been aware. Therefore, the jury reluctantly convicted Lisle, who was executed. (Her conviction was repealed by an Act of Parliament in 1689.)

One of the most celebrated examples of the English jury flexing its muscle on the law came during the trial of William Penn in 1670. Penn, a rebellious sort who would soon establish a colony in America, was charged with unlawful assembly and speaking to a gathered crowd, thereby causing great disturbance of the peace. The jury retired to deliberate but would not return a verdict that held the assembly unlawful, finding that Penn had been guilty only of speaking. The judge sent the jury back to deliberate five more times, over a period of two and a half days—no food, no drink, no chamberpot—and when they still refused to acquiesce, he fined them all about $26 and kept them in jail until they had paid.

One of the jurors, Edward Bushell, was outraged and filed a writ of habeas corpus, protesting his detainment. His action put an end to the practice of fining or coercing juries to reach a desired verdict.

Once colonization of British America began, the jury system acquired new life. It was guaranteed in some form in the incorporating charters of each colony. Massachusetts allowed jurors to get advice from anyone before reaching a verdict, and to remain silent, individually or collectively, if they could not reach a verdict. Though unanimity among jurors in criminal case verdicts had, for the most part, become English rule, some colonies had provisions for majority rule decisions.

The First Continental Congress in 1774 asserted that the colonists had the right to be "tried by their peers," and the Declaration of Independence declares among its grievances against the English king that he had been depriving colonists "in many cases" of the right of jury trial. The Sixth Amendment to the Constitution specifically guarantees the right to jury trial in federal criminal trials, and the Seventh Amendment provides for the right in civil trials. In 1968, a U.S. Supreme Court decision held that the Sixth Amendment had been incorporated into the Fourteenth Amendment and therefore applies to the individual states, so that states are not free to withhold the right to jury trials.

Throughout its history, at least in England and the United Kingdom, the jury's role expanded or contracted depending on the evolving state of common law. In most countries of the world, the jury system does not function and has all but died out in most Western European countries, though some use a system of lay judges.

Most Colonial American juries retained the right to decide both law and fact in civil and criminal cases. A classic example was the trial of publisher John Peter Zenger in 1735, on charges of libeling the governor of New York by charging him with, among other things, depriving the citizens of the state the right to trial by jury. Zenger's attorney, Andrew Hamilton of Philadelphia (whose involvement in the case gave birth to the expression "talks like a Philadelphia lawyer"), argued that if what Zenger had charged was true, he could not be found guilty. The judge counterargued that whether the charges were true was irrelevant to the question of libel and instructed the jury that only he (the judge) could decide this point of law. Hamilton proceeded to address the jury about what constituted libel, and he offered the opposite opinion, suggesting that the jury members could make up their own minds on the point. When the judge interrupted him, Hamilton persisted. When the judge instructed the jury about the law, he acknowledged that Hamilton had been taking "great pains" to show "how little regard juries are to pay to the opinion of the judges." But the judge reminded the jury that their only role was to decide whether what Zenger printed was libelous and not whether it was justified. After a short deliberation, the jury acquitted Zenger.

The jury's right to decide the law, assuming the law was constitutional, persisted in the United States until about 1835. It is still debated among lawyers, and is especially urged on juries, usually by defense attorneys, in political trials where "crimes of conscience" are involved. Indeed, to capture the conscience of the jurors is the modern attorney's biggest challenge, whether the courtroom proceedings are routine or unusual. Athena's jury innovation gave life to a format for a battle of words, wit, and money that lasted thousands of years and flourishes grandly as today's trial court.

[3]
The Law, the Trial, the Case

Delay in the court is sometimes attributed to the time involved in preparing cases to be heard before a jury. It is argued that the ground rules of what constitutes admissible evidence, the pretrial motions, and the other preparations can stretch to unconscionable lengths the time needed to make a case jury-ready. One hears also that if cases were argued before judges instead of juries, much of the manipulation and appeals to sympathy—what attorneys might call "strong adversarial techniques"—would be cut back, since few attorneys would blatantly try to woo a judge the way they often woo juries.

These allegations may be valid, but the fact is that most cases that come before juries are not clear-cut; they have snags, gaps, tangents. Cases come before juries precisely because they are not cut-and-dried. Parties to a case who do not waive their jury right expect perhaps a greater measure of fairness from juries than from judges, on the theory that jurors come to the legal system with a greater ability to think of each case as unique.

One feels instinctively that juries are less tough than judges. However, in 1966, in what has become a landmark study of how the jury works in criminal trials, the late Professor Harry Kalven, Jr., and Professor Hans Zeisel, of the University of Chicago Law School, demonstrated that that conventional wisdom did not hold. The researchers wrote: "We suspect there is little or no intrinsic directionality in the jury's response. It is not fundamentally defendant-prone, rather it is non-rule minded; it will move where the equities are." Thus, the "strong advocacy" style of some attorneys, which is intended to sway the jury, coupled with the

31

possibility that, through a crack in the case, one or the other side can slide a slight advantage for itself through to the jury, are the true determinants of the pace and clarity of the trial.

The child pornography matter proved to be a classic example of the tug-of-war nature of trial practice. The fact that any jury can be almost mercilessly tugged this way and that and still come to verdicts based on evidence alone is surely a strong argument on the jury's behalf.

In this trial, the prosecution had some strong evidence, as well as some shortcomings of evidence to explain, and the defendants believed there was a decent chance the jury would acquit them. The judge, though ruling on the law only, was, one sensed, outraged by the crimes. Some of his rulings, it could be said, were intended to close out any areas where sympathy for the defendants might develop.

Both defense attorneys told me they had been looking for an intelligent, strong jury able to spot the gaps. The prosecution, for its part, needed the same juror qualities if the gaps were not to be interpreted as evidence of nonguilt.

The younger defendant, Wyman, the middleman, offered the defense that he did not know what he was doing when he sold the films to the undercover policeman. A tug one way. However the judge ruled that "diminished capacity," interfering with a defendant's ability to intend the consequences of his actions, was not a proper legal defense in this case. He would have allowed the attorney to offer a defense based on insanity—that is, to say the defendant had not known right from wrong. But Wyman's attorney did not believe he could prove insanity, so he tried everything possible to bring information before the jury that would arouse enough sympathy among them to disagree with the judge's ruling and rise above his direction about what constituted defense.

The debate over what constituted Wyman's defense continued through the trial. Often, the jury would be kept waiting in their jury room for several hours while inside the courtroom the district attorney and the defense lawyers hammered out points of law before the judge. It was, in fact, a good example of the extra time jury trials entail.

A key element for Wyman's defense was whether or not the

unmentionable gentleman, Lewis, would be permitted to testify, and if not, whether the defense would be permitted to introduce his relationship to the defendant through other witnesses. Lewis was an admitted pedophile. He and his father operated a drugstore from which they dispersed numerous illegal prescriptions. They also had a legal videotape business. At the time of this case, Lewis's drugstore business was being investigated; Lewis was under federal indictment on other charges, and he had been granted immunity from the district attorney's prosecution once he became an informant on the matter of child pornography. The fact that he had introduced the defendant to the undercover policeman seemed irrelevant to the prosecution. But it was crucial to the defense because the defense wanted to convince the jury that Wyman only sold films to the policeman to insure a continued supply of drugs.

It was obvious that the prosecution did not want Lewis brought into the case to distract the jury. Also, since the indictment alleged specific crimes on specific dates, from the prosecution's point of view, the defendant's state of mind on only those specific dates was relevant. The defense, on the other hand, was trying to show that Wyman was a Quaalude addict during the entire period covered by the indictment. But while the judge had ruled that the defendant's psychiatrist or counselor could testify only about the defendant's capacity on the dates of the indictment, the defense attorney continued to bring up the matter almost daily during the trial anyway (with the jury waiting outside), in the hope of changing the judge's mind.

The defense tried valiantly, through the prosecution's own witnesses, to plant these seeds with the jurors, once they were back in the courtroom and the trial had resumed. Wyman's attorney repeatedly questioned the most damaging witness, the undercover cop, about whether he ever saw the defendant high and why the police officer had not been interested in the prior relationship between the defendant and the informer. The policeman's standard response was that it was not his job to question the history of informers. When the policeman was asked potentially incriminating questions he simply said he did not remember. The defense attorney was so frustrated that he took to just blurting things out. "Did you know that your informer is under indictment

facing twenty-five years in jail. . . ?" he questioned the policeman. This brought an immediate objection from the prosecution,
which was sustained, along with a reprimand from the judge. He
ordered the question stricken from the record and the jury to
ignore what it had just seen and heard.

It was not difficult to understand the defense's strategy. The
prosecutor's case was strong and there was also a political
dimension at work, given the nature of child pornography.

Child pornography is big business in the United States, accounting for $500 million to $1 billion of underground income
per year, and involving perhaps as many as 1 million children. In
relation, the Wyman case was small potatoes, but it was still
potentially a high visibility case for the Manhattan district
attorney's office.

The prosecution's case against the young middleman, Wyman,
consisted essentially of testimony from policemen and evidence in
the form of the seized films and the undercover tape recordings.
The case against D'Arazzio, the wholesaler, was entirely circumstantial, but nevertheless became the focal point of the trial—it
was his conviction the prosecutor must have wanted most.

The prosecutor's case was presented more or less chronologi-
cally; each witness, most of them policemen, described his involvement. The main undercover cop had posed as a pedophile
after having been introduced to the defendant by the informer,
Lewis. He wore a hidden microphone and asked the middleman,
Wyman, to secure some "young stuff," meaning films. Wyman,
who also worked as a cashier in his father's adult bookstore and
peep show, was, therefore, heard on tape saying he could indeed
get the films, "no problem," from someone named "Jeb." Wyman
never used a family name for Jeb, and the undercover policeman
never elicited it. The jury heard Wyman say, on several tapes, that
he could get anything the policeman needed and that films of
seven- to eleven-year-olds were easier to secure because older
children started "getting smart" and asking for a share in the
profits, so the film makers didn't use them as much. Wyman also
told the undercover policeman that these films doubled their
return on resale.

Over a two-month period, the undercover policeman arranged
several meetings with Wyman, the middleman defendant; two

purchases of films were made. The buying procedure was always the same. The policeman ordered; the middleman phoned "Jeb"; and a different team of policemen followed the middleman to Jeb's shop, another adult sex paraphernalia establishment at the other side of Manhattan. The two defendants met, came out of Jeb's shop, and entered another building nearby. When they reemerged on the street, Wyman was carrying a brown paper bag that looked like the bag which contained the films that Wyman eventually turned over to the police. On one stake-out, the police also located themselves inside the second building the middleman and Jeb entered, and observed them taking an elevator to an upper floor. The police did not, or could not, follow.

The tape recordings of the policeman and the middleman were quite incriminating. The middleman talked about how "good" one particular film, BG-1, was. (That was an abbreviation for Boy-Girl 1.) The jury also heard the middleman boasting about deals he had made in Hong Kong, transporting drugs through customs by sealing them in the lining of a grandfather clock, of making a half a million dollars, and of plowing it all back into his father's business, of a vault on the seventeenth floor of Jeb's building full of child pornography films. Wyman also laughed inappropriately and made personal statements, such as that his wife really was his "mother image."

The investigation proceeded. The policeman became a moderately regular customer, each time increasing the number of films he wanted to buy, always being sure to ask for "young stuff." The jury heard a phone call, or at least one side of it, that the middleman made to Jeb, in which Jeb apparently told Wyman he was suspicious that the buyer was "the Man"—that is, the cops. The middleman laughingly repeated this to the policeman, who did his best to laugh too. The middleman did not take Jeb's warning seriously and agreed to arrange a major purchase of three hundred films just like the films "last time," as he described them to Jeb on the phone. Jeb, for his part, seemed willing to forgo his fears about the policeman by accepting the order. Wyman said the policeman would have to return with $17,250 in cash.

On the day of the sale, however, the police, amazingly, did not have the cash on hand and sought to put off the purchase. Jeb balked. He told the middleman over the telephone, "Now or never." The police still could not secure the cash, and they sensed they were about to lose months of the investigation. They decided to arrest the middleman, even if they could not consummate the wholesale deal. Once they had the defendant Wyman in custody, they asked him to place a final phone call to Jeb to determine whether the buyer, the undercover, could still pick up the films. Wyman placed the call, which the police taped. The tape was the only piece of evidence that linked the two defendants concretely. The jury heard Jeb say on tape, "This whole fucking thing sucks. . . . It is all packed up and stashed away. . . . You are going to bring him here? I don't want to see this guy. . . ." D'Arazzio was willing to let Wyman collect the films, but by the time the police had the money and went to complete the deal, Jeb had left the premises and the cache of films was stashed safely away again where they had yet to be found.

To present this evidence, which was intended to prove that all these events took place, the prosecutor took six days. Listening to the tapes was extremely tedious because of the long silences in them while no conversation was being recorded. Once, when the jurors were recalled into court after a legal argument between attorneys, they groaned loudly in unison, knowing the tape-playing would resume. The case was beginning to try the jurors' patience and attention.

In the middle of presenting her case, the prosecutor requested a one-day recess because she was feeling ill. The jury, meantime, had been sitting in its room waiting for the day's events to begin. After they were excused for the day and the trial recessed, I walked to the subway station with two jurors who complained that no one involved with the case had been considerate enough to call, and head them off from coming to court. They resented the waste of their time, and they particularly resented not knowing the reason, for the judge had not provided them with one. One speculated that surely the defense needed the break; the other was just as sure it had been the prosecution. They did not ask me, although they might have been tempted since I never had to leave the courtroom and therefore was privy to details they were not. I did not offer them any information, for that would have constituted talking about the case, which they were forbidden to do. Also, possibly the recess had been called to handle a midtrial attempt by the defendants to plea-bargain. It was conceivable that the next day the jury would be advised the case had been "disposed of."

But no. Next morning it was trial as usual. If there had been a plea offer, the prosecutors had not accepted it. In fact, as they wheeled in their evidence, the prosecutors were accompanied by a third bearer. While the jury milled around in the hall, one juror murmured, "By now there is so much they need an extra person to carry it." Another juror remarked, while reading a newspaper article about an ongoing murder case, "That murder sounds cut-and-dried, not like our case." Opinions, however subtle, had begun to form. How can a juror remain above the instinct to come to some conclusions each day?

No trial can avoid the human need for some levity, from time to time. In this case, for example, during the long musical interludes on the tapes, recorded when the policeman was waiting for Wyman in his parked car with the radio on, the jurors could not keep from smiling. The court clerk, out of the jury's hearing but not mine, remarked that he felt he should ask the district attorneys to dance so as not to waste such pretty music. Also, outside the jury's sight and hearing, the attorneys frequently relaxed their adversary roles. The defense chided the prosecutor about a long gap on one of the tapes, and joked that she had found Rosemary Woods. They talked about other cases, what they had had for dinner the night before. While, for the jury, the child pornography case was *the* case, for the attorneys, it was one among many. But neither side wanted the jury to see them as other than pitted tooth and nail against each other.

The defendants too kidded among themselves. Outside the jury's hearing, but in front of the sour court clerk, D'Arazzio suggested to Wyman that they hire the very overweight but handsome guard as a male dancer. The clerk did not smile, the guard laughed awkwardly.

I tried to stay far from the jury, but it was not always easy. One day I rode in the elevator with a few jurors who asked me to come to lunch, promising they would not ask me about the case or talk about it. I would have loved to have gone—I was getting very tired of eating alone—but I decided against it. "Then we'll talk about you," one of the jurors joked.

The denouement of the prosecution's case was the showing of the films, which the judge had ruled admissible. The judge ordered the courtroom locked. Those of us inside at the moment were permitted to stay, though we would not be permitted to interrupt the film showing in order to leave. Both defense attorneys again objected to the showing of the films on the grounds that they could not help but be prejudicial. One of them said, "I beseech your honor to reconsider," but the judge was unconvinced. The courtroom lights were put out and the screen set up.

The films were grotesque. All but one depicted young boys in all positions of sexual contact. The infamous BG-1, however, showed a Hispanic-looking boy having intercourse with a young blond girl. They both looked about seven or eight. The films had no sound track, but the children, on some off-camera direction, mouthed obscene words to the audience, pointed to each other's sexual organs, caressed and penetrated each other.

The films were unquestionably prejudicial, since one could not help but feel that anyone who had anything to do with these films should be convicted. The notion of providing a fair trial almost seemed irresponsible, nearly perverse, in relation to the perverse exploitation of the children used in the making of these films.

If the films elicited this reaction in me, how, I wondered, could the jury possibly keep an open mind? I noticed Wyman and his attorney move to a bench behind the screen from which they could not see the films. It was partly a protest of the showing and partly a show for the jury.

I began to think that showing the films might actually harm the prosecution because after one or two, the films were unrelentingly the same; the shocking impact diminished after one had seen a few of them. The camera was often so close to sexual canals that they looked like valves in open heart surgery in a medical textbook.

I finally removed my glasses so that all I saw on the screen was moving white light. I felt dragged through the films—and since I had watched them voluntarily, how could the jury feel? The jurors gazed somberly and passively at the screen. One juror drummed his fingers on the jury box railing. The judge noted each time a film began and ended. For the transcript, the undercover policeman, who also projected the films, named the sexual acts each film had shown. The entire proceeding was grim; tension mounted among us all.

The district attorney pointed out that one of the films she was about to show had three separate parts. She did that, I think, because in one of the tape recordings, the middleman spoke about a "great three-parter." The prosecutor was doubtlessly trying to establish for the jury that the defendant knew the merchandise. She asked for a stipulation, an agreement for the record, from the defense that the same film had three parts so she would have only to show the first part. The defense attorney seized the moment. "Do whatever you want," he said brusquely. Without the stipulation, the prosecutor chose to project all three parts.

When the film viewing ended, even the judge seemed sobered. He released the jury, and repeated his admonition not to read about the case. "Particularly in this case," he said, "do not talk about the material or discuss the exhibits. Keep an open mind until you hear all the evidence." The judge agreed to a conference in his chambers with the attorneys in order to resolve the still pending matter of whether Lewis would be allowed to testify. Outside, Wyman told me he thought the film most damaging to him was BG-1. I told him he should be more careful whom he talked to in the hall and what he said.

[4]
The Ungentlemanly Gentleman

The next day, the judge's attitude seemed to have mellowed. He sustained a defense objection to a chart prepared by the prosecution, which suggested that the enterprises employing the defendants were part of a "corporate network" linked to organized crime. Also, after a very long delay in the matter, for which no one apologized to the jury, the judge agreed to permit Wyman's attorney to call Lewis, the psychiatrist, and anyone else, provided the testimony related only to the dates and events in the indictment. It was half a victory, but one which I doubt the defense would have won at all, were it not for the showing of the films.

When the jurors at last were admitted to the courtroom, they were using newspapers to fan their faces. (Newspapers, I thought, ought not to have been there, although the case was not receiving daily coverage.) The room the jurors waited in each day had no window and no ventilation and reminded one juror, as she later told me, of the subway.

When Lewis testified, he had his own attorney at his side to counsel him about whether he should answer a question or plead the Fifth Amendment—so many were the charges pending against him in various courts, and his immunity was limited. The effect of this was that Lewis seemed in such deep trouble with the law that any examination by an attorney was a potential minefield of self-incrimination. But the defense used Lewis's reticence to its advantage—even unanswered questions, put in the minds of the jurors, could possibly raise sympathy for the defendant.

The defense managed to maneuver Lewis to admit he had once

40

turned in his own father to the police to win immunity for himself, and that he patronized young male prostitutes. He admitted to having been a supplier of Quaaludes to the defendant but would not say he was the only supplier, nor that the defendant was an addict.

Lewis was a distinctly unattractive, obese man. A neck problem kept his head tilted to one side. He claimed to be thirty-four, but looked about fifty. However he seemed highly intelligent and knew exactly what he was saying and what was being said to him. On cross-examination, the prosecutor got Lewis to admit that he could not be certain that the defendant was high specifically on Quaaludes on the occasions when he had seen the defendant high.

Throughout Lewis's testimony, Wyman suggested questions for his counsel to pose to Lewis, and kept shaking his head as if to say he could not believe how boldly Lewis was lying. But when Lewis's testimony was over, the defense had been unable to link Lewis concretely to the defendant's Quaalude use.

Also, outside the jury's hearing, the defense argued that Lewis had been in contact with Wyman throughout the period covered by the indictment but the DA said that was "news" to her. If it could have been proved, the continuing use of Wyman as bait for the wholesaler would have been highly suspicious from a civil liberties point of view, particularly if Lewis had continued to present the policeman as a "friend." It would have been perhaps a strong entrapment defense. Lewis, however, repeatedly denied on the stand having had any contact with the defendant during the period of the indictment. Wyman continued to shake his head.

Overall, Lewis seemed a very careful liar. Though he was an unappealing, low-life character, the overpowering evil that the defense hoped to portray was not conveyed—at least not to me.

The judge also permitted expert medical testimony on the symptoms of Quaalude addiction and withdrawal in general. (Withdrawal, the expert testified, produced pain and other symptoms that could be worse even than heroin withdrawal symptoms.) But the judge would not permit testimony about the effect Quaalude addiction might have had on this particular defendant. The jury never knew that the witness who was giving this generalized testimony had also been the defendant's psychological counselor after his arrest. So in the end, if there was any link to be made between Quaaludes and the defendant Wyman, the jury had to make it from inference and not from any testimony in court. In any case, jurors later told me, they essentially disregarded the testimony of the counselor, finding it had no bearing on their evaluation of the evidence.

Wyman's only remaining defense consisted of testimony from car pool friends who drove to work with him during the period covered by the indictment. They testified about Wyman's addiction—how he nodded off in the middle of the afternoon, that he had taken as many as four pills at a time. There was testimony that Wyman had a car accident due to drug intoxication. This was the only testimony tying Wyman's access to large quantities of Quaaludes, through Lewis, to the fact that he actually took the pills. After this testimony, Wyman's attorney—for the benefit of the jury no doubt—ended his presentation with the words, "In view of your honor's rulings in this case, the defendant Wyman rests."

D'Arazzio's defense was much more simple. Through book-keeper's records, the attorney established that on some days there was a second "Jeb" working in D'Arazzio's establishment as a cashier. Another witness testified that anyone who did business with D'Arazzio called him by his nickname, "Bunkie," and that, at the time, the establishment was selling special European films, kept separate from the usual stock. There was also testimony that in the building where the police observed Wyman and D'Arazzio take an elevator, D'Arazzio's printer had an office on an upper floor.

When D'Arazzio's attorney summed up his case, he suggested to the jury that the "Jeb" that Wyman had been calling could have been the "other Jeb"—no one had ever used a second name—and that the "secret" transaction D'Arazzio was handling through Wyman had to do with the European films. The reason D'Arazzio did not want to meet the undercover buyer personally was because he did not want to have any direct "hassles" with a buyer. D'Arazzio's attorney argued that the sale of European films might have been a criminal action, but it was not the crime charged—i.e. wholesaling child pornography. D'Arazzio, his attorney continued, could not be held responsible for what Wyman had told the police or for where Wyman secured the child pornography films. He told the jury that without Wyman's statements on tape, the case against Jeb was nonexistent, and since the jury never heard Jeb's voice in the courtroom—he did not testify on his own behalf—it was only the testimony of one policewoman that had identified the voice of the Jeb on tape as the voice of the Jeb on trial. Remember, he cautioned the jury in his summation, you are not here to solve this crime! "If the inference you can draw from circumstantial evidence flows equally to innocence as to guilt, you are duty bound to acquit."

Wyman's attorney's summation began with a thanks to the jury for their time. Indeed, it had taken nearly three weeks to reconstruct the events of a few days. He told the jury there was no doubt his client had dealings with the undercover agent, but that the entire story had not been brought out. Here, at last, was his chance to fill in where judge's rulings had prevented him before. He called Lewis "slime who crawled out from under a rock" who should not be pitied. He described how "this piece of garbage" hooked Wyman on Quaaludes, giving him free prescriptions in return for films. He told the jurors that in their own minds they had to know Wyman was addicted and that it was his supplier, Lewis, who "turned the police on" to Wyman in return for immunity from other prosecutions. He made much of the police not remembering anything that could possibly help the defense. And he reminded the jury that they had heard the rambling in Wyman's voice on tape which showed that the drug affected Wyman's ability to make judgments. Trying again to open the door the judge had closed, he said, "You will have to decide whether this negates any element of the crime." Neither the judge nor the prosecution let that remark slide. "You know that is improper at this juncture of this case," the judge said, as he sustained the prosecutor's objection.

The attorney told the jury what they decided would effect the rest of Wyman's life. "There is not a person on this jury," he remarked, "who doesn't know what is going to happen to him if he goes to prison." Again, the prosecution objected, sustained by the judge, who reprimanded the attorney—"that comment should not have been made. The jury is not to consider punishment. I suggest you know that." The attorney then told the jurors they represented the citizens of the county, city, and state. And "I tell you that in my heart, this kid is not guilty because he could not have been guilty in his condition during the time in question." His final words were that each juror should stick to his or her own convictions. His final hope, it seemed, was that if they would not all acquit his client, perhaps one juror would, and therefore "hang" the rest.

The prosecutor then tried to put the jury back on her track. She thanked them again, alluding to the many interruptions and delays that, she said, would "try anyone's patience." To blunt some of the defense, she added that the delays had occurred to assure that "all that comes before you is competent, legal evidence." It was a skillful summation. She addressed the questions that had to be in the forefront of the jurors' minds, and acknowledged that witness testimony can be imperfect, that investigations can be conducted imperfectly, that, after all, events that happened several years previously cannot be perfectly recalled. Maybe, she said, you can feel sympathy for Wyman, but what it came down to was, as tapes had shown, that Wyman had competently and willfully sold the undercover policeman "kiddie porn." As for the "other Jeb" theory, she suggested that the jurors ask themselves if there had been any confusion in the phone calls; did anyone ever ask Wyman to which Jeb he wanted to speak? No one had said, "Jeb who?" As for the European film theory, she did the arithmetic for the jury which showed that the total amount of money that Wyman, Jeb, and the undercover cop agreed to as payment for the child pornography films did not correspond to the prices for the European films mentioned by D'Arazzio's own witness. (D'Arazzio's attorney, on the other hand, had suggested that the jury not do the arithmetic because "the numbers in this case will only lead you to confusion." At least one juror had been busy doing computations as witnesses testified about the cost of the various films.)

Then the prosecutor got tough, as if she had saved her biggest fires for the end. As vividly as the defense had portrayed Wyman as a vulnerable young man dependent on drugs, she portrayed him as "no little kid like the kids in the film." She reminded the jury that Wyman was twenty-four years old, married, responsible. He had been able to make telephone calls and complete cash register transactions simultaneously, according to the tapes. The prosecution was not required to prove why he did what he did, she said, only *that* he did. Did the defendants know the content of the material they were selling and did they agree willfully to sell it? These were the relevant questions, she concluded, nearly two and a half hours after she had began.

Though we were now well into the afternoon, the judge charged the jurors on the law and, over defense objections, intended to let them begin their deliberations that day. His instructions on the law were clear: The defendants should have intended to enter into the conspiracy to sell the films; the case against D'Arazzio was entirely circumstantial; being under the influence of drugs did not excuse having committed the crimes. If, on the other hand, at the time of committing the acts, Wyman did not, could not, know what he was doing, then he could not be guilty. The judge reread the indictment and gave several examples of circumstantial evidence, including one about how, if you are driving down a road and see all the trees blown over in one direction, you might reasonably conclude that a strong wind had blown through recently in that direction. As the judge repeated all the counts of the indictment, the aides to the prosecutor followed along, seeming to read a copy. The judge took two hours to instruct the jury, and at 6:30 P.M., the court broke for dinner. Deliberations would begin after that.

Wyman's parents and wife were in court that last day and waited with Wyman. His mother suggested that I write a book about the case from his family's point of view because "they never show the good side of his family, only the bad." I was indeed personally eager to know what made Wyman tick, what his family really thought about running a pornography store. Later, the attorney told me that Wyman had wanted to become a hairdresser but went into his father's business instead. It seemed like a caricature of a Mom and Pop store. The defense attorney said he wished the jury could have learned more about Wyman's family background.

The court clerk had given the jury a verdict sheet on which to record its decision and to reduce the three weeks of testimony and forty-three counts of the indictment to a few words written on predrawn columns.

The courthouse was empty at night, except for the juries

deliberating in various compartments of the building and the rest of us waiting, making nervous small talk. Attorneys mixed, even defendants mixed. I heard a cart rolling and turned to catch sight of the cleaning lady headed around the corner. For a minute, it had sounded like the evidence being wheeled in yet again.

Then the judge was summoned from his chambers, and he in turn summoned us into the courtroom. The jury had sent a note, which the judge read aloud to the attorneys—a system which seemed so primitive: an unclear note written on paper torn from a notebook. The jury had asked to listen to a tape but there was no tape for the date they requested. The judge summoned the jury into court. He reminded them that one tape had been mislabeled and asked them to clarify which tape they needed to hear. They all looked over to one particular juror, one of the older black men, and began to ask him. Clearly, the request has been his. The judge interrupted and suggested they resolve the question privately in their room. In the meantime, to oblige the jury, one DA had gone back to her office and returned with all the tape transcripts which had to be covered in a huge plastic garbage bag because it had begun to pour with rain. But by the time she sat down with them, there was another note from the jurors which said, "We accept your explanation, Judge. We don't need to hear the tape again." The first note had raised a defense hope that the jury wanted to review whether Wyman had sounded too "high" to know what he was doing, but with the second note, the hope was dashed. At about 10:00 P.M., the judge ordered deliberations to cease, and the jury was sequestered for a night. A bus took them to the Holiday Inn at New York's Kennedy International Airport. Being sequestered under guard was very disturbing to the jurors, they told me later. Policemen escorted then everywhere, even to the toilet, and they hated that.

There is no guide on how to deliberate. Jurors are simply sent into their room and expected to come to a verdict. The foreperson is given no instructions on how to conduct the discussion. Usually, judges give no guidance on deliberations at all, and juries, probably not used to group decision making, muddle through. It is a bit like the childhood game pick-up-sticks, where the sticks are thrown down and lie in disarray, and the task is to pick them all up somehow. The judge's charge on the law is supposed to be the map to aid the picking up.

In this case, there were interesting speculations into which the jury might easily have wandered. There was first the issue of police incompetence. I learned during this trial that, for one thing, undercover policemen often receive no special training. In this very important case, a key undercover role was played by a policeman who had no special preparation at all. He had simply been a part of the New York City obscenity squad and then assigned to a special pedophilia unit. One of his jobs, he had admitted, was to "seize films and get them deemed obscene by a judge." A quota system operated in the squad, which could have led to an overzealous investigation. Then, there was the matter of the police testimony—the back-up police seemed to undertake surveillance jobs without knowing why. They are told to trail someone; they do it, but they don't seem to receive any information about how this trail fits into any larger investigation under- way. I am told this is so the police cannot be blamed for manipulating events to make them happen in line with the goals of an investigation. But in this trial, the police looked like robots. They repeated what they saw, no less, no more. It was difficult to believe that when they followed Wyman and D'Arazzio, they had no idea what they were going after.

The biggest incompetence was police failure to seize the films because they did not have the cash on hand to make the purchase. It never became clear how this happened, although the defense chalked it up to administrative bungling. One juror told me later that she thought it was possible that a policeman, in the pay of the pornographers, had thwarted the arrest. The fact remained, however, that the police looked bad, and the defense attorneys had been able to make much of the sloppy police work, making outright fun, to the jury, of the fact that even though there was supposed to be a vault of films hidden on the seventeenth floor of the building where Jeb worked, no policeman could say how many floors the building had. (In fact, it had only six or seven.) The police never made a search for that vault; they could not obtain a warrant because they could not be specific enough about where they suspected the films to be hidden. The police never dusted the film boxes for fingerprints. They never bothered to verify any of Wyman's boasts; for all they knew, the story about importing drugs from Hong Kong in a grandfather clock was true, and Wyman was a millionaire.

A major police error, however, was never brought out in open court, and thus never known to the jury. Once Wyman had been arrested and made the last call to D'Arazzio—which was taped— the police had not properly apprised Wyman of his right to counsel, and they lost the consent form they say the defendant signed. Consequently, that tape was illegally secured. In a pretrial motion, the defense attorney had succeeded in suppressing this tape, so that it could not be used against Wyman. When the jurors heard the last tape, the judge instructed them that what Wyman said on the tape could not be used against him. They were not told why. It would have been a feat of will if they could successfully have ignored it. (The jurors later told me that they didn't feel they needed that particular tape to evaluate Wyman's guilt or innocence.)

But if the police work had been sloppy, some of the lawyering was manipulative. The defense employed the "blurt out" approach to the jury throughout the trial. D'Arazzio's attorney never, despite several requests from the prosecutor (according to standard, acceptable legal practice), gave her a list of his witnesses in advance. When his defense witnesses did appear, the prosecutor had to be the one to remind them that they should sit outside the courtroom until their turn came to testify. When the prosecutor wanted to have a second look at the employment records that had been introduced in support of the "other Jeb" theory, they were not in the courtroom, where the judge had directed they remain. But perhaps the biggest tactic of questionable professionalism came over the near arrest of a defense witness.

The D'Arazzio defense witness who testified about the European special films had a criminal record, and when his Social Security number was run against police records by computer, an outstanding arrest warrant showed against his name. While he was sitting outside the courtroom, ready to testify, a policeman came down the corridor to arrest him. The warrant had, in fact, been vacated—it was no longer valid—but it still showed on the computer.

The witness understandably protested his arrest, but the

policeman would not be dissuaded. The witness then called out to attract the attention of D'Arazzio's defense attorney, who was just coming out of the courtroom, as were some jurors headed for lunch break. Most of the jury had already disappeared down the hall, but a few remained, one in a phone booth. When D'Arazzio's attorney learned what was going on, he became enraged and told the policeman to back off. The policeman would not. Then somebody pushed the lawyer, or so he claimed. The lawyer grew even more angry; he and the policeman began yelling. The melee fell into the courtroom, now empty, except for the judge who refused to intervene, commenting to D'Arazzio's attorney, "I have no basis for telling the police not to arrest this man." And so, the witness was led away in handcuffs.

During the lunch break, the record that proved the warrant was obsolete was found by the prosecutor, but before the jury returned to the courtroom from lunch, D'Arazzio's attorney moved for a mistrial on the grounds that one of the jurors—the one in the phone booth—had seen a defense witness being arrested. Two other jurors had also seen the man being led away. When the judge heard this, he went ashen, for this truly could have been grounds for a mistrial. He called the jurors into the courtroom one at a time and asked if they had seen anything unusual at lunch. One said only that she had heard the lawyer arguing in a loud voice with someone else. She seemed to have no idea who any of the other players were. She did not mention handcuffs, nor did the judge ask about them. Several other jurors questioned were even more oblivious to what had happened. The motion for mistrial was denied.

I still wonder whether the defense attorney deliberately exacerbated the confusion in the hall because he knew a juror was nearby. He did remark, when one of the prosecutors told him to keep his voice down because of jury presence, "I don't care, let them hear."

I also wonder how the policeman knew exactly where to find this witness on that particular day—in Manhattan when the warrant in question had been issued in Queens. The prosecutor's position was that it was her obligation to inform the police where the man was when the warrant showed outstanding. She might also have warned the defense attorney, but did not. By then, I think, she was getting tired of being the "good guy," going by the book. She might also have grown tired of being belittled for her thoroughness. One defense attorney said during an interlude in the playing of the tapes, "Judge, do we have to hear all this? The way *she* tries a case, we'll be here all afternoon listening to traffic." Outside the jury's presence the two men once said outright that the prosecutor did not know the law, or that she knew the law as it was sixty years ago. In fact, that was a tactic too, and the prosecutor was always sustained when she took a legal position in this case.

At 12:50 P.M. on the first full day of deliberation, the last note came from the jury. "We the jury have reached a verdict."

The jury commanded all eyes; everybody was waiting to hear what they had to say. Everybody that is, but D'Arazzio's attorney, who was in another courtroom taking care of another matter. When he returned, the forelady stood up, as did both defendants; all three looked anywhere but at each other. It took the forelady twenty-five minutes to deliver the full verdict, speaking the word "guilty" eighty-six times, as the clerk read off each indictment count for each defendant. I felt no rush of surprise in the courtroom. In fact, Wyman had asked his mother to buy him four packs of cigarettes, just in case he had to go to jail that day. The prosecutor's expression did not change while the verdict was being read. Now she would ask the court to remand to jail the men with whom, only the night before, she had been making small talk. The defendants had changed status; they had passed from innocent to guilty.

The jurors were polled, and each said, yes, he or she agreed with the verdict. Then the judge briefly thanked them, told them their court-ordered lunch was waiting, and that they would be free to eat it and go. Most of them opted out of the lunch and left immediately.

Once the jury was gone from the courtroom, all wraps of innocence fell away. The defense attorneys told the judge that, having expected this verdict, the defendants had brought bail, which was set at $10,000 in cash, each. Wyman's family had brought their bank books, so had D'Arazzio. The attorneys left, the defendants stayed behind to sign bail forms. All of the jury tugging had now come down to paperwork.

The court reporter left, carrying the last folds of punched tape to be transcribed. He asked, "Were you surprised? Not me. Maybe Jeb, but Wyman was gone from the beginning."

When D'Arazzio's attorney came out, he stopped to comment, "Win a few, lose a few. I tried. The cops don't go around arresting innocent people, even my son thought I was breaking my head on this one." So no one, including the attorneys, had believed the defendants were not guilty. They had simply taken a chance that a jury might.

Wyman's attorney said he thought his client had an excellent chance on appeal. The prosecutors left, smiling, asking me to thank the jurors again if I talked to them. The curtain had come down; everybody was going home. The facts had been sculpted, and the guilty image left behind. The jury had been assembled, done its business, and disbanded.

Throughout the Wyman-D'Arazzio child pornography case, I lost many hours of sleep making up my own mind, then reversing my decision, depending on what evidence came into the trial that day. And then there was all the legal argument I had heard, which the jury had not, about admissibility of medical testimony. I was anxious to hear the jurors' impressions and match mine with theirs. The deliberation was both typical and atypical, and what follows is a report on what happened, based on interviews I conducted and a questionnaire returned by half the jury.

Most of the jurors claimed that the opening statements had made an impression on them, but that the evidence itself shaped their deliberations.

The forelady had first asked if there were any votes for acquittal, or any uncertains. There were four, three of them male. This led to a discussion that lasted about ten hours.

The holdouts had been concerned about two main things—police incompetence and entrapment. About the latter, they were dead on the money; legal professionals have since said they felt that in Wyman's case, considering the evidence presented and the importance placed on testimony and tape recordings secured by undercover police, an entrapment defense would have held more water than one based on diminished capacity. Several of the jurors wished to acquit, because the undercover policeman had lured

Wyman—that is, put in the mind of the defendant the idea of selling the films in return for Quaaludes. But one juror eliminated this line of discussion, drawing on his personal view that had entrapment been involved, the defendants would not have been indicted. He was not absolutely correct about that, but he was correct in that the jury was not supposed to deliberate on matters not charged to it. The word "entrapment" had never been used during the trial, so it was a nonissue for this jury. But had one juror not intervened and spoken out, the entire jury might have gotten hopelessly sidetracked on the entrapment question.

However, several jurors still had problems getting past the idea that the conspiracy had been a setup, and here is where individual juror psychology entered the deliberations. One man said he had been "screwed by the system" when he was younger and did not want to do the same to the defendants. (This bias ought to have come to light during voir dire, but did not. In fact, this juror was a Romanian exile who bantered a bit with the defense attorneys about freedom of speech in and outside Romania, and one wonders if his staunch acquittal stemmed from some political ideas about authority and the state.)

The holdout jurors felt that some of the police had lied on the stand, that they had made severe errors of judgment, that they had bungled the investigation. This incompetence, they felt, called the entire case into question. (The skepticism these jurors felt about the police is interesting in that it is said among attorneys that urbanites, especially minorities, tend to be suspicious of the police. However, in this case, the holdouts were all white except one.)

Once the holdouts had thrashed around their concerns, the definites, mostly women, moved in. For them the case boiled down to the tapes and what they had heard. They agreed that the investigators had bungled, but this, they argued, did not diminish the guilt of the defendants. To their minds, Wyman consciously engaged in the sale and never sounded "high" enough to be excused on the basis of his addiction. Though they had some reservations about certain counts, they were able to convince the holdouts that the defendants did indeed willfully sell the films the jury saw in court. They sent a note to the judge asking him to reread the legal definition of "promote," and when they heard the last words of it, "or offer for sale," they decided Wyman was guilty of promoting.

Where D'Arazzio was concerned, it was more open and shut for the jury than it was for me. Throughout the trial, I kept thinking it was possible, though unlikely, that D'Arazzio had not known what kind of film Wyman was promising the police officer. And there was no eyewitness proof that the bags of films Wyman gave the police were the bags D'Arazzio had given Wyman. I had not been sure that there was proof beyond reasonable doubt in D'Arazzio's case. But I had forgotten something important that the jury together had not.

In one taped conversation, Wyman had said to Jeb, "Just like the last time, yeah, same guy." This, the jury believed, definitely linked the two defendants and all the transactions.

I found it intriguing that all the attorneys' tactics simply never impressed the jury enough to make a difference in the deliberations. The defense's best attempts to portray Wyman as a helpless addict had failed. While the jurors felt some sympathy, none finally felt that sympathy excused him. After all the debate about whether Lewis would testify, the jurors paid almost no attention to anything Lewis said, finding him pathetic but incredible. His testimony, from their point of view, might as well not have been given. They never gave a moment's credence to the "other Jeb" theory, nor to the European film theory. And they felt that the policewoman who identified D'Arazzio's voice—the same policewoman who periodically inspected his store and knew him quite well—was the most credible witness they heard on either side. They disliked watching the films, even resented it, but believed the experience was necessary to decide on each count. They also felt that the tactic of defendant Wyman and his attorney sitting behind the screen was a little silly.

There were problems of keeping an open mind after hearing the tapes, and several jurors simply could not refrain from discussing the case with their friends. The fact that the last tape could not be used against Wyman presented no problem for the jury, since they could convict him on all the tapes that had come before. That neither defendant took the stand in his own behalf did seem indicative of guilt to the jury, but that opinion did not interfere with their deliberations, they said.

They intensely disliked D'Arazzio's attorney, largely because of his condescending attitude and because his arguments seemed unbelievable to them. They strongly sympathized with Wyman's lawyer but felt there was little way he could have won. Of the lead prosecutor, they had mixed opinions. On the whole, they thought her case and presentation were extremely well prepared and that her handling of the evidence was excellent. However, they felt that in her dogged attention to detail, she condescended a bit to their intelligence. They especially resented the maps the prosecution used to orient the jury as to the locations of the establishments mentioned in the case. New Yorkers feel they know their city—certainly east side from west.

The jurors thought the defendants should have worn suits to the trial and that the presence of Wyman's family in court was too dramatic. In fact, one juror confessed to having felt a bit of anger when she saw Wyman's mother brush away a tear during the concluding arguments: "It is too late for that—she could have stopped Rod's bad behavior years ago."

As for the personal effect of their jury service on the jurors, few could say they enjoyed the experience, though most found it fascinating. All were greatly inconvenienced by the time they spent away from their jobs, and though they seemed willing to sit on a jury again, none wanted to do it anytime soon. One juror said she felt dirty, inside and out, at the end of every day of the trial. "The entire things sticks in my throat," she told me, and that seemed to sum up the way most of the jury felt.

Interestingly, nothing of what was discussed outside the jury's hearing would have influenced their verdict. What distressed those jurors who were indecisive had little to do with what the defense was so gallantly trying to include as evidence.

And, of course, the jurors were deeply irritated at the many times they were kept waiting with no explanation. Loss of time was caused by the attorneys disputing the rulings of the judge and by lingering questions about the law, by defense arguments in favor of diminished capacity, by much debate over questionable police practices. It seems incorrect to blame this jury for "the law's delay."

And in the end, the verdict depended not on tricky legal technicalities or esoteric evidence or ornate oratory by the various attorneys. It depended on the jury's common sense and the ability of individual jurors to follow the judge's instructions and come to a group decision, despite differences. It came down to twelve jurors trying to determine what was justice.

[5]
Shooting the Messenger: Does the Jury System Work?

When the ancients received bad news, they sometimes put the messenger bearing it to death. Rising crime is bad news, so are the inefficiencies of the justice system. But putting the whole blame for them on the jury is like slaying the messengers of bad news.

Whether the jury system can be said to be working properly depends on what we expect a jury to be able to do. Juries can and do make errors, of course, but they are not the exclusive source of their own bad judgment.

Much of the criticism of the jury system has to do with whether ordinary people can really understand the evidence and the legal concepts before them. Doubtless there is a problem of terminology, given the low level of education common among jurors. But on the other hand, it is true that the jury gets the dirtiest work, since usually only the complicated cases—complicated from an evidential and legal-principles point of view—ever come before a jury. The open-and-shut matters are usually weeded out.

Some studies have attempted to probe inside the jury jar to see what impressions and abilities in fact lurk there. But the jury in general remains inscrutable, especially in actual deliberation processes.

The fact that this deliberation process cannot be brought under control as neatly as the trial, puts it beyond reach of the judge and attorneys, a frustration that may account for continuing jury system criticism.

The law amounts to rules; the jury system does not. Its first service is to itself and thereby to the larger community. Attorneys tend to view the jury as a convenience for them—great until it backfires. The attorney who commented that "smart" juries are wanted only by the side that is right, also mentioned that "only the side that is looking at its last chance wants a jury at all." Whether the jury system works, and for whom, is a kind of black box debate that seems to grow darker the more you get into it.

The classic study on the workings of the American jury (though not the first) was the Kalven-Zeisel report from the University of Chicago Law School, a pioneer work in the field of law and sociology. In 1966, Henry Kalven and Hans Zeisel published information on 3,576 criminal trials, having questioned 555 trial judges around the United States. Their findings (though their methodology has been criticized by some) have been cited ever since. Recalls Zeisel now, when asked what attracted him to the jury, "That is easy to say—we had to find a study about something important in what was then the new field of law and social science. . . . It was a good study, still alive, and it will remain alive for a long time."

Because of the logistical problems involved in talking to jurors in such a large number of trials, the study used the rate and quality of judge-jury disagreement as a means of measuring jury efficiency. The study found that in about 70 percent of the cases, the judges who heard the cases would have reached the same verdicts as the juries. Disagreement was no more frequent in easy cases than difficult ones—a finding which Zeisel and Kalven call "a stunning refutation of the hypothesis that the jury does not understand." The researchers concluded, using the judge's responses, that 86 percent of cases on trial are easy enough for the jury to understand and that jury misunderstanding rarely causes judge and jury disagreement. It found that when evidence is clearly for acquittal, the jury acquitted 95 percent of the time; it acquitted only 10 percent of the time when evidence for acquittal was weak. The overall conclusion was that "verdicts move basically with the weight and direction of the evidence." Kalven and Zeisel also cite informal studies by individual judges of their own trials between 1930 and 1960, that show the rate of judge-jury disagreement was similar to the rate they (Kalven-Zeisel) found.

According to the Chicago study, about 20 percent of the jury-judge disagreement was due to juror sentiment about the law or the defendant. In other words, when there was doubt about the facts in the jurors' minds, they made room for sentiment to enter into the resolution of the dispute. Strong sentiment might even stimulate a juror to look for weaknesses in the facts or perhaps even oppose the law. In the Wyman-D'Arazzio case, it was exactly this dynamic that the defense wished to engender, hoping the jury would be moved by the drug addiction argument to a different interpretation of the facts.

As the Chicago study put it, "We know from other parts of our jury study that the jury does not often consciously and explicitly yield to sentiment in the teeth of the law. Rather it yields to sentiment in the apparent process of resolving doubts as to evidence."

But disagreement between judge and jury also derives from other bases, and the Chicago study suggests two. One basis is witness credibility—a jury may award more or less credibility to witnesses than a judge. If so, this may be because attorneys, in voir dire, emphasize that testing credibility is part of everyday life. Judges too are more jaded about lying.

An even more prevalent basis, the study suggests, is that juries probably have different standards for "reasonable doubt." Juries tend to hold higher standards concerning how much proof overcomes the presumption of innocence in a criminal case. This too is partly because attorneys plunge the jurors in the concept, and partly because the layperson is perhaps less cynical than a judge, on this point. There is no threshold to signal when "reasonable" has been reached, so the jury does the best it can. A judge's view is one person's view of reasonable; the jury's, in theory, is the average of what the community defines as reasonable. That the two views do not always line up is not indicative of a weakness or inefficiency in the system, but a tribute to it and part of its inherent value—in effect, precisely the point of the jury system.

One of the Chicago study's findings was that when the judge and jury disagreed, it was usually over cases in which the jury had found in favor of the defendant. Using a very widely circulated questionnaire, the study attempted to quantify the bases for disagreement, and unsurprisingly, the study concluded that approximately 21 percent of the disagreement derived from such factors as feelings of sympathy for the defendant or a conviction that the victim contributed to the fault. Only 2 percent of the disagreement was based on information the judge knew but the jury did not, such as the defendant's prior criminal record, which is usually not admissible evidence on the question of guilt or innocence in a specific case. However, the study did conclude that the jury has suspicions about a defendant's record. When a defendant takes the stand, his previous court record may be used by the jury in evaluating the defendant's credibility as a witness, though it is usually instructed not to take the record into consideration when deciding guilt or innocence in the specific case on trial. The Chicago study concludes that in most cases, if the record of the defendant had been made available to the jury, the jury and judge would probably still agree on the verdict. The researchers call this the "price" in "unjustified acquittals" which the system is willing to pay for avoiding prejudice in other cases where shared information could lead to an unjust conviction.

While the jury tends to be more lenient on matters of reasonable doubt, neither judge nor jury, on balance, seemed more skeptical or gullible. The study concluded that the jury was more susceptible to being swayed by a strong prosecutional case, though it was also more likely to acquit in protest of what it perceived as police or prosecutorial abuse. Still the jury often fails to give the benefit of the doubt in close cases, if it does not like the behavior of the defendant—such as use of offensive language or style of dress in court. These "little things" can and do make a difference. In the 1983 federal Brink's conspiracy case (not to be confused with New York State's Brink's cases tried the same year for armed robbery and murder), courtroom watchers believe that the behavior of one defendant in court—in particular, her falling asleep during the trial and badgering witnesses as they testified—helped the jury convict her.

Even given obvious disagreements, judges let jury verdicts stand in 56 percent of the cases where a jury reached a verdict the judge would not have. And considering how much effort trial lawyers expend in wooing the jury, it is notable that the Chicago study found only 4 percent of the disagreement could be justifiably attributed to lawyer's performance—that is, something lawyers did or did not do, their personality as far as the jury was concerned, and so forth.

For the most part, a juror's mind is made up after the trial ends and before deliberations begin, according to the Chicago study. The initial majority opinions usually carry the verdict. Kalven and Zeisel conclude, "Deliberation is the route by which small-group pressures produce consensus out of the initial majority." The deliberation then is the forge of the decision, not its ingredients, and according to Zeisel, only 5 percent of juries hang—that is, remain unable to reach a verdict.

Overall, from this study, one could conclude that insofar as juries base their decisions on the evidence most of the time, the system is, in fact, working.

Given its power, what keeps the jury from being a "wildcat" operation—to use Kalven-Zeisel terminology—is the legal system itself. As Kalven and Zeisel noted, there is little gap between what the law prescribes and what the average juror believes. Presumably, were this gap to grow too wide, the jury system could not function. Finally, the group enterprise will almost naturally neutralize outlandish ideas. It is hard to push a large group of common sense types against common sense—a frequently used argument for maintaining the jury of twelve, rather than reducing the size.

Although the study could not conclude objectively whether the jury system is worth keeping, it did characterize the system as a "daring effort in human arrangement to work out a solution to the tensions between law and equity and anarchy."

The research in the Chicago study gave rise to more research. Dr. Rita J. Simon of the University of Illinois in a 1980 report entitled, "The Jury: Its Role in American Society," tended to corroborate the Chicago findings on deliberation, although she concluded that among 55 percent of the jurors she polled, there was "no conflict between the opinions they held before they entered the jury room and the subsequent group decision." Still, 16 percent of the juries she questioned "hung," and for 23 percent of the jurors, the group deliberation process caused them to be swayed to the majority view. However she concluded that "in slightly more than one out of three juries, the group verdicts differed from those which the jurors would have reported, had they been polled individually, immediately following the trial."

A third of the verdicts seems enough to justify saying that the deliberation process earns its keep. While it may be difficult, and rare, for one person to sway an entire jury, two persons can argue and hold out for a long time. There is little way to know how often holdouts give in simply to avoid a hung jury, and less way to know who correctly determined the facts.

A friend of mine sat on a murder case jury, and was convinced of the defendant's guilt, even though the evidence was entirely circumstantial. A cynic about the efficiency of the state, he nevertheless believed the case an open-and-shut conviction and was shocked to see, during deliberations, that he was the lone vote against acquittal. He tried to argue, but could not beat back eleven opinions. He began to doubt himself and, in the end, succumbed. Later, he talked to the prosecutor, who told him that not only had the defendant committed the crime charged, the defendant had had a long criminal record which, of course, the jury knew nothing about. My friend did not think that knowledge of the record would have swayed his jury, but there is no way to know. Here, of course, was an "unjust acquittal" with which the rest of us have to live.

In 1983, a case of one bold jury member forcing an incorrect civil verdict came to light in a libel suit involving highly visible entities, the Mobil Oil Corporation and the Washington *Post*. The president of Mobil, William P. Tavoulareas, sued the *Post* for $50 million, on grounds that articles the *Post* had published about him had damaged his reputation and that of his son, Peter. The *Post* articles alleged that in 1974 Mobil's president established his son—"set him up"—in a shipping business which thereafter did exclusive business with Mobil. A second article alleged that Tavoulareas violated securities laws by failing to report the relationship between Mobil and his son's company. A key ingredient for libel, in the legal sense, is that the material must have been published with "actual malice"—that is, despite knowledge that the articles were false or likely to be false. In this case, it was not enough to prove the articles damaged Tavoulareas' reputation; his attorneys had to prove the *Post* intended to damage his reputation by printing falsehoods.

A six-member—three male, three female—jury found the *Post* had, indeed, committed libel; it awarded Tavoulareas $1.8 million in punitive damages and $250,000 in compensatory damages. Nine months later, a federal judge set aside the verdict because, he concluded, no evidence had been presented to prove the *Post* knew the articles to be false. Willful malice, or reckless disregard for the truth, were not proved, according to the judge.

As it turned out, most of the jury had not agreed with its own verdict, but two jurors—in particular a young man with ambitions to be a lawyer—had hounded the other four into accepting a libel vote. This was no mindless "runaway" jury, but one which was a victim of group dynamics; its good sense might not have been as easily overturned if the jury had been larger, or if jury selection had weeded out the aspiring lawyer. Also, since federal juries are questioned rather superficially by judges, the voir dire procedure did not expose the potential juror's ambitions clearly enough to signal attorneys that one juror might be eager to maneuver the deliberations. The judge had asked only if the man had ever studied law, not whether he wished or intended to study law. Especially unfortunate was the fact that the points of law that the juror pushed on his fellow jurors were incorrect and contrary to the judge's charge.

The jury's first ballot, according to Steven Brill writing in *The American Lawyer* magazine, was 4–2 in favor of the *Post*. But the would-be lawyer, aided by one other juror, succeeded in convincing the rest that the *Post* had had the obligation to prove the stories correct. In fact, under the libel law, the burden was on Tavoulareas to prove them false and to prove that the *Post* knew them to be false. After eighteen hours of deliberation, the jury turned in its verdict. When the jury was polled, each member said he or she agreed, when in fact, several members later admitted they had given in just to end the ordeal of deliberation. Brill quoted one juror as having said, "It was go with him [the aspiring lawyer] or go and be a stupid hung jury."

To be sure, there were other factors at work here: unclear instructions on the law from the judge and unclear legal battling by the attorneys, which failed to keep the jury focused on the essential legal question—did the *Post* know the articles were false? The case flies in the face of all empirical research: One jury member *did* convince the rest; deliberation *did* change an initial majority opinion; the jury *did* fail to understand the evidence and *did* fail, in the end, to deliberate in maximum good faith by allowing individual jurors to give in rather than stick to their convictions. Given the notoriety of the plaintiff and defendant, the verdict also drew national attention, damaging the *Post's* reputation and credibility at least until the verdict was overturned. But the *Post* cannot sue the jury; the jury went wrong, but it has no responsibility for doing so. It is a case often used to point out the potential for breakdown inherent among juries.

In Atlanta, Georgia, in May 1982, one juror raised the ire of the entire city. Mr. Beoties Emory, a thirty-nine-year-old metal finisher for the Ford Motor Company, was on a jury which convicted "Amp" Wiley of murder. Wiley, a twenty-two-year-old black man, was accused of brutally stomping to death a white woman while she and a friend were having lunch in a park. It was a gruesome crime, which justifiably horrified the community. After a trial that lasted a week, the jury took only one hour and forty minutes to vote Wiley's conviction.

However, Georgia is a death-penalty state, and when a defendant has been convicted on a capital charge, the jury must also vote unanimously on whether to recommend execution. During jury selection, all potential jurors are "death qualified"—that is, they are asked if they could, in conscience, invoke a death penalty should there be a conviction. Those who, at this juncture, say that they could not under any circumstances invoke capital punishment, may be excused from the jury panel by the prosecution, for cause.

Emory had said that he had no objection to the death penalty. However, when the time came, he could not vote to invoke it, even given the heinous nature of the crime. The jury deliberated another nine and a half hours, but Emory would not give in. Though the first ballot had been 6—6 on the death penalty, all jurors but Emory eventually agreed to the death penalty. The foreman reported the deadlock to the judge, who was so incensed that he ordered the foreman to identify the holdout juror in open court. The judge thus exposed Emory to public scorn, and even suggested that Emory had committed perjury when he had said he could invoke the death penalty.

Emory's position was that he could, in principle, invoke death, but not in this case. Others jurors reported that he talked about love and mercy in the deliberation room and about how he did not feel the crime warranted death for the defendant. Another juror quoted him as having said, "After all, he let the other girl live." Emory, a black man, was suspected of harboring sympathy for Wiley, because the defendant was black. Emory had acid thrown into his locker at work and received anonymous death threats over the telephone at home. The ACLU of Georgia brought the judge before a Judicial Qualifications Commission hearing, charging he had acted unethically by exposing secret jury deliberations in public. Emory, in turn, sued the judge in federal court for damages, on the grounds that the judge's action had caused Emory "humiliation, embarrassment, and mental distress." Emory lost his suit and has since refused to discuss the events. In the meantime, "Amp" Wiley was sentenced to six consecutive life sentences, plus forty-five years. Still, somehow, he will be eligible for parole in seven years. When, during the deliberations over the death penalty, the jury asked what Wiley's parole status would be, the judge refused to answer the question and told them to continue deliberating.

While the Emory case demonstrated the power of one person, it also exposed weakness in other people, including the judge. And although some may call it a failure of the jury system, the case simply showed that in extraordinary circumstances, people can behave unpredictably.

One of the interesting questions about jury system workings, raised by the original Chicago study, was whether agreement between judge and jury was per se a measure of jury efficiency. That the two agreed said nothing really about why they agreed or if their reasoning was the same or even similar. Also, even a high rate of agreement is not perfection; if there is agreement in 75 percent of the cases, and these represent "correct" verdicts, then 25 percent is an awfully high number of "incorrect" verdicts.

In 1979, in London, researchers John Baldwin and Michael McConville published results of a fascinating study, in which judges and police officers participated in evaluating jury verdicts. (The Senate of the U.K. Bar refused to let any individual lawyers participate in the study because their statements might "impair the close relationship between client and counsel," and because "the jury might be less likely to give credence to the arguments of counsel if they knew that counsel might privately hold a different view of the case.") The project had been stimulated by, among other things, statements by a leading British police officer that the jury's acquittal rate was excessive, especially in cases where the defendants were professional criminals. But the empirical research did not bear this out.

The report concluded that professional criminals—although they were quite successful in eluding capture and harsh penalties when convicted—were only rarely acquitted altogether and only "exceptionally" in questionable circumstances. As for rate of acquittal, the researchers concluded, "There is no proper rate for the job." Still, they found more "questionable" acquittals than did previous research in the United States, and on this basis they suggest that "trial by jury is a relatively crude instrument for establishing the truth." However the researchers were much more worried about questionable jury convictions than questionable acquittals. Worse, because of the sacrosanct nature of the jury, its verdict is difficult to overturn. If the trial was conducted fairly and properly, then a wrongfully convicted person has no remedy, because there are no points of law on which to appeal, and the jury has no obligation to explain the reasons for its decision. Baldwin and McConville contend forcefully "that the questionable conviction of those charged with serious offenses, resulting in devastating social consequences for the defendant and his family, in circumstances which effectively pre-empt any review, is sufficient to raise doubts about the very basis of trial by jury."

The talk is strong, but it sharply focuses the discussion about what jury efficiency really means and what can and cannot be known about it.

Few people have been able to report on what transpires in deliberation rooms. The Chicago Jury Project did once put tape recorders into the deliberation room, with the consent of the federal judge involved in hearing the cases, but they were strongly criticized for this and desisted. In fact, Henry Kalven was called before the U.S. Senate Subcommittee to Investigate the Administration of the Internal Security Act and other Internal Security Laws of the Committee of the Judiciary. After Kalven's death,

Zeisel wrote in an article that the committee, in a McCarthy era mood, "seemed anxious to show that the research effort . . . was a Communist-inspired plot to subvert the American jury system." But since then, to my knowledge, no one but sworn jurors have been privy to deliberations. And only when jurors are willing to talk after the deliberation can any part of the picture emerge.

The jury defies definitive study since no two juries are alike. For example, Rita J. Simon described results of studies with experimental juries which confirmed that, on balance, it is rare for one person to be able to convert eleven people or to hold out under pressure for a different verdict. Kalven-Zeisel questionnaires, sent to jurors, suggested the same pattern. Yet, as we have seen, on occasion this can and does happen.

The public does not hear or care much about trends and empirical results, but rather about exceptions. Exceptions stick in the mind; exceptions attract coverage. And when people hear of "travesties" of justice, the jury system is blamed and the jury system is said to have failed. However, jury verdicts do not derive from thin air, and blaming the jury perhaps misfocuses fault. We can either shoot the messenger, or we can examine the source of the messages.

[6]
Nuts and Bolts: How Big, How Long, How Come?

We speak of *the* jury system when in fact there is no one way of doing things where juries are concerned. Each state and local jurisdiction varies, and the federal courts are something else again. Most of the framework currently applied to the jury system has been defined by Supreme Court rulings.

The right to trial by jury in federal criminal matters is guaranteed by the Sixth Amendment to the Constitution and has been held by the Supreme Court, in *Duncan* v. *Louisiana* (391 U.S. 145, 1968), to be incorporated into the Fourteenth Amendment definition of "due process" of law. Therefore, state courts are also obliged to provide jury trials to defendants, though states are essentially free to adopt their own rules as far as jury workings are concerned. However, juveniles on trial in juvenile court, even those over sixteen, have not been held to have adult rights to jury trial. Petty offenses, usually misdemeanors that do not carry a penalty of incarceration, may also be tried without juries. The Supreme Court has ruled that defendants may waive their right to a jury trial, and that plea bargaining—promises of more lenient sentencing recommendations made by prosecution offices in return for a guilty plea—is not an unconstitutional violation of the defendant's right to trial by jury.

In many state courts, the consent of the prosecutor is not needed for a waiver of jury trial rights by the defendant, but this is not true of cases tried in federal courts. The Federal Criminal Code states that a defendant may waive a jury trial only "with the approval of the court and the consent of the government." Currently, however, lawyers are debating whether the trial court judge may overrule the government's refusal to waive a jury trial. This debate received some prominence in the trial of the Rev. Sun Myung Moon and Takeru Kamiyama in July 1982. Moon, a Korean resettled in the United States, is well-known as the leader of the Unification Church, whose disciples are nicknamed Moonies. He and his associate were charged with federal income tax fraud, obstructing justice, and perjury. Moon's attorneys sought a waiver of jury rights, on the grounds that Moon would not be able to secure a fair and impartial jury because of extensive publicity about how Moonies are kidnapped or brainwashed into joining the Unification Church. Moon's attorneys argued in court and on appeal that Moon's jurors would almost necessarily harbor a religious hostility toward Moon, and thus a jury trial would be akin to religious persecution. The United States prosecutor in the case, Jo Ann Harris, refused to consent to a waiver of the jury because, as she explained to me, "The government believed that it was in the public interest to have a jury trial here, and it has nothing to do with punishing anyone for anything." She continued: "In our judgment, in this case, like a lot of cases with high visibility, it is very important that the process appear to be normal and regular. . . . It is important for community acceptance, particularly in a case where there is controversy."

Mrs. Harris' decision has been criticized by attorneys who believe the government refused the waiver because it thought Moon was likelier to be convicted by a jury than by a judge. (In fact, at the U.S. Court of Appeals hearing on this case, March 23, 1983, Judge Ralph K. Winter commented to Mrs. Harris, "I would almost prefer to have you say 'we had a right to it because we thought we would do better with a jury' which is the reason I think you chose it anyway.") Mrs. Harris denies that and emphatically argues that if it had been clear during voir dire that an impartial jury could not be selected, she would have consented to a bench trial, that is, a trial before a judge alone.

As it happened, after seven days of jury selection, sixty-three out of two hundred venirepersons were questioned to secure the panel of twelve, plus seventeen more to obtain six alternates. The presiding judge, Gerard G. Goettal, stated that he was satisfied that the jury was impartial. The trial proceeded, and the defendants were found guilty on all counts.

The defense appealed the verdict, maintaining before the U.S. Court of Appeals—and subsequently in a petition to the U.S. Supreme Court—that Moon's trial before a jury "doomed" him to "conviction based upon religious prejudice" and that it was a "constitutional error of the first magnitude."

Jury verdicts are all but sacrosanct. In criminal cases, it is only convictions that can be appealed to a higher court—an acquittal cannot be questioned. (However, if new evidence leads to new and different charges—sufficiently new and different to avoid the double-jeopardy protections—a defendant could face a new trial; this is what happens when defendants acquitted of murder in state courts are retried in federal court on conspiracy charges.) Even convictions can be overturned in appellate court only on points of law—often, in fact, on errors in the judge's charge to the jury. But the jury's verdict, itself, is never the basis for an appeal.

Civil cases are somewhat different. The right to trial by jury in civil cases is guaranteed by the Seventh Amendment; the original language calls for jury trials when the amount "shall exceed twenty dollars." Both parties in a civil suit must agree if the jury right is to be waived. However, the judge may set aside a civil verdict on appeal, on the basis of points of law or a review of the evidence; he or she may also change or reduce the amount of monetary damages awarded by the jury.

Nevertheless discrediting a jury verdict is never undertaken lightly. Even if jurors themselves have second thoughts, they may not impeach themselves by publicly seeking to undo what they have done. Attorneys—as in the Moon case—may impeach a verdict by alleging juror misconduct during the trial, but this is often difficult to prove.

Normally, jury deliberations are not subject to dissection after the fact, especially not officially by a judge and the attorneys involved. However, in the Moon case, trial judge Goettal held a highly unusual posttrial hearing with three of the jurors. This hearing derived from the fact that one juror, by giving a posttrial interview to a local newspaper, attracted the attention of a private investigator, who paid a call on her. He discussed the deliberations with her—"leading her down a garden path," according to Mrs. Harris—so that she described comments the jurors made to each other throughout the trial. Among other revelations, she mentioned that there had been newspapers in the jury room—which may have carried articles about the Moon case the jurors could have read—and that another juror had commented during the trial that the defense might have been trying to intimidate her. Apparently, this juror speculated to her colleagues that a hole had been found in a window in her home and that it might have been caused by a BB shot by agents of the defense. She also suspected that the back-ending of her car might have been the doings of the defense as well.

The private investigator, who himself had a criminal record, sold a tape recording of his conversations with the juror to an attorney for the Unification Church. Apparently some hints were also given that money would be paid for juror statements that would help the defense discredit the verdict.

This tape recording was presented to Judge Goettal, who referred to the methods as "sleazy and unattractive," and he called in the jurors involved for questioning. Goettal eventually dismissed the defense motion for a new trial, concluding "the credible evidence established that there was no basis for the proceeding." He also issued an order preventing the defendants, their agents, and their attorneys as well as the government's attorneys or agents from "communicating with, or contacting in any manner whatsoever any juror."

Though twelve-member juries are still most common, dating at least to the time of the ancient Greeks, the U.S. Supreme Court has held that the Constitution nowhere states that a jury must be of this size. In *Williams* v. *Florida* (399 U.S. 78, 1970), Justice White wrote in the majority opinion that the number twelve had been an "historical accident, unrelated to the great purposes which gave rise to the jury in the first place."

As of 1983, seven states permit juries of less than twelve in some felony matters, though all states require twelve in capital offenses. Twenty-four states use juries of less than twelve in misdemeanors. In civil cases, twenty-two states permit juries of less than twelve. In 1981, a man charged with criminal mischief in Boulder, Colorado, requested a jury of one and cited wording in the Colorado statute: "The defendant in any felony or misdemeanor may with the approval of the court elect to be tried by a number of jurors less than the number to which he would otherwise be entitled." The defendant's attorney believed one person would be less likely to wish to assume the burden of conviction alone, and the trial judge agreed with the defense's request. The Appellate Court, however, ruling on a writ filed by the prosecution, reversed that decision and ruled that six was an absolute minimum.

There is inconsistency in the law about whether verdicts must be unanimous. The U.S. Supreme Court ruled that the Constitution did not require unanimous verdicts in criminal proceedings, but in practice all federal verdicts, criminal and civil, must today be unanimous. All states still require unanimous verdicts in felonies, but five states permit majority verdicts in some misdemeanors. In civil cases, thirty-one states permit nonunanimous verdicts.

The American Bar Association, while calling for more research on the effect of jury size and the unanimity requirement, made the following recommendations in its Standards Relating to Juror Use and Management, issued in July 1982: .

• Criminal juries should consist of twelve members if a sentence of more than six months' confinement is at stake, of at least six members if sentence would be six months or less, and that all verdicts in capital cases should be unanimous.

• Civil juries should have no fewer than six members and no more than twelve, and nonunanimous verdicts are acceptable so long as they do not represent the opinion of less than three-fourths of the jury.

The idea that a jury could consist of fewer than twelve members was established only in the 1970s, in a series of U.S. Supreme Court decisions which went to the heart of prevailing customs where juries were concerned. In 1970, in *Williams* v. *Florida*, the Supreme Court ruled that Williams' conviction for armed robbery by a jury of only six had not violated his rights under the Sixth Amendment. In his majority opinion, Mr. Justice White wrote that not only had the number twelve lasted for several thousand years through accidental tradition only, but that the jury's role "to prevent government oppression" was "not a function of the particular number of the body that makes up the jury. To be sure, the number should probably be large enough to promote group deliberation, free from outside attempts at intimidation, and to provide a fair possibility for obtaining a representative cross section of the community. But we find little reason to think that these goals are in any meaningful sense less likely to be achieved when the jury numbers six than when it numbers twelve— particularly if the requirement of unanimity is retained."

This decision opened the door to other modifications in jury tradition. In 1972, a Supreme Court decision in *Johnson* v. *Louisiana* (406 U.S. 356), held that when the defendant was convicted by nine out of twelve jurors, rather than unanimously, the due process guaranteed in the Fourteenth Amendment had not been violated. Johnson argued that since the standard of proof in a criminal case is "beyond reasonable doubt," three dissenting jury members meant reasonable doubt had lingered in the jury room. A 5–4 U.S. Supreme Court majority ruled that disagreement among jurors did not necessarily mean that there had been reasonable doubt of guilt. Also, in 1972, in *Apodaca* v. *Oregon* (406 U.S. 404), the Supreme Court ruled that a non-unanimous verdict in criminal cases did not violate Sixth Amendment guarantees to jury trial. In 1973, six-member juries in civil cases was upheld in the case *Colgrove* v. *Battin* (413 U.S. 149). Then, in 1978, the Supreme Court in *Ballew* v. *Georgia* (435 U.S. 233) ruled that a five-member jury, at least in criminal trials, was a violation of the Sixth Amendment.

There was no real agreement on why five was bad and six was good, except that the Court did cite statistical studies of group dynamics, which tended to suggest that the reliability and representational nature of this size group would be diminished enough to suggest a Constitutional violation. The dissenting view, however, referred to the statistical work as "numerology." Then, in *Burch* v. *Louisiana* in 1979 (441 U.S. 130), the Court ruled a majority 5–1 verdict in a six-member jury for criminal matters was also a violation of defendant rights under the Sixth and Fourteenth Amendment.

Thus, since then, the U.S. Supreme Court has ruled for criminal cases that six-member juries are constitutionally the minimum size and that juries of this size must reach unanimity. Juries of larger size in criminal cases are thus constitutionally able to submit majority verdicts, as are juries in civil cases. State courts are free to implement jury procedures that the federal government does not.

Behind the argument to reduce jury size and eliminate unanimity is the concern for greater efficiency. But there is no research to show that smaller juries make trials move along more quickly. In fact, once the jury is in place, no delay can reasonably be blamed on them. Deliberation time is but a fraction of trial length. There is some data to support the contention that smaller juries deliberate less long, and if it is true that deliberation smooths out doubts among jurors, then there will be fewer doubts to smooth among fewer jurors.

A 1973 study by the Center for Jury Studies, now based at the National Center for State Courts in Williamsburg, Virginia, investigated the change from twelve-member to six-member juries in Washington, D.C. The study showed there was no time savings with smaller juries, just with smaller jury panels. Professor Hans Zeisel remains a strong critic of both reducing jury size and nonunanimity, arguing that verdicts will necessarily be different. He suggests that smaller juries in criminal matters would lead to "fewer hung juries, more findings of guilt, and among them relatively fewer convictions for lesser included offenses." In civil cases, he suggests that when a jury of twelve deliberates, it is much more likely to reach a verdict reflective of the community's view of fair damages than a jury half that size. Other studies have shown that while verdicts in civil cases do not change much with jury size, monetary awards can be erratic. This is because a small jury's decision is more likely to reflect the view of the most persuasive members. Other researchers, most often using statistical models, have provided evidence that jury size makes no difference. And still other researchers refute that conclusion and question the methodology. The only real conclusion that one can draw about the effect of jury size on verdicts, has been that the effect is subtle. There has yet to be a study whose results stand, on either side of the debate, without severe criticism from the academic and legal community concerned.

Research is a little clearer on unanimity questions. Rita J. Simon of the University of Illinois, a prominent figure in the study of the jury, recently issued a report comparing criminal trial juries—those deliberating with a five out of six majority rule against those deliberating with a unanimous rule. Results show that unanimous juries have been "marginally more likely to hang," and "significantly less likely to convict when given multiple conviction alternatives."

In civil cases, unanimity does not seem to make a difference either in verdicts or in the size of awards for damages. Researchers attribute this to the fact that arriving at an amount of monetary damages almost always requires compromise discussions, whether juries have twelve or six members.

One of Chief Justice Warren Burger's most oft-repeated suggestions is that jury trials should for all intents and purposes be eliminated in civil matters. He also advocates the elimination of juries in long, complex trials. Often now, lawyers do waive their jury right in these cases. However, the U.S. Court of Appeals has consistently refused to recognize that complexity per se defeats the right to a jury trial in civil matters. The Court pointed out that it would become difficult to "draw the line between those cases which are, and those which are not, too complex for a jury." After all, who is to say what is complex for whom, and decision rule depends on completeness of discussion. Though the research is fraught with contradiction, some general patterns have been discerned, according to Dr. Michael J. Saks, who reviewed the literature in a book entitled, *The Psychology of the Courtroom*. Saks suggested there is little doubt that under unanimous decision rules, "deliberations took a longer time, juries were more likely to become hung, minority factions shared more equally in the communication, more communication occurred in total and jurors were more certain of the correctness of their verdict." Also, members of minority factions were more satisfied with the deliberations, more conflict was generated, more opinion change occurred, more jurors felt "justice was done," and there was more minority influence.

Another key question has to do with composition of smaller juries. It would seem clear that the smaller the total number of players on a team, the less likely the team is to include representatives from the widest possible number of different ethnic and minority groups that comprise the community. In fact, in a dissenting opinion in *Colgrove* v. *Battin* in 1973, which upheld the six-person jury in civil cases, Justice Thurgood Marshall wrote: "It is, of course, intuitively obvious that the smaller the size of the jury, the less likely it is to represent a fair cross section of community viewpoints." Fear that smaller juries would not represent the broadest possible spectrum of the community is what led the Federal Judicial Conference to reject the idea of six-member juries for federal criminal trials. Of course, one must infer that the federal government had decided to accept less broad representation in civil trials, since the six-member jury there is by now the virtual rule.

Though in 1971, Chief Justice Burger stated that $4 million per year would be saved if all federal juries consisted of six members, a later report by the Administrative Office of the U.S. Courts reduced the projection to $1.8 million. In theory, half the number of jurors means half the amount of dollars paid in juror fees (and support funds should jurors be sequestered). But other jury costs do not necessarily decrease, as Professor Jon M. Van Dyke, of the University of California's Hastings College of Law, pointed out in his book *Jury Selection Procedures: Our Uncertain Commitment to Representative Panels.* Whether the jury panel will be hewn down to six or remain at twelve, the judge must provide the same general instructions to the jury and pose the same general questions during voir dire. Voir dire time might be reduced, but deliberation time, though perhaps shorter when smaller juries are involved, is not entirely wasted time for the court system, since almost always judges and attorneys go about other business during the period.

The suggestions that juries be smaller and majority verdicts be accepted may have political implications. They seek to move the system faster and to give the public the idea that the justice system is cognizant of public worry about crime and that crime is being punished. Both smaller juries and majority verdicts are publicly perceived to be proprosecution modifications. In fact, in dissenting in *Apodaca* v. *Oregon*, which affirmed that nonunanimous verdicts in criminal trials did not violate the Sixth Amendment guarantee to jury trial, Justice William O. Douglas wrote that he wondered how the presumption of innocence would fare after the decision had been handed down.

Moving the system faster leads to moving the system "surer," and there seems to be little real debate about the fact that smaller juries would tend to hang less than the present approximately 5 percent "hang" rate. The system wants decisions, not equivocation. But a "hung" jury is not a failure of the jury; perhaps it is the opposite—a case where a minority viewpoint is able to hold the majority at bay. Though the majority is probably most often right, the recognition that the majority is not *necessarily* right underlies the very rationale for preserving the jury system. Also, juries do not always get hung because of the obstinacy of one person—there may indeed be a substantial question of fact, a reasonable doubt, a lack of preponderance in the evidence. If juries can deliver verdicts based on majority view, then those questions of fact are left aside in the interests of bringing in a verdict, almost by hook or crook.

The Supreme Court has ruled in *Johnson* v. *Louisiana*, that where reasonable doubt is concerned, the presence of dissent does not by itself mean that the standard of proof-beyond-a-reasonable-doubt has been sidestepped. But when a unanimous verdict is required, the presence of dissent means dissent must be heard and reacted to. Under majority rule, especially if the majority is large enough, dissent can be ignored as irrelevant and inconvenient. Once there is enough opinion for a majority verdict, deliberation can stop. In the Wyman-D'Arazzio trial, for example, the initial vote was 8–4. That four-person minority had legitimate doubts, not about guilt necessarily but about whether the case had been proved beyond reasonable doubt. Four out of twelve is, of course, one-third, which would seem to indicate reasonable doubt, yet a majority rule would have let the doubt through. A few hours more of deliberation brought the group into unanimity. Several jurors told me that simply knowing they would have to agree helped them deliberate in maximum faith. Though majority verdicts might be more practical, they represent an erosion of the principle that the whole community—that is, a whole cross section—decides what is reasonable.

If one of the jury's functions, at least in criminal cases, is to prevent the conviction of innocent people, then, it is argued, the jury's function must also be to let every voice be heard. Majority rule is not as dependable a safeguard as unanimity. Also, dissenting jurors might be extremely dissatisfied and publicize their dissent, perhaps creating an uproar over what would otherwise be routine cases. Defendants convicted by majorities would perhaps have grounds for appeal that they would not otherwise have had, thus extending the time expenditure far beyond that of an unanimous jury trial. A unanimous jury is a unit; a mixed jury is split into two camps, making a battleground of what is supposed to be community justice. Cases may well split community opinion, but a verdict that intractably splits a jury ought to be unsatisfactory.

Finally, changing the operations of the jury, without changing the operations of the larger legal system, nets only superficial results. Blaming jury size for court delay does not attack the deeper causes of slow pace. It is the ameliorable, concrete inefficiencies of the jury system that yield unrepresentative and uninformed juries. Altering jury size and deliberation style without making other changes is a bit like trying to fix the music after it has come out of the horn.

[7]
Many Are Called . . .

The jury selection process is one of the most controversial aspects of the jury system, because of the relationship it has to the movement of cases through the courts. The prevailing idea among jury reformers is that jury selection, no matter how long it takes, takes too long and could take less long. How the selection works and whether it does take too long is a matter that can be decided only on a case-by-case basis. But it is true that there are significant differences between the theory of jury selection and its practice.

The first step in jury selection, for both civil and criminal trials, is the "wheel" or venire. This lists eligible jurors—drawn, in theory, from the population of those citizens of the United States, age eighteen or older, who can communicate in English. How jurisdictions gather the venire varies greatly, but most common is the use of voter registration lists. Voter lists are the most convenient source of names from an administrative point of view. But since only about 60 percent of eligible voters register, any jury list drawn from a voter's list will, by definition, exclude 40 percent of potential venire persons, often minorities, who tend not to be registered voters. To improve the reach of a jury list, in an increasing number of jurisdictions, voter lists are supplemented by drivers' license lists, tax rolls, welfare rolls, telephone directories, census, and other civic lists which tap populations the voters list would miss. These lists are pooled, and then names are randomly drawn, now often by computer, and summonses are issued. In theory, in a truly random selection, all names have an equal chance of being chosen, and no name should be chosen more frequently than every two years, at least not within the same tier of the legal system—county, state, federal.

In a random pool, every one is theoretically a "peer," and, indeed, a jury composed of peers is at the heart of the system. However, there is substantial debate on what "peers" means. The concept of peers or *pares* derives from the use of these words in the Magna Carta, conferring the idea that the King's authority was second to the right of the accused to a trial by "peers."

Originally the word meant "equals." A baron's peer was another baron. In 1224, according to Lloyd Moore in his book on the history of the jury, Botun, a Jew, and his wife, were accused of murdering a Christian servant. Two juries heard the case—one consisting of twelve Jews and the other of eighteen Christians (peers, apparently could be unequal in number). The Jewish jury acquitted, and when the judge questioned the Christians, they too thought Botun innocent, though they had doubts about his family's innocence. In 1302, a knight objected to a jury due to try him because it did not have knight members. He succeeded in having a second jury of knights impaneled. Under Edward I, foreign merchants living in England involved in other than capital cases were entitled to juries of six foreign merchants and six other peers from the venue of the trial. By 1352, another statute required that in matters where both parties were foreign, the jury would consist of only foreigners. Merchant juries, in cases involving merchants, continued in England until the early 1970s and, according to Jon Van Dyke in *Jury Selection Procedures*, the English had also regularly called juries of specialists. Van Dyke's example is a jury of cooks to try cases of persons accused of selling bad food. Peerage thus implied knowledge on the part of the jurors of the general area in question in the trial.

In modern United States, it has even been argued that, in criminal cases, knowledge of the circumstances of a defendant is so crucial that only members of his or her class, even ethnic group, are fit jurors in the case. Thus, whites would try whites, blacks blacks, etc. This argument, however, is not only extreme, it is also destructive, because it erodes what surely is the most appropriate definition for "peer"—one of the community.

In an essay published in 1852 called "On the Trial by Jury," the writer Lysander Spooner put significant emphasis on the fact that trial by peers actually means trial by "the country" and that the decision reached should not be substantially different from what the entire country would agree on, were it present at the trial. Spooner, writing in Boston, said that "now, in every criminal trial, the jury are told that the accused 'has, for trial, put himself upon the country, which country you (the jury) are.'" This instruction is still frequently used in courts. In that we depend on the jury to provide a distillation of the country's view, we rely on a representative cross section—supposedly pulled through random lists—to be present. But this idea has evolved in fits and starts.

In its 1880 decision in *Strauder* v. *West Virginia* (100 U.S. 303), the U.S. Supreme Court stated, "The very idea of a jury is a body of men composed of peers or equals of the persons whose rights it is selected or summoned to determine; that is, of his neighbors, fellows, associates, persons having the same legal status in society as that which he holds."

But in practice, discrimination—racial, sexual, and economic— has narrowed jury lists throughout history, so that mostly the names of affluent white males appeared on the panels until well into the midtwentieth century and, in some jurisdictions, even today. Spooner called every jury in the United States in 1852 "illegal" because the universe of the eligible had been whittled down to property owners and those appointed by the state. By restricting the eligibility lists, Spooner wrote, "Government has usurped the authority of selecting the jurors that were to sit in judgement upon its own acts."

Blacks were granted rights to be jurors through the *Strauder* decision, but theory eluded practice, as civil rights battles became implicit in jury selection challenges. The *Strauder* decision found a West Virginia law, which explicitly limited eligibility to "white male persons," unconstitutional in view of the Fourteenth Amendment. However, the court allowed that states could establish "qualifications." A state, the court said, may "confine the selection to males, to freeholders, to citizens, to persons within certain ages, or to persons having education qualifications. We do not believe the 14th Amendment was ever intended to prohibit this." Those confines effectively continued racial and sexual discrimination. In 1909, in *Thomas* v. *Texas* (212 U.S. 278), the Supreme Court gave further support to discriminatory selection procedures. Thomas, a black man, had been convicted of rape in Harris County, Texas, where 25 percent of the population was black. His plea to the Supreme Court was based on the fact that state procedures, upheld by the Appellate Court of Texas, were unconstitutional because no more than one black had ever sat on a grand jury in the county and no blacks had been called on the venire from which Thomas' jury was chosen. Other material showed that throughout Harris County, roughly only one black a week was ever called for jury service. The Supreme Court declined to overturn Thomas' conviction because it accepted testimony from Texas jury commissioners that they had not willfully discriminated. The lack of blacks was seen by the Supreme Court, in effect, as coincidence.

In 1935, the political climate had progressed a little, as evidenced in the Supreme Court ruling in *Norris* v. *Alabama* (294 U.S. 587). The State of Alabama had heard an appeal from a defendant named Norris, who showed that no blacks had served on juries in the county where he was tried. According to Van Dyke's book, Norris even presented statements from elderly black men, who testified that no black had *ever* served on a grand jury that they could remember, and statements from the jury clerk that notes about race were put next to every juror's name on the venire list. Still the Alabama Court rejected Norris' appeal because the jury commissioners denied intentional discrimination. But instead of accepting their remonstrations of good faith, the Supreme Court ruled that jury commissioners' statements could not suffi-ciently explain the absence of blacks and reversed Norris' convic-tion. By 1940, even Texas could not count on Supreme Court acquiescence. *Smith* v. *Texas* (311 U.S. 128) was a twin case to *Thomas* v. *Texas* from 1909, but this time, the Supreme Court found for the defendant. According to Van Dyke, this was the first time the Supreme Court stated that the jury must be a "body truly representative of the community," because it was not only a legal instrument but also a democratic institution. Then in *Glasser* v. *United States* (315 U.S. 60), in 1942, the Supreme Court ruled that jury selection procedures, even though intended to secure compe-tent jurors, had to "comport" with the concept of the jury as a cross section of the community. From decisions such as these, law evolved that stated essentially that underrepresentation of "cognizable classes"—groups perceived by the community as having definable common experiences—was grounds for reversal of verdicts, provided that it could be proved that those who prepared the list had "opportunity to discriminate, as well as intent." Statistics showing underrepresentation have not been enough to move the Supreme Court to rule that a jury of one's peers had been denied. Racial and ethnic groups, and women, have gradually been held to be unquestionably cognizable; other categories—such as the young, poor, religious, undereducated— are still legally arguable and therefore argued.

In 1968, Congress passed the Federal Jury Selection and Service Act, which removed "special" requirements, such as that a juror must be of high intelligence or known to be morally upright, from federal juries. The law underlined the belief that jury selection should be random and that the Sixth Amendment guarantee of an "impartial jury" also binds the states and their courts to the idea that an impartial jury can only be a representative one. How representative, in what proportion, remains open to dispute.

At the courtroom level, one does not always find randomness and broad representation in the jury pool. A notorious underrepresentation was uncovered in Boston in 1968 by attorney Leonard Boudin at the trial of Dr. Benjamin Spock and others (including Marcus Raskin, Codirector of the Institute for Policy Studies in Washington, D.C., and William Sloane Coffin, then chaplain of Yale University in New Haven, Connecticut). The charge was conspiring to help young men avoid the draft during the Vietnam War. During jury selection, Boudin pointed out to the court that only five women appeared on the list of eighty-eight potential jurors. This seemed not only flagrant underrepresentation, but in view of how many mothers and others raised their children on Dr. Spock's seminal book, *Baby and Child Care*, also suggested to Boudin that perhaps the list had been reviewed by the government with an eye toward screening out jurors possibly favorable to Spock. Boudin called the jury clerk to the stand, who then testified that he had drawn up the jury list by looking up at the ceiling before allowing his finger to come to rest next to a name on a city street-address directory. He could not say whether it was "probable" that he had deliberately avoided choosing women in order to save himself the extra paperwork of excusing a woman who claimed pressing responsibilities to children and home. According to author Jessica Mitford's book *The Trial of Dr. Spock*, published in 1969, a Harvard mathematics major in the courtroom audience calculated the odds as one in a trillion that the selection had been random, given sexual demographics in Boston. Still, the trial judge denied Boudin's challenge to the jury panel, and the defendants were tried by all white males.

In 1983, notoriety for jury discrimination came to a tiny hamlet in Georgia called Wrightsville, a town of 2,600, dominated by a large white courthouse with creaking sloping wooden interior stairs and voters' boxes lined up along the walls. With gauzy white privacy curtains across each one, each looked more like a confessional than a place to cast a ballot. The courtyard is a popular, public gathering place; blacks chat on one stone bench, whites on another. Whites in Wrightsville will walk through a group of blacks and not look at them, evidently preferring not to see them. A local Baptist preacher called Wrightsville "one of the most racist places in Georgia," and the claim was tested during the trial of the local sheriff. He had been charged with, among other counts, violating the civil rights of a group of blacks who had been protesting the hiring practices in the sheriff's office in 1980. The peaceful protest, it was alleged, was disrupted by the sheriff and his armed deputies. Protestors were beaten. Violence threatened the town, and several blacks were shot, allegedly by sheriff's men.

Johnson County, where Wrightsville is situated, has a 33 percent black population. Yet, in February 1983 when jury selection began in this trial, blacks constituted only eight of sixty-four in the original jury pool, or 12.5 percent. In Wrightsville, jury lists are culled from voter lists, which still, it is claimed, seriously underrepresent blacks. Then, according to the town clerk, the jury list is "revised" by jury revisers—a half-dozen local people who, going by their personal knowledge of the community, remove the names of people who have died or moved away, and add those they think would make good jurors. There is nothing to prevent them from tampering with the list, consciously or unconsciously; their meetings are secret, and they will not talk about how they do their job. Their existence is legal, and yet their work could well account for the underrepresentation of blacks in the pool.

The skewed distribution was not lost on the jury. One of the female jurors told me, "I've served several times before in heavily black areas, and usually the juries are about half and half. I knew something was wrong in that courtroom as soon as I saw that [12.5 percent] pool. There is no way that could have been a random sample of that area." The sheriff and his men were acquitted.

While in principle the jury system in the United States has evolved to encourage maximum randomness and representation, what happened in Wrightsville happens in other small towns still, especially in the South, but elsewhere in the country as well, where few questions are asked about the legality of it. In 1977, after an exhaustive study of venire procedures, Van Dyke wrote, "Most courts in the United States still have a long way to go before truly representative juries are the rule." In 1983, the American Bar Association continued to call for randomness to be the standard at every stage of jury selection. In short, if what is poured into the top of the funnel is all the same, one cannot expect much mixture at the funnel's mouth.

[8]
...Few Are Chosen

Once the list has been culled and the summons sent out, the next phase of selection begins. "Think of an excuse," reluctant summonsees are advised by their friends. And, according to Van Dyke, about 60 percent of those summoned do think of an excuse good enough at least to postpone their jury service. In my case, before being called for the Wyman-D'Arazzio trial, I had been traveling on a variety of projects and had asked that my jury service be postponed five different times. On the fifth occasion, I was told by the jury clerk that I had had my last postponement: "We are tired of fooling around with you, Miss DiPerna," the clerk reprimanded me. There was a computer record of my postponement history should I try to misrepresent it. The system had caught me.

Of course, there are many reasons—personal and professional—for wishing to be excused from jury duty. But plain old not-wanting-to-serve is not good enough, unless one is willing to give a judge the idea that one's antagonism about serving amounts to bias.

Jurisdictions vary on granting exemptions, and though the American Bar Association recommends that all automatic exemptions and excuses be eliminated, they persist. Only twenty states allow no occupational exemptions. Attorneys, physicians, firemen and women, pharmacists, embalmers, dentists, nurses—in general those concerned with life and death, can be excused in many states, and in some, they are automatically exempted. Some states also exempt teachers, veterinarians, and telephone operators. Virginia exempts ferry boat operators, but states like Michigan and Washington—also big users of ferries—do not. New York, which offers quite a few occupational exemptions, does not exempt Staten Island ferry operators in New York City, though the ferry is the primary way of reaching Staten Island, and ferry boat operators are very important. Virginia also exempts tobacco pickers during harvests, but major agricultural states like Kansas, Ohio, and California maintain no exemptions at all.

Females with children, provided the children are no older than sixteen, can secure exemption in fifteen states, and in four of them, exemption can also be claimed by a man caring for young children.

The effect of exemptions is to eliminate whole categories of people, usually professional, thereby significantly narrowing the representation of lists. Obviously, wholesale elimination of professionals greatly shapes the sociological composition of the jurors who remain.

Then comes the economic factor. The average juror fee is $10 per day, with a low of $5 and a high of $30. Most courts now also provide a mileage allowance for drivers and some out-of-pocket expenses. Theoretically, employers should not penalize employees who are called to jury service, and the ABA has urged the passage of state laws to prevent employer harassment of jurors who must miss work. Most large-scale employers do continue to pay employees' salaries, or at least the difference between the salary and the paltry jury fees. But many small businesses cannot afford to. According to the Center for Jury Studies, total juror fees paid out by governments at all levels is approximately $200 million per year, and jury-related work absence costs approximately $1 billion, 68 percent of which is borne by employers.

According to research compiled by the Center for Jury Studies, courts bear only 16 percent of the overall cost in jury fees, and jurors who lose income during jury service bear another 16 percent. However, given a depressed economy and budget cutbacks, court systems are hard pressed to meet their jury fee obligations, and some courts have begun to reduce calendar time for jury trials to distribute jury costs over a longer time. Some court systems, like Wayne County, Michigan, considered adopting a four-day trial week to hold down expenses, at least in the short term.

Economics not only affect the flow of trial traffic; it affects the composition of jury panels. According to the Center for Jury Studies, about 25 percent of all jurors who report no income lost due to jury service are not employed—retired, unemployed, students, homemakers. Also, while most employers pay employees during jury service, most self-employed persons and blue-collar laborers have no such protection. Economic hardship is an acceptable exemption in most states, and judges tend to release any juror who claims he or she will not receive a salary other than the jury fee. This, plus the fact that low-income people tend to be underrepresented anyway on voter registration lists, can skew the jury pool away from the blue-collar worker.

Mary Timothy, who wrote *Jury Woman* in 1974, about her stint as a juror in the trial of Angela Davis, the black economics professor who was tried for murder in California in 1972, easily noted the waves of exemption that washed over voir dire in that trial: ". . . the next to leave were the workers. Those whose income depended on day to day employment were allowed to present evidence to show that remaining on the panel would cause them undue hardship. . . . Over 40 people disappeared without ever being called down to court. The group remaining was far more homogenous than the original 116. The students had gone, the workers, the poor, the old and the weak. Those left were largely middle-aged, middle-class people employed by the large industries of the area—industries large enough to absorb the financial loss of an employee's long absence. . . . Economics had a great deal to do with the composition of the jury. . . . With this early exodus, most of the minorities also disappeared."

This preliminary cut, on the basis of economics, had also taken place in the Wyman-D'Arazzio trial, when the judge had excused those who could not serve three weeks to a month. Had not one attorney told me the final jury was middle-class and professional? In a 1983 federal conspiracy trial of political radicals in New York, accused of several robberies of Brink's armored trucks, among other crimes, economic hardship was a frequent plea for excusal because the trial was projected to last five months. The defense attorneys challenged the judge's ruling on this point, especially when he excused minority group members, having failed to inform them that they could receive their jury fee checks weekly, and that the fee increases after one month of service. The final jury had only one self-employed member. Almost all of the rest were civil servants or retired; two worked for private enterprises.

The same hardship culling took place when John Mitchell, Attorney General under President Nixon, and Maurice Stans, Secretary of Commerce in the same administration, went on trial in New York City in the spring of 1974 on charges of impeding a Securities and Exchange Commission investigation of Robert Vesco, who had made a $200,000 contribution to Nixon's reelection campaign. This case provides a potent example of the effect the economic status of jurors can have on verdicts.

According to Hans Zeisel, eighty-five panel members were excused for hardship, twenty-four for employment-related reasons. The final jury was, in fact, nearly all blue collar, consisting entirely, according to Zeisel, of poorly educated, poorly informed persons, save for one alternate—an educated man, a vice president of a major international bank—who became a full-fledged jury member when one of the original jurors became sick and could not continue. This alternate had not disclosed to the court, when originally asked if he had any personal or business relationships that might affect his ability to be impartial, that he had an acquaintanceship with the assistant U. S. attorney trying the case. Still, when this information was brought out by the defense, the judge allowed the alternate to join the regular jury.

More significant, however, was the manner in which his background, so different from his "peers," apparently influenced the verdict. The jury was sequestered during the trial—that is, they did not go home at the end of the day's proceedings but went instead to a hotel, eating all meals as a group, with U.S. marshal protection. According to a report in the New York *Times* on May 5, 1974, after the verdict was announced, the juror used his bank perquisites to entertain his fellow jurors: access to a private auditorium where he showed them films; access to a bank-building office window from which they could view the St. Patrick's Day parade; a supply of pocket cash to cover unexpected expenses. During deliberations, a first ballot was taken: 8–4 for conviction.

The banker-juror, however, then persuaded the jury to listen again to parts of the testimony and to reread certain documents.

Also, although sending notes to the judge is the foreperson's responsibility, the banker-juror apparently wrote the notes, and the forelady merely signed them. In the end, the jury reversed itself and acquitted.

It should also be mentioned that this juror was a Republican, a conservative, and a contributor to Nixon's campaign himself. During questioning for jury selection, he had said he felt the case was one where the "administration are powers on one side, and members, former members of the administration, are powers on the other side." He also seemed to be more informed about what Watergate was than any of the other jurors. Interestingly, the defense in this trial had developed a profile of the jurors they wanted—low level of education, low level of information about Watergate—and the banker-juror distinctly did not fit it.

Zeisel described the interaction and final effect of this juror on deliberations: "The eight 'profile' jurors who eventually were to be persuaded to give up their guilty vote were perfectly selected for such persuasion. Their coming throughout from the lower and middle social strata, only one of them with as much as one year of college, made it easier for the one nonprofile juror who came from the upper class and was at home in the world of high finance to explain to his fellow jurors that the evidence in the case did not warrant conviction."

I contacted the juror in Hong Kong where he now works and he replied to the charge: "My major role was to keep the jury focused on the judge's instructions." He admits he used his bank privileges to make sequestering more bearable for the jurors: "I did what I could to facilitate recreation." But he denies that his position or class accounted for the verdict. "I came out of the experience with a great respect for the jury system—there were many strong views of different things—" When I asked if he was looked up to by the other jurors, he answered, "I don't know— who knows? After a while each person had different influences. The jury came to a decision on an intuitive basis, which is as powerful, if you will, as someone trying to influence or steer the group, which was the implication in the discussion of my role."

Whether the banker's privileges or his personal style had an impact, or whether the evidence did warrant conviction, is no longer an issue. But the case does highlight what economic shaping can mean in terms of jurors' views, even their understanding. Had another alternate, one who more aptly fit in with the rest, become a juror, the verdict might well have been different, as it might have been had the jury been properly representative economically.

What the complexion of the jury means for the verdict is only one prong of the question. The other is a matter of how society at large is affected when responsibility for deciding is relegated to only the moderately socially enfranchised or the less active members of the society. Who remains on a jury says quite a bit about the workings and goals of the adversary system of justice.

The composition of the ultimate Mitchell-Stans jury, for example, was not just the result of an exemption system, or the mere fact that many potential jurors preferred not to serve for hardship reasons; it was the result of lawyers' selection. The voir dire process leaves many potentially good jurors behind. While jury lists may be much less than ideally representational, and excuses more broadly allowed than ideal representation can stand, it is the scrutiny, questioning, challenging, and selection of jurors, by lawyers or judges or both, that finally shapes the jury's character, flavor, and group dynamics.

And here is where the idea of an impartial jury of one's peers takes the most abuse, for here is where, in fact, the selection process is used by lawyers, not to select the most impartial, or the most representative body, but the one most likely to be amenable to the lawyers' view of the case.

The lawyers for both sides in Wyman-D'Arazzio told me they wanted a "smart" jury. Another very experienced attorney once told me, "The side that has a chance of winning usually wants a smart jury." As attorneys follow their selection plan, if they have one, each side inches toward the quality of "smartness" it seeks. The jury that emerges might be the result of a plan, or it might be there for reasons which are anybody's guess. Well-known defense attorney Herald P. Fahringer, who has defended such notables as Jean Harris and Claus von Bulow, calls the selection process the "valley of the blind."

Voir dire is king of the valley. And it is this time in the selection process that the court system most begrudges. In New York City, it is said to account for 40 percent of the total trial time in state courts.

The voir dire is a discovery process, a probative excursion in which attorneys try to match a name on a slip of paper with a face and personality. They ask questions and then "challenge," that is, dismiss the jurors they don't want. In most federal courts around the country, questioning of jurors is conducted by the judge who may, using judicial discretion, supplement the session with questions lawyers have submitted in writing. Generally, however, the judge poses all the questions to the potential jurors. In federal courts, the average voir dire takes 2.5 hours; in state courts with lawyers conducting the voir dire, the process takes an average of 12.7, but some trials can take as long in voir dire as in the actual trying of the case. As of 1983, approximately thirty-six states permitted attorneys to conduct voir dire, and it is a right they jealously guard. However, given the assault on it, the right may be lost by the end of this century.

Voir dire has a relatively murky history, but we know that the right to challenge jurors was awarded by the Crown in England to "triers," who were either attorneys or coroners. When in the sixteenth century the order to summon a jury was given, the sheriff rounded up males twenty-one to seventy years old who were not outlaws or aliens (unless an alien was being tried), who were respected members of the community. People involved in the case could challenge the jurors as a group or individually, and the triers made the final decision as to the juror's fitness. Challenges presumed biases, such as blood relations to a party in the trial or reasons to suspect a juror had something to gain economically from a particular outcome in the case. If at the end of the selection there were not enough jurors left to comprise a jury, the sheriff was authorized to go around picking up "tales," that is, anyone who was hanging about, and press them into jury service.

In the young United States, the Sixth Amendment, which guarantees jury trial, originally also guaranteed the "right of challenge." However, these three words were dropped, apparently because the word "impartial" was deemed to protect that right adequately. However, the oft-cited case which firmly fixed the challenge right involved Aaron Burr, Vice President from 1801 to 1805 under Thomas Jefferson. Jefferson charged Burr with treason. Burr's case received a good deal of publicity, not least of all because he had killed Alexander Hamilton in a duel and was himself a public figure. Burr's trial in 1804 tested the law regarding the rights of attorneys to select jurors. The prosecutors in the case argued that jurors could not be disqualified just because they had preconceived ideas about the case. However, the trial judge, Chief Justice John Marshall, ruled that if jurors had some kind of prejudice in mind, they would not necessarily be fair weighers of the evidence and that a biased state of mind was as firm a ground for challenging jurors as blood relation, close or remote, to a litigant in the case.

Marshall's ruling, which may have been at least in part motivated by his own ill-will toward Jefferson, stimulated state courts to follow suit, thus opening the area of potential juror bias to voir dire. This had not been heard of before, certainly not in England where even today voir dire is barely permitted. In a sense, Marshall's ruling made suspect terrain of the juror's mind and gave license to attorneys to prospect, as well as cultivate there. Once this was done, it was very hard to undo.

Today, the voir dire process is three tiered. Usually, the judge asks basic questions of the entire panel in the box—sixteen or so jurors from the larger pool whose names have been drawn from some kind of selection. The judge, who at this point has no more idea what the specific evidence will be than the jury has (unless there has been some pretrial motion pertinent to it), asks preliminary questions about jurors' occupations, relations to those involved in the case, familiarity with locations involved, or with any of the witnesses due to testify. He may ask whether any juror has served on a jury before. Then the lawyers ask more specific follow-up questions about what jurors do in their spare time, if they belong to clubs or organizations, if they know any lawyers, etc. Then, the lawyers may ask more specific follow-up questions and, on the basis of their answers, may challenge jurors. On the other hand, I have seen trials where lawyers, though they have the right of voir dire, do nothing more than verify the potential juror's name and address.

Challenges can be for cause—that is, concrete, discernible bias, such as a juror saying, "Most defendants are guilty in my mind," or "I think people who are dumb enough to slip on sidewalks do not deserve any settlement if they break their legs." The trial judge rules on whether a "cause" challenge is legitimate, and attorneys may make an unlimited number of them. Peremptory challenges are those which the attorney need not justify, even explain. They are the challenges based on the attorneys' gut reactions, the good or bad vibrations which they perceive. When a juror is not chosen and doesn't know why, usually he or she has been peremptorily challenged. The number of peremptory challenges are fixed, depending on the matter at trial, the number of parties, and the judge's discretion.

In-depth voir dire can be amazingly revealing, depending on the participants and how comfortable they can manage to be with each other. After all, the jurors are being asked to bare their souls, to step out of them like zipper suits and reveal their prejudices to people they have never seen before—lawyers, judge, other jurors. A juror, for example, would be expected to admit to biases ("I distrust long-haired men") or preconceived notions ("If he's on trial, he must be guilty") or honest reactions ("How can I put aside the fact that the newspapers have been headlining this case for weeks?"). Although there are a variety of theories about what tactics are best for attorneys to use in voir dire, it seems to me that if attorneys want truthful answers, it is best to put the jurors at ease as soon as possible.

First-time jurors are easily intimidated. Often they will not speak to the judge or anyone until spoken to, no matter what. At one voir dire, I observed a moderately elderly woman, who was hoping to be excused from the trial, wait two days to give her reason to the judge. The pool had been large (the trial was expected to last several months, and the jury clerks had assumed many people would not wish to serve), so it took several days for the judge to work his way down to the woman's name. When he finally did, she told him she had interrupted dental work to answer her summons and that she had not been able to eat since she had been coming to court. "All the other people here eat lunch," she complained. "Not me. I have to sit with no teeth. If you don't believe me, I'll show you." And she opened her toothless mouth for all in the courtroom to see. The judge excused her, no further questions asked.

A woman wrote me a letter in which she said the jury voir dire experience had been a severe hardship for her because she is "painfully" shy. Since she is self-employed, she had hoped to be able to postpone her jury duty and had brought some letters from clients explaining how they were in the midst of their busiest season and needed her services. She wrote that she still had nightmares from the experience. "I still have not recovered from the trauma, only buried it. . . . Herded among hundreds of people, I was terrified—had no idea of what to do or how to speak to the judge. After a morning of watching others, finally my turn came. I showed the judge the letters and asked to be excused. Suddenly he started yelling (other interviews had been in hushed tones), furious at me for asking such a thing. When he did read the letters, he granted me a postponement, but sternly told me I could not ask for another. . . . I felt like a criminal being sentenced." This woman did do her jury duty stint later, when her work had its slow season. "I was asked to speak but could not. The whole process was so intimidating for someone who had never been in such public places. I nearly blacked out from the stress."

Probably this woman was more uncomfortable than most people would be in the same situation; but nevertheless inexperienced jurors can shrink before courtroom authority. Attorneys, in my experience, don't do much to relax jurors during voir dire. Even when he is trying to woo jurors or get to know them better, the average attorney fails to reach out to them. It is surprisingly common for attorneys and judges to condescend to jurors. Consequently, the juror, perhaps with reason, feels he has no allies in the courtroom, and that he or she had better make no false move.

Ironically, alienating jurors is precisely what voir dire is *not* about. Herald Fahringer, a champion of lawyer-conducted voir dire, has written and said frequently that "jury selection is the most important part of any criminal trial." He believes that "in most cases the defendant's fate is fixed after jury selection." Hans Zeisel, on the other hand, contends, "If this were true, our justice system would be in real trouble."

The truth lies somewhere in between. One juror or two can make a considerable difference, if not in the verdict itself, at least on the length and substance of the deliberation. Often, attorneys are looking for the one juror who will hang, or hold out, depending on which side has the stronger case. Still, most of these quirks lie outside an attorney's ability to predict—probably beyond anyone's ability to predict—although the more detailed the voir dire, the more insight the jury selection team will gain. But despite voir dire, certain less desirable jurors slip through, eluding even the most professional efforts to pick and choose them in a controlled, knowledgeable fashion.

Fate put the banker-alternate in the Mitchell-Stans trial and placed him in the jury almost despite the attorneys' opinions. According to Zeisel, this was the juror for all seasons. "When he was first questioned, the defense had challenged him for cause, the routine challenge it had raised against all prospective jurors well-informed about Watergate. By the time he was to become a juror, and the government suspected his veracity, the defense fought tooth and nail to retain him, in spite of the fact that he did not fit the profile of the good defense juror in four important respects: He was college educated; he probably knew more about Watergate than any other member of the panel; he regularly read *The New York Times*; and he was clearly a member of the upper class."

Perhaps defense lawyers suspected that the banker-juror would be on their side; maybe eventually the feelings the juror radiated accounted for the defense's change of heart; or maybe the fact that the government did not want him was enough to signal the defense that the juror might be a boon to them. In the end, he was, but it was fortune, rather than conscious selection skill on the attorney's part, that put the banker into the picture.

In the Wyman-D'Arazzio matter, the four skeptics tending toward acquittal were only half predicted by the attorneys involved, according to my reconstruction of the deliberations, based on interviews with the jurors and lawyers involved. One of the strongest proconviction voices was not at all anticipated by the prosecution. One of the staunchest opponents of conviction was a soft-spoken older black man who owned his own business; his skepticism of the police surprised the defense side. Though each side clearly tried to select a "good" jury—that is, one favorable to its side—there finally seemed to be a catch-as-catch-can aspect no amount of speculation could avoid.

Voir dire takes on additional importance in so-called political trials. Mitchell-Stans had that political hue, given the charges and the general post-Watergate climate. Voir dire was quite important during the 1960s and 1970s, in the trials of activists like Spock, who broke the law in order to oppose the war in Vietnam. A major "political" trial in the 1980s—and exceptionally important voir dire—took place in the 1983 federal Brink's trial. Jury selection was fascinating, not least of all because the jurors were questioned anonymously, and chosen jurors' names and addresses were kept secret throughout the trial from all but the jury clerk, who had to mail them their jury-duty checks. They were even told by the judge they need not share their names with each other and that the anonymity system was to protect them from being hounded by the press.

The case involved charges lodged against political radicals—some of them members of the Black Liberation Movement—of racketeering and conspiracy to commit armed robberies and murder. The case was so named because several of the robberies involved Brink's armored cars. One such robbery, in Nanuet, New York, about forty miles north of New York City, gained special notoriety when two policemen and a guard were killed, and it was announced that one of those apprehended was Kathy Boudin, daughter of Leonard Boudin, the leading attorney for liberal and progressive causes, who had defended Dr. Spock.

Ms. Boudin had been a member of the radical Weather Underground, which was born in the social tumult of the 1960s. She had been living underground since an explosion racked a brownstone hideout and presumed bomb factory in Greenwich Village, New York City, in 1970. Boudin and others escaped, not to be heard from again until they were captured after the Nanuet (Rockland County) shootout. The federal government then indicted members of the gang on a variety of charges, leaving Ms. Boudin an "unindicted coconspirator." She was tried separately by the state of New York in spring 1984, for her role in the Nanuet robbery.

The federal prosecution charged that, using a system of safe houses and proceeds of the robberies, which were as high as $1.6

million in some cases, the group, while managing to evade capture for several years, sold drugs and operated small-scale prostitution rings on the side.

The defendants, on the other hand, contended that they had been hounded by the government for their political beliefs and investigated for those beliefs through the racketeering laws. Some of the defendants advocated, among other things, that several states in the southern United States rightfully belong to black people and only the establishment of the Republic of New Afrika in these states could rectify the situation. Five of the six defendants in the federal case—Sekou Odinga (also known as Nathaniel Burns), Cecil Ferguson, Edward Joseph, Bilal Sunni-Ali (also known as William Johnson), and Silvia Baraldini—were charged with being members of the racketeering group; a sixth defendant, Ileana Robinson, also on trial, was charged only with being an accessory after the fact, having aided the team after a getaway.

For any jury, the case presented serious challenges. It was complicated, involving defendants on trial, defendants named in the indictment but not on trial because they remained at large, and defendants named in the indictment not on trial in federal court but in state court instead. There were nine counts to the indictment, alleging not only conspiracy but over two dozen specific acts. The case alleged seriously violent acts, including murder, which had received a certain amount of publicity. An unmistakable political quality was ascribed to those acts by the defendants. The trial required the jury to forgo normal life, including summer vacations, for nearly six months. It required them to observe a varied and large cast of characters. There was a prosecution team of three attorneys, a legal assistant, and an FBI agent. There were six defense attorneys—one defendant had two attorneys—and one defendant acted on his own behalf. Some of the defendants wore Palestinian shawls and Muslim caps—what the judge called "distinctive garb."

The anonymity factor required that eighteen people—twelve jurors plus six alternates—interact every day, eat lunch as a group in the company of federal marshals, be driven home at night in chauffeured limousines with blackened one-way glass windows, and not discuss the case, nor be afraid that their identities would be discovered by the defendants or the press. For reasons well beyond their control, criminal events, probably well beyond their imagination, were swept into their lives every day supposedly to be swept out again each night and when the trial was over. The voir dire in the case was both extraordinary and ordinary, and it showed how the best laid plans about jury selection may not, in the end, make any significant difference.

[9]
Anatomy of a Choice

Security was tight at the federal courthouse on April 5, 1983, the day jury selection for the Brink's trial was to begin. Guards checked my purse and briefcase—even my newspaper, lest some weapon or recording device be hidden in its folds. I chatted with the marshals, who were polite enough in doing their job. One of them, it turned out, had been a guard in the federal trial of Lewis, the "ungentleman" from the Wyman-D'Arazzio trial. "One way or another," the guard said, "we see everything down here."

The New York Times and other newspapers reported that day that one thousand potential jurors had been summoned. The judge, Kevin T. Duffy, when discussing, during voir dire, pretrial publicity and how people ought not believe everything they read, used the "1,000 people" item as an example of inaccurate reporting. "You don't see 1,000 people in here, do you?" he chuckled, trying to put the potential jurors at ease. Yet Judge Duffy himself had cited the number in his memorandum granting an anonymous jury: "Here, the jury commissioner has summoned a special panel of 1,000 veniremen." And in fact, the jury commissioner had done so, summoning twice the number he had normally summoned on an average week, according to his office. In the end, they used far fewer than 1,000 people. The highest number called into the Brink's courtroom was 225, and of these about 160 potential jurors were actually questioned. The last ninety were called into the courtroom simply because one last alternate remained to be chosen. Jury selection took ten days.

Duffy first filled the courtroom with potential jurors, who had been given numbered cards. He asked all who wished to be excused to give their number to the court clerk, who made a handwritten list of them. Then, all the numbered cards were put into a metal box that spun, and groups of eighteen numbers were drawn. These eighteen people sat in the box and were asked general questions in front of everyone. Then, the entire pool retired to the jury room while the judge questioned the eighteen, one at a time.

Judge Duffy had told the panels in court that the one thing they could expect from him was the unexpected and that he was somewhat unpredictable, though he seemed to relish that reputation more than deserve it. He had a boyish look, and his style in court was alternately tough and folksy; he was both judge and television talk-show host. He tried to put the potential jurors at ease by seeming to be one of them, calling them "folks" or "you guys."

Of the two hundred or so to be summoned into the Brink's courtroom, about forty asked to be excused and were, on the basis of hardship due to the length of the trial, the nature of the crimes, or the fact that the potential juror had some type of connection to the case—employment by a bank or a law enforcement agency, for example. One young man asked to be excused because he was due at National Guard camp in a few months. "And you'd rather be there than here?" the judge jibed in partial jest.

Duffy asked general questions of groups of eighteen at a time—county of residence, occupation, number of children, marital status, education background, previous jury experience. Had the basic information Duffy elicited in general questioning been available in advance from a questionnaire, jury selection might have taken two full days less. The judge also asked those who had previously served on juries what verdicts that jury had reached, which was unusual; most judges, in fact, tell jurors they do not have to reveal the prior verdict if they do not wish to. However, it is useful for attorneys to know whether a potential juror had served before on a convicting or acquitting jury. Duffy did not permit attorneys to put questions to the jurors, in keeping with standard federal practice, but he did accept written questions from the attorneys and also allowed some follow-up questions.

The first round of excuses reflected how jury duty slices into people's lives and how jurors become public property for a time.

A member of the Rockefeller family received special treatment, asking to see the judge privately and winning an excusal because she did not feel her identity would long remain a secret. She was right. There were not many medical excuses—only one for glaucoma, out of the first hundred. Length of trial and the hardship it would impose were the most common excuses, but the judge was a relatively soft touch for lots of other regrets as well. He excused a woman who had to plan her daughter's wedding and a man who said he had a job pending after a long period of unemployment. A woman's husband needed her constant care because he had had a stroke. Another juror brought a letter from a therapist stating that jury service would "accelerate" the juror's anxieties. Another woman honestly said, "I'm prejudiced. My heart goes out to the people killed."

Just as the defendants hoped to weave American history into their defense, a juror wove world history into voir dire. She nervously told the court she was opposed inexorably to violence of any kind, and the mere thought of it made her nervous. It seemed she had lost her entire family in the Holocaust in Europe. "It had a great effect on me," she said quietly, not looking at anyone in court, not even the judge as he excused her.

Since Duffy posed all the questions, his was the only voice the potential jurors heard throughout jury selection. If the attorneys wanted follow-up questions to their written questions, they requested them outside the jury's hearing. Also, most of the questioning was done one juror at a time, so no juror could have the benefit of hearing a previous answer. This meant that the full panel, save one, was being brought in and out of the courtroom several times a day and spent most of the day waiting.

Still, jurors quickly learned that a sure way out of the trial was to admit to being "partial." When Duffy asked, "Do you think you can be impartial," and a person said no, Duffy dismissed him quickly. He obviously didn't want to waste time on these jurors, but he also accepted the answer "yes" quite easily, with little probing. I am not convinced all potential jurors know what the word "impartial" really means, but they do know it is what a juror is supposed to be.

There is definitely a problem concerning juror literacy. One man said he didn't need "corrective lenses," even though he had glasses on. When Duffy asked what industry jurors worked in, two jurors in a row said "out of state." One man in the jury pool I watched was either practicing penmanship or learning to write.

The trial, like most, seemed primitive because except for microphones, electric lights, and the security apparatus outside, the courtroom was empty of technology. In fact, trials may be one of the few institutions left where the only error made can be human. All that happens is based on human interactions, wants, needs, frailties, prejudices, communication, and lack of them. This, plus the general pomp and circumstance, makes trials seem anachronistic. In most jurisdictions, trials are chronicled by artists, instead of by television and photography. To get a closer view, without moving up, the artist uses opera glasses. There is a human secretary, instead of a tape recorder, and a metal spinning box, that is as basic as the wheel, from which the jurors' numbers are drawn. These old-fashioned touches remind one that no matter how fast the world outside is going, inside a courtroom the pace is only as fast as a human being can think, say, and do. Perhaps, one day, a computer will be fed the case "pattern," add up the points each side has made, and come to a mathematically correct verdict. For now, courts are wonderfully tuned to the limits of the human race.

Many argue that the federal, judge-conducted model voir dire should be adopted by state courts in order to save time. Jay Schulman, a well known sociologist who pioneered the use of sociology in jury selection and helped the defense choose jurors in the Brink's case, believes Duffy's voir dire was 98 percent more probing than most federal judges', even allowing for the special character of the case. At a seminar given by the Practicing Law Institute in New York City in December 1983, seasoned trial lawyers from around the country lamented the depth of the average federal voir dire. One attorney complained, for example, that a judge declined to ask a potential juror whether he belonged to a union, in a case involving crimes allegedly committed with union funds. It was the sort of question that would seem justified to uncover a legitimate preconception and source of a challenge for cause.

One advantage, it is argued, of having the judge conduct voir dire is that the lawyers cannot use the time to ingratiate themselves with potential jurors. The judge, then, can act as a buffer between juror and lawyer personality, as well as lawyer tactics. So, to the jury in the federal Brink's case, the nine attorneys who sat on the opposite ends of the rail were mystery people who never spoke until the trial actually began. Probably this gave the prosecution a slight advantage, since the defense attorneys were, on the whole, more personable that the U.S. attorneys and this would have come through in voir dire as it eventually did in opening statements. All of the attorneys were young, none over forty. The government team had two males, one female, all white. Although I am sure part of her facade was necessary in her official role, the female seemed remote, cool, and tough. She told me she thought "any twelve" would do as far as jury selection was concerned. The lead male, too, seemed a bit overconfident. The second male, the most personable of the three, also seemed to resist the urge, or the need, to relax. The only time the team loosened up was when they came to the back of the courtroom to look at the artists' renderings of their movements through the trial.

The defense, on the other hand, was more animated, possibly in part because they had more to gain by creating the best possible impression on the press and any other observer whose interest they could catch. The defense team was a motley group, all with political activist backgrounds: five white, one black; four men, two women. There was a serious-looking male attorney who wore thick, wire-rim glasses and 1930's double-breasted suits; a wide-eyed feminist who liked to banter mildly with the judge; another woman who had been a schoolteacher for eleven years before going to law school and who did not waste any words or anyone's time; her cocounsel, a tall stately black man, who was also "Minister of Justice for the provisional government of the Republic of New Afrika" and who bantered unmildly with the judge; a shortish man who looked like a legal-minded Jerry Colonna; and finally another amiable male who seemed to be coming and going at the same time.

This team of attorneys had put together a set of follow-up questions aimed at uncovering racial prejudice. Such questions have been held to be valid and within the scope of voir dire only since 1973 and the U.S. Supreme Court decision in *Ham* v. *South*

Carolina (409 U.S. 524), though the decision was based on lower court cases involving the question since 1880 or so.

Among the questions were these: "Have you ever moved away from a neighborhood because you felt it was changing; have you ever had a negative experience with someone of another race; have you ever been a victim of a crime perpetrated by someone from another race, etc." A "yes" to any of these questions elicited follow-up. These questions and those about pretrial publicity, whether a juror had been exposed to it and whether the juror could put that exposure aside, accounted for most of the voir dire time.

The answers were sometimes unpredictable. To the question about moving away from a neighborhood, one man answered that he had moved once because of witchcraft. The judge allowed as how witchcraft might well change a neighborhood, and the man was excused eventually on an unrelated hardship basis.

The judge was somewhat unpredictable about the "cause" challenges he allowed. A young Hispanic man who had told the group he had no feelings "for or against" the government was seen at a lunch break by a prosecuting attorney at the local FBI office asking for a job application. The attorney reported his sighting to the judge. When questioned later in court about why he wanted the job, the potential juror said the trial had piqued his interest and "if I am good enough, they will take me." The judge himself dismissed the juror for cause. Yet, when a man replied to the changing-neighborhood question that he had moved because of an influx of "Spanish, colored and Albanian or whatever the hell they were," Duffy denied a defense challenge for the cause on the basis of racism.

Duffy also refused defense urgings to question potential jurors about what effect, if any, the anonymous selection had had on them. The defense believed that anonymity, regardless of how the judge explained its rationale, frightened jurors. Further, the defense believed anonymity could frighten jurors out of impartiality. But the judge was unrelenting on this point, even when several jurors volunteered that back in the jury room, where the jurors were waiting their turn to be questioned, many were talking about the case and speculating about why they were given numbers and not allowed to reveal their names. The defense, on learning this, moved to strike the entire pool of jurors on the basis that they had been irrevocably biased against the defendants, a motion which Duffy summarily rejected. Later, when the defense made a similar motion because it had become obvious that many of the jurors had read or heard something about the case, Duffy told the attorneys that if they wanted to waive the jury, he would give them a fair bench trial. The defense rejected the bargain.

What the jury supposedly did not know, but probably did know, was that Duffy had granted the motion for an anonymous jury because he had been persuaded by the government's argument that there could be "danger to trial participants." Indeed, the prosecution had appended materials—posters, flyers, and such— which suggested that supporters of the defendants had advocated rubbing out informers or harassing grand jurors at home or at work. There had been some precedent for anonymous juries; the government cited other cases involving major drug-trade rings.

The defense had argued that they could not pick an impartial jury if they could not know who the potential jurors were— specifically by name, address, and place of employment—but Duffy was unconvinced. He wrote, "It is true that the defendants will be unable to get the exact jury they want. That is not required by law."

The defense, nearly giving up but not quite, tried to turn the anonymity to its advantage, by alluding to it in opening statements. "They [meaning the government] have taken your names from you," one defense attorney stated. The judge sustained all prosecutional objections to that line of comment, but by then, the jury had heard them. Mission was accomplished, thanks to the blurt-out approach.

The supposition that being kept in anonymity for five months and escorted to and from court, meals, and home by federal marshals would not frighten jurors seemed a bit naive to me. I think the judge realized that too, which is why he would not question jurors about it. Too much questioning uncovers too much; had it become obvious that anonymity was indeed hampering the defense and the presumption of innocence, the trial could not have proceeded.

The selection plodded on, the racial question looming from

time to time, causing a wide variety of distractions. The defense attorney-Minister of Justice objected to what he perceived as the judge's too willing acquiescence when a black potential juror asked to be excused for hardship. Duffy, the attorney alleged, did not probe black jurors as much as the whites, giving the impression that Duffy wanted the whites to stay. Duffy listened to this accusation but ignored it and told the lawyer to sit down. The lawyer refused unless the judge said, "*Please* sit down." The jury panel was outside the courtroom during this interlude. Lawyer and judge locked wills, until finally Duffy threatened the attorney with a contempt of court citation. The attorney still would not sit down, so Duffy simply said, "O.K., marshals." Several tall men swung into action, coming up behind the attorney. Metal glinted. Someone, perhaps the wide-eyed feminist attorney, screamed, "A gun!" All the feminists in the audience, supporters of the defendant Baraldini, shrieked shrilly, like cartoon-character women who had just heard the word "mouse." I think the glinting metal was handcuffs, but as Duffy left the courtroom to allow a five-minute cooling-off period, the feminist attorney yelled that she wanted the record to reflect that a marshal had pulled a gun on an attorney in this case. All this happened in minutes, and though the jury panel was outside the courtroom, they may have heard the shrieks. When the cooling-off period was over, Duffy returned to the bench, and the jury came into court soon after. Most of the excitement had passed, the lawyer had sat down, but continued a bit of verbal back and forth with the judge. Then decorum returned, and jury selection continued. (After the trial, the lawyer was cited for accumulated contempt of court.)

Duffy used a system in which attorneys could exercise one challenge after each full round of questioning. In this way, the jury panel became like a poker hand in which one throws out a card in hope of getting a better one. The attorneys rarely saw the entire panel of eighteen again before it challenged, so they relied on charts and collective memory. Once, toward the end of the challenges—the prosecution had six and the defense ten—the attorneys asked to see the full hand again. "That will be awkward to explain," the judge replied. But he called the jurors in, and when they arrived, he told them, "We called you in here so you wouldn't think we had forgotten about you." As the attorneys panned each face, trying to match it with the notes they had taken and the memories they had, how could the jurors not know they had been summoned only to be looked at, sized up, one more time?

The defense seemed to want the most proletarian jury possible, for political reasons, but I wondered if they realized how hard it is for a poor man with little money in the bank to think of bank robbery as "expropriation for liberation," which is how the defendants characterized the charges.

In fact, jury selection in this case, as in most cases, was a reflection of the social and political attitudes of the attorneys. The defense was not monolithic, of course, and each lawyer had his or her own standard of radicalism to apply. There were some universals, however, like the defense referring to any ethnic, minority group members as "Third World persons." The defense occasionally split opinions over a juror. A young Hispanic woman was being questioned and was one of the jurors who mentioned to the judge that the jurors were troubled by having to remain anonymous and that they were discussing that among themselves. She was attractive and straightforward, not in the least intimidated by the judge. About her dealings with the police, she simply said she had once been a candidate for the police academy. She did not say, and the judge did not ask, why she had not ultimately taken the course. I'd have pegged her as a good defense juror, but I was told later that most defense attorneys had felt that the fact that she had once wanted to be a policewoman made her "too sympathetic" with "the system." They did not challenge her, however, because they felt sure the prosecution would, because she was young, "Third World," and independent. The prosecution did challenge.

The young woman and I talked awhile outside the jury room as she was leaving. She confessed that she had not expected to be picked. "I am not afraid to say what is on my mind," she said. Also she had been offended by the fact that the attorneys were not introduced by name and by the fact that the jurors were left to sit in the jury room for hours at a time with no information about when they might be called or whether their excuses might be granted. She added that many jurors who had been frightened by the anonymity had simply made up reasons to be excused, and that many jurors were discussing the case against the judge's instructions because "who listens?" I found her to be proud and thoughtful, probably one of the best jurors for such a case—if a fair trial had been the only goal of the attorneys. But nobody wanted her.

How attorneys choose to spend their challenges announces clearly where their own biases lie. The prosecution ran no risks. It used four out of its remaining five challenges to excuse young minority group members—three black, one Hispanic. One of the blacks was a factory worker who worked double shifts and said all he did in the evening was play with his children. The prosecution did not believe him. I overheard one say to another, "When does he sleep?" They suspected he had an ulterior motive for giving the impression that he had no familiarity with the case. They thought he might have wanted too much to be on the jury, so they challenged him. Perhaps three young middle-class white lawyers simply could not accept the man's simple life-style. The prosecution also challenged an attractive, middle-aged white man with a master's degree in mathematics. He seemed well educated, perhaps liberal. He reported during voir dire that a family menber of his had once been called to give grand jury testimony. The prosecution waived its sixth peremptory challenge.

The defense, predictably, dismissed all who seemed too affluent or middle class, including the man who thought his neighborhood had had an influx of Albanians.

Having been unable, because of the anonymity requirement, to learn the jurors' addresses, the defense tallied the counties potential jurors lived in, counties having been the maximum address jurors had been permitted to provide. When the defense had nearly exhausted its peremptory challenges, they moved to be granted additional peremptories, on the grounds that the jury pool contained a disproportionate number of people from the upstate counties in which the alleged crimes had been committed. The motion was denied.

Finally, there were twelve jurors and six alternates, not as much acceptable as they were unchallenged. However, one of the twelve returned to court one afternoon with a letter from his employer stating that the employee's job could not be held open for five months. The juror, a young white man, told me he had wanted to serve but could not afford to lose his job. This bumped alternate number one, a black man, onto the jury. The defense offered to waive choosing a sixth alternate but the prosecution would not. So jury selection continued for two and a half more days.

The final jury consisted of eight blacks and four whites: six women, six men. It included two college graduates, two U.S. Postal Service clerks, three retired people. The alternates were two whites, four blacks: two men, four women; including one retired person and one middle-aged woman who had just finished college the year before.

When the final jury had been selected and returned to the courtroom to be seated and given its preliminary instructions, the defense attorneys rose. The prosecutors did not. Judge Duffy commented, after the jury had been excused, that he noted the defense had elected to use an uncommon but acceptable custom to acknowledge respect for the jury. Thereafter, every time the jury entered the courtroom, the attorneys rose, including the not-to-be-outdone prosecutors.

There was no professional among the jurors, no obviously well-informed person, no perceptible leaders. Among the basic twelve, however, was a woman whom courtroom watchers dubbed "the general's wife." She had a master's degree in English, was then unemployed, and the recent widow of an armed services career officer. She was blond and well-coiffed—the epitome, I would have guessed, of a "bad" defense juror. The defense had not challenged her, however, because of the attitude she displayed toward the judge during voir dire. Judge Duffy was fond of referring to any woman juror as "young lady," regardless of age. He did not seem to think of the expression as patronizing. When he questioned the general's wife one day, he called her "young lady," and she let it pass. But the next day, when he asked if she was retired, she quipped, "Yesterday I was a young lady, today you think I'm retired."

Anyway, Jay Schulman, the sociologist, had recommended to the defense that she not be challenged. He viewed her as a good risk; she remained. Several months after the trial ended, he reflected: "I had never seen ejaculations like that in any court-room on the part of a juror toward a judge. This woman thought of herself as above authority in some way, and either she was crazy

or she had some ideology which was not possible to be seen. . . .
The government of course wanted her. That she was a general's
wife was enough for them; usually the government is simple-
minded. More often than not it backfires on them. Either way,"
Schulman added, "I thought that the rest of the jurors would not
like her and that could help the defense."

But about four months into the trial, she missed two days in a
row, claiming her father had had a heart attack; when the judge
had the clerk phone her, the juror would not come to the phone.
Anxious not to lose time, Duffy dismissed her from the case and
put alternate number one in the box. Apparently the general's
wife's attitude toward authority enabled her to quit the jury, just
like that, something that is rarely done.

Alternate number one was an older white man who had retired
after many years of working with what he described as a state
insurance fund. During voir dire, he had brightened the days
with his brisk, straightforward answers: He didn't know the
defendants "from Adam"; their names and all the witnesses'
names were "Greek to me." The only part of the newspaper he
read was the racing page, but he never went to the racetrack; he
"only went to the bookie." The judge and everyone laughed—
bookmaking being illegal in New York—and then Duffy added, "I
guess you mean Off-Track Betting"—that is, the official state
betting parlor. Then, the activist feminist lawyer suggested tartly
that the judge advise the juror of his right to remain silent.

The defense was delighted to have him join the full-fledged
jury, especially because they had become disillusioned with the
"general's wife." Writer John Castellucci, who covered the entire
trial for the Rockland *Journal News*, an upstate newspaper,
reported that one defense attorney spotted the general's wife
winking more than once at the prosecutors. She was also seen
mouthing the words "shut up" to one of the defense attorneys
during a long statement. And when the attorney suggested, while
cross-examining a government informer witness, that the government must have highly valued this witness's testimony because it
was willing to spend a lot of taxpayer's money putting him up at
hotels, the general's wife was seen mumbling to the juror next to
her, "This is costing a lot of taxpayer's money too."

In the end, after five months of trial including testimony from

117 witnesses, the jury deliberated three days through a very hot
Labor Day weekend. Their verdict was mixed. Two defendants
were acquitted completely—Ileana Robinson, who had been tied
to the case loosely, and Sunni-Ali, who had had two attorneys,
including the "Minister of Justice" who had played a recording of
his client's saxophone playing to conclude the summation statement on his behalf. Only two defendants, Sylvia Baraldini and
Sekou Odinga, were convicted of the conspiracy and racketeering
charges that were the heart of the government's case. The
remaining two, Ferguson and Joseph, were convicted of being
criminal accessories only. (The armed robbery and murders that
took place in Rockland County [Nanuet and Nyack] were the
bases for a state trial later in the year.)

It has been impossible, so far, to gauge what effect the dismissal
of the general's wife may have had on the final deliberations. The
verdict disappointed the government and probably surprised the
defendants. Apparently, the jury rejected key assertions made by
informers—juries generally do not like informer testimony. Without the informant testimony to glue events and people together,
most of the government's conspiracy allegations would come
apart. It's also possible that the jury reacted positively to the
defendants' political arguments, or that they disagreed with the
law or perhaps simply did not understand the law as the judge
instructed them. Perhaps the jury simply got tired, or found that
the charges had not been proved beyond a reasonable doubt. All
of it, some of it, or none of it could have happened.

Hans Zeisel believes it was possible that the anonymity had, in
fact, helped the defense: "When a jury does something surprising, one must look first at some unusual factor." Federal prosecutors may think hard about invoking anonymity again.

Regardless, after the verdict, Judge Duffy was widely quoted as
having remarked, "I have never understood juries." As far as I
know, it was his last public word on the subject. He declined to be
interviewed for this book or to allow the court clerk to forward a
request to the jurors, should they be willing, to contact me to
provide an interview. The jury's deliberative process is probably
lost to scrutiny for now. But what is clear is that the outcome of a
major trial of this decade derived not only from hunches and
tactics and gambles played to the jurors during trial, not only

from evidence or its lack, but from a selection process which began with a chance computerized list and ended with the questioning of several hundred people whose names we may never know.

[10]
The Goat Situation

Attorneys, said an Atlanta judge to a panel of potential jurors, are an unpredictable lot, and there was no telling what they wanted in jurors. He himself, he added, could not "make rhyme or reason" of their choices, and perhaps attorneys themselves could not either. His opinion was borne out by the very action he was about to try, for after a half day of careful jury selection, the defendant pleaded guilty, and the case was over.

What do attorneys want in a jury? In theory, they want an impartial representative group of people who will listen to and consider all the evidence fairly and bring in a verdict. In practice, they want people who have some disposition, some tilt, toward their client, or who can be tilted. Jury selection is, in the end, the manipulation of bias.

Fahringer has called the attorney's style in voir dire "guile" and points out the essential contradiction: "Lawyers announce they want only jurors who will decide the case impartially while, in fact, they want partisan jurors. Counsel is obliged to pick people who by reason of their background, personality, or attitudes might be expected to find in his client's favor. This insincerity is quickly detected by the jurors. We lie to them and they in turn to us: this is a bad beginning for a project designed to discover the truth."

Indeed, attorneys seem to choose not the best and the brightest of the pool but the least offensive, independent, and informed.

In the Wyman-D'Arazzio case, the attorneys claimed they broke the usual mold because they realized that the "usual" jury would get bogged down and not perceive the nuances of the evidence and the case.

But in the Mitchell-Stans trial, Hans Zeisel wrote, the major achievement of the defense during jury selection was to "reduce the number of jurors well informed about Watergate from 32 percent in the total panel to 8 percent, a single juror." And, he added, the attorneys were able to change dramatically the composition of the jury itself: "45 percent of the original panel had some college education. On the jury, their proportion was reduced to 8 percent—one juror with one year of college. In their stead, the middle group—white collar occupations with at least some high school—had expanded from 36 percent in the original panel to 76 percent on the jury."

How much the attorneys are able to manipulate jury composition depends on what they are able to learn in voir dire, and that is determined by how extensively attorneys can use voir dire. What attorneys want is very much linked to how much they think they can find out about a juror.

Among the most interesting, exceptional, and manipulative voir dires I have observed involved the second trial in the case of the *People of the State of New York* v. *Ricky A. Knapp*, which took place in September 1983 in Cooperstown, a village of 2,500 people, known to all the world as the home of baseball's hall of fame. Several exceptional factors at work made the voir dire unnecessarily long and arduous. It was a good example of how the jury system gets blamed for delays and costs that are really due to attorneys' agendas, questions of judicial competence, and other factors quite separate from the right to trial by jury.

Cooperstown sits in a fold of rolling hills in upstate New York, several hours from any city of size, where it preserves a turn-of-the-century look and a turn-of-the-century pace. It is a pastoral tranquil place where crime is a dirty face of the outside world. However, because Cooperstown is the Otsego County seat, now and then the village must host trials, including murder trials.

Any murder in Otsego County would be a major public event, but the Knapp case was especially notorious. Ricky Knapp, aged thirty-two, had been arrested for the murder of Linda Jill Velsey, a seventeen-year-old freshman at the State University of New York at Oneonta, who disappeared in December 1977. Police, acting on a tip from an informant, seized Knapp as he prepared to move Velsey's frozen body from a shallow grave in which she was buried. At some point during his interrogation, Knapp allegedly confessed to the murder. He later recanted, claiming the police pointed a gun at him and told him he would be shot trying to escape if he did not confess. Also, at the burial site, he had allegedly blurted out: "Shoot me, shoot me, I killed her. I am sick." But this statement too was later disputed. Knapp is a low-life character with a history of social maladjustment related to women. At the time of his arrest for the murder, he was out on bail awaiting trial on unrelated charges of sodomy and rape.

Knapp's side of the Velsey story, told at his first trial in June 1978, was that he picked up the young woman when she was hitchhiking and offered her money to have sexual intercourse with him. She agreed, they did, and he paid. But, he claimed, as he was driving her home, he began to begrudge himself the money and asked for it back. When the girl refused, a struggle ensued. According to Knapp, the woman fell out of his car, and when he stopped to pick her up, she was unconscious. Then, he testified, he did not remember what happened next, except that the girl died and he buried the body. A friend of Knapp's, Arthur Hitt, who later became a police informant on the case, testified that Knapp told him that he had murdered the girl and where he buried the body. Hitt then called the police.

The case aroused extensive publicity in the area—a missing coed story blights a town where colleges are a major industry—and the police were under a good deal of pressure to solve the case. The investigation, arrest, and trial were front-page news in the region for several months. However, there were many evidentiary problems with the case—which the jury recognized—and Knapp was convicted in June 1978 of only one count of murder in the second degree for failing to get the unconscious girl aid that might have saved her life. Though Knapp had been charged with intentionally causing the girl's death, the prosecution never proved Knapp had actually killed the girl. Knapp was sentenced to life in prison, to be eligible for parole after twenty-five years. Knapp was also tried and convicted on the sodomy charges; the sentences were to run concurrently.

However, a bad case is like a bad penny, and the Knapp case

came back. John Owen, Knapp's attorney, then public defender, appealed the verdict in the first trial, citing many questionable rulings by the trial judge, Joseph A. Mogavero, and contending that Knapp's confession had been inadmissible because it had been extracted without the presence of an attorney and without the defendant's having been informed of his right to remain silent. The appeal also argued that the testimony of Arthur Hitt was inadmissible, because he had been acting as a paid agent at the time he secured incriminating evidence against Knapp, although Knapp had no knowledge that he was a police agent.

The Appellate Division of the Supreme Court of New York denied Knapp's appeal, citing the admission of the confession as a "harmless error" on the part of the judge. Owen, however, went on to the U.S. Court of Appeals, which stated that no error on the confession could have been harmless since the confession was at the heart of the case. The Court of Appeals overturned Knapp's conviction in October 1982 and voided his sentence on the Velsey murder charge. The reversal was a stunning humiliation for Judge Mogavero—he and Owen had been bitter rivals in the election for judge, and there was little love lost between the two. And it astonished the community, mainly Republican and conservative, where legalities such as the controversial exclusionary rule—which prevents admission of evidence obtained in violation of the Constitution—does not cut much ice. The community believed that the defendant did it and had said he did, and that was that.

So, in this highly charged climate, the prosecution retried Knapp in 1983, now precluded from using the confession and most of the key Hitt testimony as evidence, since both had been ruled inadmissible. Jury selection began anew. This time, not only did a jury have to put aside what it had read and heard about the original trial, it now also had to forget that Knapp had been convicted. Most of the evidence from the first trial now no longer applied. As far as these jurors were concerned, the events—as previously told—did not happen.

Retrials present challenges to any jury, but in a rural setting where word spreads like wildfire, securing an impartial jury can be virtually impossible. In fact, the defense hired a sociologist from a nearby private college in Oneonta who surveyed community attitudes and found that 87.5 percent of the people in the county believed Knapp guilty, regardless of the Appeals Court ruling. Citing these survey results, the defense understandably moved for a change of venue, but the Appeals court denied the motion. The original trial judge, Mogavero, would also hear the retrial, a circumstance which would have much to do with the way the retrial voir dire went. In fact, many judges in Mogavero's shoes would have disqualified themselves. To begin with, he had had a bad year of reversals. Second, he had to face his nemesis, Owen, again, as well as a community that now questioned his judgment. Third, he had been the presiding judge when the police made an immunity arrangement with Arthur Hitt, in return for his becoming an informer to gather evidence against Ricky Knapp. For a judge, that is a considerable amount of personal involvement in a case, leading to a considerable amount of pressure. In my view, Mogavero's desire to save face and be vindicated had much to do with the way voir dire went and how long it took. But the attorneys too saw this case as a battle of lawyerly skill—"knee-jerk liberalism" and "pandering to defendants" versus "bringing the guilty to justice." The district attorney was a lame duck who had chosen not to run again and probably wanted to end his term by reconvicting Knapp. Owen, the defense attorney, who had judicial ambitions, probably wanted Knapp clearly acquitted so that the lawyer would not be thought of as a quick-talking lawyer who got a murderer "off" on a technicality. With all these possible personal agenda on, or under, the table, voir dire began.

Jury selection was long and grueling, and cost the county approximately $31,000 in juror fees and reimbursed mileage, but not because of any particular juror or the jury system per se. It also served as a dramatic statement about the kind of juries some attorneys want.

Approximately 3,000 summonses were sent out to veniremen and women for this case, accounting for approximately one-third of the county's eligible jury pool. Then all but eight hundred potential jurors were excused by phone for reasons such as personal hardship or professional exemption. Of these eight hundred, all but 682 were excused by the judge during a prescreening process, either because they had overt biases, links to the case, or other readily identifiable cause challenges. Had a change of venue motion been granted—it was denied four times—this large number of people, higher than the number used in the federal Brink's case, wouldn't have been necessary. Had the judge supported the change of venue motion, it might have been granted. The practical effect of all the excuses was to reduce to 118 the number of those apparently qualified. As might be expected, almost all professionals and white-collar workers disappeared in the process. Otsego County has an impressive number of wealthy citizens, corporate executives, and college graduates in its population, but true to statistical trends, the final pool contained almost all blue-collar workers, the unemployed, and the retired. Doubtlessly, this was, in part, because the professional types knew what to say in order to be relieved. Some people remaining in the pool did not understand such words as "relevant," "absolute," "instrumental," "indictment," "felony." Most did not know the difference between civil cases and criminal ones. One man did not know the difference between an "award" and a "reward." Vocabulary problems haunted this jury right through deliberations.

The pool was also predominantly male and all white, the black population of Otsego County being less than 1 percent. Of the first group of sixteen venirepersons to be questioned, all were over the age of fifty, I would say; three were women, and nine of the men were at least age sixty.

In what a local newspaper called "a move perhaps unprecedented in the history of Otsego County court," the judge agreed to allow voir dire to take place *in camera*—that is, in the privacy of the judge's chambers. However, because the town's landmark-designated courthouse was undergoing renovation, the trial was being held in the County Office Building, which meant the judge had no chambers. Individual voir dire took place in the Family Court Hearing Room, while the rest of the panel waited in the larger County Board of Supervisors meeting room. The *in camera* proceeding had been granted probably because the judge was doing his best not to deny defense motions that could be hinged to yet another appeal. The defense moved for *in camera* proceedings so that jurors could be questioned about the extent of their knowledge about the case from pretrial publicity or the previous trial, without tainting the other jurors by letting them hear something they may not otherwise have known.

However, the judge denied a motion by the defense to bar the press from the *in camera* voir dire. Therefore, the defense felt precluded from probing specifics of what jurors had previously heard because it feared the press would report details that the other jurors might then absorb, even though the potential jurors had been instructed by the judge not to read or listen to anything about the case. Consequently, although the point of questioning jurors individually was lost entirely, the judge persisted with it, thereby wasting many hours and days and money. Though the defense clearly stated it would not probe regarding publicity and no longer considered the voir dire to be *in camera* due to the presence of the press, the judge played safe, probably assuming he would bar an appealable point on jury selection if he stayed with the individual questioning. The attorneys, not having anything to lose by the practice of individual voir dire, did not protest and, in fact, turned the events to their advantage.

Only two jurors were selected after two days were spent interviewing twenty-three people. The chosen were respectively a local postmaster and a railroad engineer. Here was the first taste of what the lawyers wanted. During questioning, the postmaster voiced few opinions. His most staunch position was that he would take a second look at testimony given by a convicted perjurer. Though he had two daughters of college age, he was not deeply probed, as others would later be, about whether his sympathies would lie with the victim by virtue of fatherly feelings. As first chosen, he became foreman, but nobody told him that until much later.

The railroad engineer smiled a lot; he did not seem to register exactly what he was being asked to do, except that it would be a break from work. Having established that the juror would not lose salary during his jury service, the DA asked if his mind would wander to his employment should he be selected. "Oh, no," the man replied with a laugh. He told the attorneys his wife might be a cousin of the local sheriff, but he was not sure. He had had previous jury service a few years prior—"they" found him guilty, he said. When asked what the case had been about, he replied, "I don't know. I just sat on the jury." He could not even say whether it had been civil or criminal. There was a strange detachment about him, for someone who had been through the process before, and yet he was not challenged by either attorney. He would turn out to be a staunch voice for acquittal during deliberations and, on balance, a very thoughtful juror, though nothing in the voir dire could have tipped the lawyers to that.

After the questioning that day ended, both jurors were sworn in, and the judge instructed them to have their phone calls and mail screened. The railroad engineer continued to smile, but when the judge stopped speaking, the engineer told him he had vacation plans to "go to Pennsylvania all paid for" and would it be all right if he stayed being a juror for a few days and not the entire trial? This might have been a signal to the judge and the lawyers that the man truly did not get the point, but the judge simply told him he would have to cancel his vacation and "be with us." The engineer smilingly said, "O.K."

The attorneys seemed pleased with their choices. Then instead of dismissing the selected and sworn jurors until the trial actually began, the judge ordered them to sit in the waiting room with the next panel of prospective jurors; the chosen would mix with the called. The defense, however, seized an opportunity here by objecting to the fact that there was no jury room where sworn jurors could be kept to themselves. Since the judge required the presence of the sworn jurors in court every day while the rest of the jury was selected (and theoretically, once they were chosen, they had no role in the proceedings until the trial actually started), and since there was no jury room, and since, in the defense attorneys' view, the proceedings were no longer meaningfully *in camera* due to the presence of the press—then, the defense argued, "I want those sworn jurors in the courtroom which I deem to be where we are." Incredulously, the judge asked if the defense realized that would mean the sworn jurors would hear all the answers of the potential jurors. "Yes," the defense replied. The judge then asked the district attorney if he had any opinion to voice, and the DA replied, "It matters not to me, your honor." So, two chairs were added to the non-*camera* camera, and as new jurors were selected, more chairs were added.

For the sworn jurors, this meant having to listen to days and days of the same questioning, over and over again, as one potential juror after another came and went through voir dire. In this way, the selected jurors gained unusual insight to the selection process. Though they were sent out of the room when the lawyers exercised the challenges, they had heard all the answers of all who had been picked and all who were not. Speculation is exactly what jurors are not supposed to engage in, but the temptation to speculate, at least about why the lawyers wanted whom, was doubtless irresistible.

One of the main criticisms of lawyer-conducted voir dire is that they use the time to "educate" the jury, to introduce them to the case, to float ideas, to test difficult aspects of the case, in other words, to prime the pump. However, this can and ought to be controlled by the judge. When it is not, surely the jury system cannot be blamed.

The presence of the sworn jurors in the Knapp voir dire courtroom gave the lawyers a unique opportunity not only to "seed" ideas, but to help them bloom. Normally, when voir dire is conducted in a group, veniremen do not know they will be picked, and the lawyers get only one chance to question them. In this case, the lawyers performed in front of the sworn jurors over a hundred times. The defense attorney was very skillful at making questions out of statements by ending with "right?" spoken with interrogatory intonation; essentially he used the voir dire time to make points normally reserved for an opening statement. Through questioning potential jurors, he immersed the already selected in the elements of his case. Among the seeds he planted were these: Just because the prosecution calls this a murder case does not make it a murder case; a murder case has a main question and subquestions, the main question being, Was a murder committed? The prosecution allowed the body of the victim to be cremated before the defense could have it examined (one potential juror could not have said better what the defense attorney wanted to hear: "I would call that destroying evidence myself.") Police can lie, doctors can lie, anyone can lie under oath; key witnesses can have prior criminal records and maybe even convictions for perjury. An especially key witness in this case was being kept out of state prison in return for his testimony. At best, a trial is only a re-creation of events—a prosecution witness who perjures himself on behalf of the prosecution probably will not be prosecuted for the perjury; an informant who waits five years to do his civic duty to inform might be a bit suspicious; police are pressured, by politics and public opinion, to solve crimes and might even fabricate evidence; family hatred can be a motive for testifying against a family member; there are three kinds of evidence: direct, circumstantial, and worthless; there is ore and gold, and the prosecution might have mined a lot of ore in this case and still have a very little gold; a defendant who may not be exactly innocent can still be not guilty of the charge. (The ore/gold analogy stuck well; when I interviewed the jury foreman after the trial, he recalled that "we disregarded a lot of evidence, a lot of it was that ore the lawyer was talking about and not much of it was gold.")

Owen accomplished his seeding with words, half questions, and body movements. He was constantly in motion—pulling up his trousers, arranging his tie, repeatedly switching from a pair of thick, plastic-framed, long-distance glasses to a pair of close-in glasses, stroking the back of his head, flipping through papers. This tended to attract the attention of potential jurors who may have listened better because they had to keep their eye on this man on the move. Then he would say something like "You don't think that just because a person comes into court and takes an oath"—he put up his right hand in swearing position, twisting his face into what he imagined would be that of a sullen liar—"he has to be telling the truth, do you?" Or, "If you find Ricky Knapp not guilty, you are going to be able to tell your neighbors 'I was there and heard the evidence,' right?" But Owen's best performance by far came on the matter of the goats.

From the district attorney's questioning, we learned that one potential juror's previous experience with law enforcement involved a mysterious poisoning of some of the dairy goats on her farm. The police never found the perpetrator, but that failure, the hearty widow farmer believed, did not reflect poorly on the police—"goats are so low on the social scale that nobody would call that a crime, but I make my living from them." The district attorney let the matter drop, but Owen moved in later. "Now on that goat situation," he began, one pair of glasses on and one pair dangling in his hands. "Suppose," he said, "that the community was up in arms about your goats. Everybody was talking about how awful the event was, goats dead or disappearing everywhere, and why didn't the police find the guy. The guy who did the crime [an attempt to cast suspicion on Arthur Hitt, the prosecution's star witness] sees a good opportunity, so he calls the police and tells them he knows who did it and, what is more, he can get the person to show him where the poisoned goats' bodies are buried. Now this volunteer also has some charges pending against him for other crimes [Hitt had a criminal record] so he makes a deal with the cops to stay out of prison in return for his help in solving the goat case." Owen embellished, describing in detail how the informer asked his friend for help moving a dead goat at a specific time and place, then called the cops to be at the same place so the friend could be caught red-handed with the goat. It was a tour de force.

"Now," Owen finally asked, "you can see how a totally innocent person could be set up in such a situation, can't you?" The widow said, "Of course." Who couldn't? Even the district attorney was enraptured by Owen's version of the crime and, amazingly, had not objected once. Although neither side selected this farmer, she beautifully served her purpose as fertile ground for Owen's parallel. The sworn jury, by then eleven people, sat captivated by the entire tale. Here, at least, had been a story to which anyone could relate.

The district attorney, for his part, seeded too. Since he was the first to question prospective jurors, the greetings to the jury fell to him, as did an explanation of what voir dire was all about. He used this chance to be cordial in order to dispel Owen's implication that the prosecution would stoop to anything to convict Ricky Knapp. He tried to put the jurors at ease, giving each a big "good morning" or "good afternoon." His main seed was the matter of reasonable doubt, perhaps one of the most elusive terms the jury must try to understand. Judges give an instruction about what it means; the most acceptable wording is "a doubt based on reason and doubt of the kind to suggest a reasonable person acquit." However, jurors still have difficulty knowing where "reasonable" begins and ends. Civil trials are somewhat simpler since the standard is "a preponderance of the evidence," and the juror can picture the scales of justice and see on which side most of the evidence lies.

In the Knapp case, the prosecutor had to be sure the jury could grasp what reasonable doubt was, without being able to tell them. First he asked each potential juror if he or she remembered the judge's instruction that the prosecution had only to prove its case beyond a reasonable doubt. Whether the juror did or did not remember, the DA asked if the juror could return a verdict of "guilty" and still have a doubt. Most said "no." They did not want to convict a man without being absolutely sure; it was logical that all doubt would have to be removed. However, the sworn juries sitting off to the side could observe that anyone who could not convict on something less than absolute certainty was never chosen. Even the one juror who could put the concept in his own words—"I guess reasonable doubt is like a gray area"—was rejected. "Gray area" was about the clearest explanation of reasonable doubt to be heard during voir dire, but neither the judge nor the lawyers picked it up to use with other jurors.

Nevertheless the concept that guilt must be proved beyond all reasonable doubt was pounded into the minds of the sworn-in jurors through hearing the same questions put to over a hundred people. And though no one ever gave them a decent example of what reasonable doubt might be, they did learn that "all doubt" was different from "reasonable doubt," and that all doubts were not reasonable doubts. Above all, that was what the DA wanted them to know, and though the defense tried to redress by saying, "You don't take reasonable doubt to be an invitation to be casual, do you?" the sworn jury went into deliberations with a much sharper than average exposure to the idea that it was all right to be less than sure about a guilty verdict.

The effect of the physical arrangement of sworn jurors watching the selection process was, to my mind, indelible. First, potential jurors came and went from the stand like witnesses—the attorneys questioned them, and their remarks sounded like testimony. One potential juror, eventually disqualified because of his acquaintanceship with someone on the real witness list, came across as a character reference on that witness' credibility. When the judge asked, "Is there anything about your relationship with him which would effect your ability to be fair and impartial," the juror said, "Well, I have never had any reason to doubt him. He has always been straight with me." The fact that the potential juror was likable enhanced his comments all the more. Would the jury be able to put this aside when and if the witness he described came up?

Now there was the ever-present, ever-closer, danger of a mistrial. All a potential juror would have to say is "I think he is guilty," or "I have heard he confessed," and that would be that. Of course, the judge warned people not to disclose what they thought they knew, but mistakes are inevitable.

Once the judge, in one of his numerous interventions on the reasonable-doubt issue, asked a potential juror if there was any doubt in her mind that, as the defendant sat there, he was innocent. She responded surely, "No, he wouldn't have gotten a new trial if—" The judge cut her off. So much for what the sworn jurors may not have known.

Though I could understand completely the need for extensive voir dire in the Knapp case, and though I believe lawyer-conducted voir dire should be preserved, the Knapp voir dire seemed a clear abuse. It was fascinating that the district attorney never once objected to the defense's questions; indeed, the DA was no match for Owen when it came to seeding. And though the judge once admonished Owen for making questions out of statements, the judge never intervened again. Possibly his hands-off approach intended to limit Owen's possible avenues of appeal, but I also think neither the judge nor the district attorney understood the potential impact of what Owen was doing. He was stacking toward a hung jury, massaging jurors' minds, for all he would need was one holdout or a few strong voices for innocence. He was writing the setup scenario, and the district attorney and the judge did not appear to care. Perhaps they thought it would not make any difference, so strong was the prosecution's case. If so, it was the kind of taking-for-granted of juries that is rather common among lawyers and judges.

This judge not only took jurors for granted, he was plain rude to them, never even greeting them or thanking them for their time—instructing the bailiff to "bring 'em in, bring 'em out," as if they were furniture. An additional chair, an additional juror—it was all the same to him.

It was obvious that these attorneys wanted the blankest jury they could find, the most easily manipulable. Consider a man they rejected.

T. W. MacDowell looked like a typical liberal—bearded, young, wearing jeans and plaid shirt. A self-employed carpenter and sheep farmer, he was building a cabin in the woods. On sizing him up, the DA went immediately for a cause challenge, trying to get MacDowell to say he would suffer financial hardship during the trial because of being self-employed. But MacDowell would not say it: "It won't break me. I could have easily gotten out of it but I thought I would do my civic duty." When hardship appeals didn't work, the DA moved on reasonable doubt. MacDowell was one of the few who remembered the judge's prescreening allusion to reasonable doubt. The district attorney tried then to make him say he would require removal of all doubt but MacDowell said, "Not all doubts are reasonable doubts." When the district attorney tried again to confuse him—often the DA would rephrase the juror's answer so it sounded like an answer the DA did not want—MacDowell said simply, "I think we are into a semantic problem here." People who can tell a semantic problem from any other kind are not usually welcome on juries.

The DA eventually used a peremptory challenge to remove MacDowell, but the defense had also intended to challenge him, because Owen had interpreted MacDowell's willingness to serve as wanting to be on the case—that is, to "get Knapp." The idea that anyone might simply want to do his civic duty seemed lost on both attorneys.

The unselected jurors reflected on their failure to be chosen. One man in particular put his finger on what he thought was going on: "They spend a lot of time picking someone they think will jump one way and that person might just as well jump the opposite." So much for the value of an average of sixteen minutes spent in voir dire time per person, with the record held at forty-seven minutes for a juror no one chose.

The Knapp jurors seemed to wend their way through the case quite well, despite gaps in evidence and conflicting crucial testimony, according to the half dozen jurors I spoke to, including the railroad engineer who, during jury selection, seemed so uninvolved in the gravity of the endeavor. At first a few jurors were ready to vote for outright acquittal on the murder charge.

The defense had succeeded brilliantly in its main strategy, which was to make the prosecution's star witness a defendant, in the eyes of the jury. "We all felt that Hitt had something more to do with it than came out in the trial," the foreman told me. This doubt that the defendant had acted alone nagged some jurors into a readiness to acquit.

During the trial, the prosecutor asked Hitt point-blank if he had committed the murder. Naturally, he denied it, but he had an unsavory criminal record and was a generally unappealing person. Yet, if one were to have heard only the trial testimony, one would not have thought the defense's aspersions were enough to so influence the jury. Thus, it is probable that pretrial seeding had quite a bit to do with the jurors tying what they had already heard about Hitt during voir dire to what they heard on the stand. "We knew who Hitt was when he came up there," one juror told me. Of course, it is completely outside the jury's province to consider whether a witness may have done the murder; their job is to decide whether the prosecution has proved its case against the defendant, period.

All the jurors felt they had been denied evidence that would have made their decision easier, and all knew they were sitting on a retrial of an old case. The medical evidence was also conflicting. The prosecution's expert claimed that the victim had lived for a while after being struck, thus aggravating the charge against Knapp—namely that he had not even bothered to take her to a hospital—whereas the defense's expert said she had died instantly. Moreover, over defense objections the district attorney was allowed to recross-examine on a new question of whether the cold weather might have slowed the victim's lethal brain hemorrhage. Confused by these tactics, the jury discounted both arguments and ignored the time of death as a factor in the decision.

Also, the rereading of the medical expert's testimony had some unexpected bearing on other evidence. A key contention of the defense was that it was not proved that Knapp had said "I killed her" at the scene of his arrest. Some police officers at the scene heard it and testified to it, but other police officers did not—at least, they had not included those three words in their testimony at the first trial. The court stenographer, the county's only one, then became a major figure in the retrial. (She takes all trial courtroom proceedings down in shorthand at 200 words per minute, using an ordinary pen and pad; I myself have seen her write for three or four uninterrupted hours.) It became extremely important to the defense whether she had perhaps missed those three particular words during the testimony of two different policemen. She was called to the stand and testified that her transcripts were as accurate as it was humanly possible to be, though she could have made an error. According to the jurors, they had decided it was unlikely that a trained stenographer would miss such important words not once but twice. "I figured he [Knapp] never said it," one juror recalled, "until we asked for a rereading of the medical testimony."

Although the secretary reread the medical experts' testimony smoothly on very short notice, she did occasionally stumble. The jurors heard her hesitate on words such as "skull" and "hematoma," and some concluded that it was possible, after all, that she had dropped the "I killed her" words from the transcript. However, the verdict did not hinge on whether or not Knapp had said the words—the jury had simply concluded there was enough other evidence on which to base a decision.

The jurors did not credit, they said, a word of testimony from the defendant's cousin who admitted on the stand that he had committed acts of violence, including the beating of his own mother. They also claimed that the fact that the trial was held in a church-affiliated building—the judge had moved the proceedings to a church hall, over objections by both defense and prosecuting attorneys, because it was the only space in town large enough to accommodate the spectators the judge expected—had no effect on their judgment. They tended to base their verdict on the fact that the defendant had been found with the body and that he had no real alibi for the time of death. The verdict was guilty of manslaughter.

Like most jurors I've talked to, the Knapp jurors lingered a bit after delivering their verdict, talking in groups in the parking lot as if trying to get used to lighter weight. Each felt relieved that the ordeal was over, but in retrospect they clearly felt they had mastered some difficult task. Nearly an entire summer had passed while they had been indoors. The foreman, Sweet, returned to his job as postmaster. He reminisced in rural fashion about the time he had given up: "I felt like when we went in there, the corn was green, and when we came out, it had all been picked." Just before the jury announced they had come to a verdict, a cheer could be heard from the deliberation room.

[11]
Behind the Jury Box:
Behavioral Science in the Court

About three days into the Knapp trial jury selection proceedings, the judge reprimanded the attorneys for taking too much time to ask potential jurors routine questions—address, occupation, and marital status. "You've had ample time to check these people out," the judge remarked. The defense immediately objected. "Your honor, we are not obliged to hire investigators. The defense has no money for that sort of thing."

"That sort of thing" is called "jury investigation," an element of the growing, costly field of jury research, intended to improve a lawyer's chances of getting a jury favorable to his or her side, and to aid the lawyer in shaping his or her case for maximum impact on the jury. This can mean questioning individual potential jurors and sampling their attitudes in order to develop a profile of the "desirable" juror—the juror, in other words, who is, at minimum, fair and, at optimum, disposed to deliver the verdict the researching side wants. Jury research can also call for using mock juries, who listen to evidence on a dry-run basis, so that attorneys can practice their case, or having shadow juries sitting in on the actual trial, advising lawyers on how their case is going over and helping to prepare charts and exhibits especially intended to clarify arguments for the jury. Jury research is aimed at improving communications between attorneys and the jury, but it becomes controversial because of the thinness of the line between communication and manipulation.

There are no real controls on jury research; no guidelines except one—no one may talk to a potential juror directly before the case begins, or to a sworn juror during the case. Apart from that unbreachable barrier against jury tampering, jury research may roam as far as its practitioners will take it. Litigants who can pay for jury research or who know how to obtain it free avail themselves of it. The rest do not, as nowhere in the guarantees for due process is there any rule regarding jury research—at least not yet.

As a new partner in the adversary system, jury research makes a marketing exercise of jury selection. Selling soup, selling the case—some of the same sampling and survey techniques are used. The marketing goal here is a favorable verdict. As of 1983, the jury research field was growing, involving approximately fifty specialists—they included lawyers, psychologists, sociologists, market experts—who can earn from $500 to $1,500 per day for their services.

Dr. Jay Schulman, sociologist and former professor at the City University of New York, is generally considered to be the father of jury selection research. He first used his academic training in sociology to help select a jury in Harrisburg, Pennsylvania, for the 1971–1972 trial of the anti-Vietnam War activist Berrigan brothers. Schulman assembled a team of students and designed a questionnaire that asked general questions about social protest and probed local attitudes toward the Vietnam War. After 840 telephone interviews plus 252 personal interviews were conducted, the data was analyzed.

There were some "surprises," Schulman recalled, according to an article in *The New York Times Magazine* in November 1982. For example, according to Schulman, the defense learned that "college educated people were not likely to be liberal in Harrisburg. Liberal college graduates, it seems, leave Harrisburg for other places, and those who stay support conservative norms." The implication here, of course, being that had the survey not been done, the defense attorneys would have assumed that college graduates would have been desirable jurors by definition.

Schulman, a tall, hefty man, wears a bushy white beard, and when I first saw him in court, I thought he looked a little like Father Christmas moonlighting in off season as a lawyer. (The courtroom artists enjoy drawing him.) He is not particularly pleased that jury researchers have proliferated and that something loosely called a profession has formed. "I did not start out to create a profession but to help my friends try to survive," he told me. "The proliferation is inevitable in a capitalist society where opportunity merges with money. . . . Some of the work is good, and a lot of it is terrible."

The main problem, in his view, stems from eagerness, "when social scientists and psychologists attempt to transfer their skills from the university directly to juridical work, as if there was substantive knowledge as to the interplay between law and social science." In Schulman's view, there is no such easy jump over, but instead a need for the social scientist to integrate him- or herself with each case.

The results of this are that "the client may pay good money for poor services; lawyers may elect to take poorly conceived strategies; the 'business' may have its reputation damaged. . . ." Hence, Schulman refers to himself as a "jury worker," which means he not only conducts investigations of potential jurors, but actually works with lawyers throughout the case on every aspect that can have juror consequences. This can range from producing movies to be used to demonstrate a point—for example, the slam effect of a motor boat coming to a halt beside a pier—to the preparation of the opening and closing statements. His ideal is the holistic approach, the strategy and the range of jury work services being dictated by the dimensions of each case.

In a small town with local lawyers on limited budgets, jury research amounts often to not more than phoning around town, asking friends if they know so-and-so, one of the potential jurors. In the Knapp case, after the lawyers had had the list of jurors' names for some time, I noted they had jotted down notes next to the various names and had indeed come up with a little background information. Still, they checked their information with the juror, using such already answered questions as, "You live in the Worcester area, don't you?" Often the answer would be "Yes, all my life." Sometimes jury investigations can be little more than gossip or folksy information gleaned from conversations held on the sidewalk or in the local café.

But where jurors are just names to attorneys, and where the stakes are high, or where there are political elements to a case, jury research takes on very sophisticated form indeed, crossing into areas of sociology, psychology, anthropology, even scientology. Jury researchers conduct telephone surveys, in-person interviews with community members, read local newspapers—even sometimes talk with friends of potential jurors and take photos of potential jurors' homes.

Do these methods serve the interest of obtaining better justice, or do they squeeze out the randomness that is the keystone of the jury system? Also, does jury research create a two-tiered system for trial, calculated versus spontaneous, researched versus unresearched?

Schulman rejects the idea that investigating potential jurors should be de rigueur. There are tactical reasons, in his view, that should override any theory about improving the odds. For example, in civil cases "where the plaintiff is an individual against a corporate defendant, juror investigations are simply not dictated." At the same time, the defendant who would presumably have much to gain from jury research may not wish to investigate jurors, because, Schulman noted, "word gets out that jurors are being investigated" and that can dispose potential jurors to resent the side doing the investigating.

Of course in very celebrated cases, about which most jurors cannot help but have some preconceptions, lawyers need to be able to screen for those who can be the most open-minded. The rub comes when they depend on standardized juror profiles rather than on the time they spend with the juror and their own instincts. In short, instead of improving their own jury selection abilities, lawyers are developing a dependence on simplistic, broad-brush thinking. A jury chosen through formal jury research has been chosen largely by reinforced stereotypes.

As pressure grows to limit voir dire time, lawyers will have less contact with potential jurors and will be able to learn less about them. Jury research may be needed to fill in the gaps. If judges do the questioning, as in most federal courts, or if court procedure so circumscribes the questions that an attorney may ask on voir dire that he can learn little about a prospective juror through his or her answers, then jury research may become increasingly necessary. Schulman lamented a case he was working on in which the federal judge picked a jury in thirty-two minutes: "We learned almost nothing about those people." Indeed, the average voir dire in the federal system in New York consumes about half an hour.

In some jurisdictions the jury clerk's office collects basic information from potential jurors on a questionnaire sent to jurors before they actually report for jury duty. This information—name, address, occupation at least—is then made available to the case attorneys in advance, and so when they actually face the jurors for the first time, they have already had a chance to do some homework about them. One lawyer in Georgia told me he routinely sends a team to the homes of potential jurors to take photographs from the outside. "Amazing," he reflected, "what you can tell about a person just by looking at where he lives. Not only the obvious, like the degree of affluence, but also style, taste, neatness, all parts of the personality puzzle we would never get otherwise."

I wondered how the attorney would feel knowing another lawyer had driven down his street, snapped a photo of his house, and concluded that because the grass needed cutting, a lazy family lived there. "It wouldn't matter. I don't care if someone thinks I'm lazy. What matters is, does the fact that I'm lazy make any difference to my service as a juror."

When Mark David Chapman went on trial in 1981 for shooting Beatle John Lennon, his only defense was insanity. His attorney wanted a jury that would be impartial enough to overcome the effects of pretrial publicity and any personal sense of loss they may have felt over Lennon's death. He tried to hire a psychologist to help pick jurors, but since Chapman was indigent, his court costs were paid by the City of New York, and the judge in question would not approve the psychologist's fee. However, the cocounsel in the case was also a social psychologist, and he spent much of his energy during jury selection interpreting body language.

In her book on the 1981 trial of Mrs. Jean Harris for the murder of the "Scarsdale Diet doctor," Herman Tarnower, writer Shana Alexander described the jury selection methods used by the first attorney in the case, Joel Arnou. The panel for the Harris trial consisted of 750 people. At the defense table sat a "mysterious, mustachioed young man" who scribbled notes on a pad. The man turned out to be a professional psychic who, Alexander reported, "sees an aura around every living thing, including prospective jurors. Blue or green indicated emotional calm and well-being; anxious persons have a red aura that in moments of unusual frustration he observes to pulsate."

According to Alexander, the defense attorneys did not always take the advice of the psychic about which jurors to accept or reject. Arnou apparently admitted he had hired the psychic to shake up the prosecution more than anything else.

In the end, the jury convicted Mrs. Harris—not to her surprise, for she had said all along that the jury would never believe her story, which sounded "too crazy." But she continued to have faith in the "truth"; to her, she could never be guilty because she had never intended to murder Tarnower. She would tell the jury that. Who the jury was did not seem to matter.

But despite the psychic, Arnou had apparently made a crucial error in judging jury attitudes. He failed to gauge the negative effect that Mrs. Harris herself—her chic dress, her aloof manner, her vindictiveness toward the "other woman" in the case—would have on the largely lower middle-class jury. (Alexander called them a "row of Edith and Archie Bunkers"—in itself an indication of class prejudice—as though this sort of a group could never give a woman like Jean Harris a fair trial.) Surely one need not have a doctorate in sociology to know that such a jury of ordinary people would have trouble identifying with Mrs. Harris' life-style, set as it was amongst the wealthy and powerful of New York's Westchester County. Indeed, Mrs. Harris' appeals by a new set of lawyers have emphasized that she ought to have been advised not to take the stand. All appeals, however, have been denied.

Also, it is claimed, the defense introduced too much technical evidence, swamping the jury in details which swept them away from the crucial question of whether Tarnower's death was accidental or whether Mrs. Harris intended it. Finally, the defense rejected an option to have the judge charge the jury on lesser included offenses, such as involuntary manslaughter, so that even if the jury had had doubts about Mrs. Harris' intent, it had no lesser verdict to choose from. It would seem that the poor judgment of those close to her—and not the poor judgment of the jury—convicted Mrs. Harris, and no amount of formal jury research could have helped that.

All lawyers maintain the right to know at least the names of the jurors in advance. In the Sacco-Vanzetti case, in Dedham,

Massachusetts, in 1921, a preliminary panel of five hundred was called and exhausted after only seven jurors had been selected. A great number of potential jurors had been dismissed because of age or hearing problems. When the first panel was exhausted, the defense attorneys argued that they had the right to a list of the names of potential jurors who would comprise the second panel. The prosecution maintained the court could simply pick jurors off the street. The judge left it to the sheriff to decide, and within twenty-four hours, another two hundred men sat in court to be voir-dired. After these new jurors had been brought into the court, the defense questioned the sheriff's deputies and found they had used almost no jury lists at all, but instead relied on names of people they knew and on acquaintances and men they thought fit to serve. This was a kind of primitive jury research intended, no doubt, to pick jurors with which the sheriff's deputies were comfortable.

In the main today, jury research techniques are employed when the stakes at trial are high, either monetarily or legally or both. The Ford Motor Company hired jury expert Hans Zeisel to help select a jury when it went on trial in January 1980 for allegedly having been careless in its design for its subcompact Pinto, particularly in regard to the safety of the rear end (where the gas tank is), and then failing to warn consumers of the potential dangers. The case was based on the death of three young women who were passengers in a Pinto when it was hit from the rear and burst into flames. Reportedly Zeisel was paid $1,000 per day, and Ford spent a total of about $1 million on its defense. Ford faced only $30,000 in fines—$10,000 per woman—should it have been convicted, but a conviction would have opened the door to dozens of civil suits by Pinto crash victims with settlements pushing well into the millions of dollars. Ford was also anxious to avoid setting any precedents in product-liability law, because this was the first time a corporation faced criminal charges in connection with product liability. The jury, seven men and five women, found Ford "not guilty" of reckless homicide.

Zeisel, an active and prolific professor who has not lost a shred of enthusiasm for the jury system since he began studying it almost twenty years ago, keeps a relatively humble perspective on the process to which he contributed. "That case was extremely important for Ford," he recalled. "No stone was left unturned." Zeisel conducted an indirect survey of attitudes—not in the area from which the potential jurors would be drawn but in states bordering on and similar to it, "in order to avoid being accused of jury tampering." There were three types of questions. First, all the standard types of demographic inquiry: age, name, address, occupation, etc. Then there was a set of questions exploring community attitudes toward the Ford company, toward vehicles, and toward driving habits. Third, Zeisel asked whether or not the respondee thought that use of criminal homicide charges in the case, as opposed to civil negligence charges, had been a good or bad idea.

From an analysis of responses, Zeisel concluded the best possible jurors for Ford would be, not surprisingly, older men, "mainly because they remember the Ford Motor Company put American industry on the map." The next best jurors, he concluded, would be middle-aged men and young men, then older women, then middle-aged women. Young women—also not surprisingly, since the victims were young women—were the worst possible Ford jurors, except "women who drove trucks who," added Zeisel with an impish smile, "tended to behave like men, in terms of the survey."

The test of the survey came during the actual voir dire. At one point a young woman told the court that she and her husband ran a small trucking business. One of the attorneys turned to Zeisel and said, "Well?" meaning, "Shall we choose her or not?" Zeisel replied, "My theory is that such a survey should never overrule the instinct of a good trial lawyer. But if it is all the same to you—if *you* don't know—then let her sit." According to Zeisel, "This juror ultimately proved very active in the acquittal." But Zeisel is quick to add, "We must ask whether any jury in rural Indiana would have convicted Ford in this case, given the facts—namely that these three young ladies filled their tank, they forgot to put the cap on, they stopped on a two-lane highway where there was no shoulder. . . . One woman got out to get the cap, and they were hit from behind by a van driven at fifty miles per hour by someone with a long record of traffic violations." Zeisel's impression was that the survey had been worth doing but that "given the uncontroverted facts in this case, I cannot call it my greatest success story."

The truck-driving woman juror, Janet Olson, has good memories of her jury experience by and large, and tends to corroborate Zeisel's estimation that the facts as presented were the determining factor. For a living, Mrs. Olson, thirty-one at the time, drives forty-foot eighteen-wheel trucks called semi's, so she knows something about driving and highway accidents.

The Pinto case was Mrs. Olson's first time in a courtroom, let alone on a jury. Her "activity" in the deliberations, she said, had mostly to do with convincing a lone male holdout that the court would never accept a hung jury in such a major case. "He kept saying they would let us go, and I kept telling him there was no way we would be able to tell them we could not come to a decision. . . . he finally gave in."

Interestingly, Mrs. Olson's sway with this juror may have derived from their voir dire experience. They had both requested to be excused on the grounds that they were self-employed, and both had been unafraid to speak out about their disinterest in serving. However, neither was excused, though Mrs. Olson had argued that she had no one with whom to leave her child: "I didn't have her so someone else could raise her." But eventually Mrs. Olson began to come around: "They started saying that when my daughter grew up she might need a jury to be fair to her for something, and when they got through with the speech, I felt an inch tall." Perhaps their initial resistance to serving set up a mutual trust between Olson and the holdout from the beginning. And she added, "He wasn't holding out because he saw the facts differently than we did. He was holding out because he thought there was more to the story than we were being told. I convinced him that that wasn't our problem. We were just supposed to handle what they gave us."

Mrs. Olson believes her profession influenced her thinking somewhat. "When you drive trucks you are used to worrying about liability and that kind of thing. And since we own our business I can see things from a company point of view, but then I also know big companies can do a lot of underhanded, illegal things." As regards her knowledge of car mechanics, Mrs. Olson recalled only one point at which it might have been directly relevant: "They were trying to say that gas cap popped off and rolled from one side of the road to the other. [The cap, which was shown in court] looked perfect to me, and I said to people that cap had not taken enough beating to have rolled the way they said [that is, the rolling should have battered it more]. . . . Some of the others did not pick that up." However, the main element that influenced Mrs. Olson to acquit was the case itself: "There just wasn't anything brought up that proved they [Ford] were liable."

In Chicago in 1980, the market research firm of Leo J. Shapiro and Associates conducted surveys of potential jurors for the law firm of Jenner and Block. The firm had been retained by the MCI Communications Corporation in an antitrust suit against American Telephone and Telegraph Company. The jury, after deliberating three days, awarded $600 million to be paid to MCI, finding that MCI had been damaged by AT&T's monopoly. The award was automatically tripled, because in antitrust suits, such is the manner of calculations, bringing the total to $1.8 billion.

Using market research, the attorneys ran a mock trial with mock juries, replaying the evidence this way and that to see which type of juror would be most likely to be predisposed, or tiltable, in the direction of MCI. According to an article on November 28, 1982, in *The New York Times Magazine*, Jenner lawyers also presented what they expected the AT&T case to be. Then the mock juries deliberated while the Jenner attorneys watched through one-way glass. According to the article, the jurors had not responded well to the idea that the law required AT&T to share the lines it had owned and built with other communications companies. On a rerun, Jenner lawyers hammered at the idea that fairness was not the issue and that it didn't matter if the jury thought the law was unfair to AT&T. What mattered was the prescription of the law. This, of course, denied the power of jury nullification—the act of a jury in defying the law as charged—which in this case would have operated against MCI.

MCI lawyers also practiced on the amount of money it could expect a jury to award, by eavesdropping on the mock deliberations and hearing a mock jury fix the award exactly at the level mentioned by the attorneys as profit lost, $100 million. When MCI dropped any guidance on amounts, the mock jury awards rose to $900 million, presumably because the ordinary jury has no real grasp of such an amount and a sense that corporate wealth is unlimited. When given no limitation, this ordinary jury awarded as high as its imagination could articulate, and the judge permitted the alternate jurors to deliberate on the portion of deliberations pertaining to fixing the award, on the request of the attorneys.

Also, the MCI attorneys used a "trailing jury." A trailing jury consists of eight to ten ordinary people, as similar to the actual jurors sociologically as possible, who are hired by the law firm or the jury consultants to sit in court each day. They then meet with the attorneys in late afternoon to describe their reaction to the evidence and argument they heard that day. Thus, the lawyers get a kind of running check on their performance—what is and what is not making an impact on the jury.

In Chicago, in 1983, the chemical industry was jarred by the conviction of several scientists and officers of the Industrial Bio-Test (IBT) Laboratory, which had been based in Northbrook, Illinois, and had operated from 1952 to 1978, making it the oldest such laboratory in the United States.

The federal government charged that the defendants had knowingly falsified data on tests conducted by the laboratory for companies seeking to comply with federal government regulations, which govern approval of new chemicals—that is, that the IBT men said these clients of theirs were in compliance when they weren't. Lawyers for the defendants hired psychologists to conduct a telephone survey of people who had previously served as federal jurors in the district and—according to one attorney who asked not to have his name used—"tried to determine what motivated them and how they would react to this kind of lawsuit." The defense team also ran several mock-jury dry runs of their case. On two occasions mock juries acquitted a defendant who was convicted eventually by the real jury. Before the mock juries, the defendant took the stand. Before the real jury, he did not. His lawyer, still visibly dismayed and depressed at having lost the case, looked down at the sheath of glass that covered the fine wood of his desk and said simply, "Those are hard judgments to call." On the other hand, the one defendant who did take the stand in court was convicted on the most counts.

The attorney acknowledged the debate about whether pretrial rehearsal of a case is ethical, but "since these practices intend to improve the way lawyers communicate, I don't see anything unethical about them."

In the IBT case, the telephone survey tended to confirm common sense. The demographic profile of the desirable defense juror—white male between forty and sixty, conservative, affluent, secure—was what the defense attorneys would classically expect the government's attorney to select. In this case, the government's point of view preferred "environmentalists" as jurors. The government's attorneys—who did not engage in any kind of formal jury research in the IBT case—challenged a male potential juror because he told the court he used a highly toxic pesticide in his garden, and the government surmised he probably had faith in chemical testing procedures.

In any case, despite the formal jury research and the informal guessing, there were six women in the jury panel, contrary to what the defense profile had called for, which perhaps just goes to show that neither side can easily negate the effect or will of the other in jury selection.

Yet, the surveys, telephone, mock juries, consultant's time add up to thousands of dollars. The 1982 *New York Times Magazine* article quotes a jury researcher as having said, "If it isn't worth spending $50,000 for jury research for your case, forget it. And a full-scale workup for jury research can run as much as $500,000."

Starting a new, expensive form of market research was not what Schulman and others, of course, had had in mind. Their goal was to uncover hostilities and biases an ordinary voir dire would not. People do not admit biases—for example, that they believe any defendant to be guilty. According to Schulman most of the general population believes that the defendant has the burden to prove innocence.

Occasionally, the value of jury research can be to probe jury attitudes and expose a community-held bias, to try to convince a judge that a field of bias exists and that questions about it are in order. Also, through jury research one might learn that a potential juror favored gun control or had married someone of another race or was active in civic organizations or, conversely, that the potential juror approved of handguns, disapproved of integration, and stayed at home when local controversies came to the fore. Any of these details could shed light on a juror's personality and might not necessarily be exposed in voir dire.

If a seriously well-done study on community attitudes can be presented, it can sometimes lead to useful changes of venue. Zeisel won a change of venue for Ford fromthe county which had been the scene of the Pinto accident; Schulman won a change of venue for Kathy Boudin, daughter of attorney Leonard Boudin, who was arrested in connection with the Brink's murders at Nyack, New York. But a very convincing study of juror attitudes around the Knapp trial in Cooperstown failed four times to win a change of venue, and had it been changed, jury selection may have been over in a matter of a few days.

Jury research is not available to the average client, who has neither the money nor the connections to pay for it. Schulman, with others, realizing that jury research could be particularly helpful in political cases, founded the National Jury Project in 1975, a nonprofit organization which uses volunteers and sociologists and lawyers to make the benefits of jury research available to those who cannot pay. It is a kind of poor people's market research, and its sympathies are liberal to left-wing.

One of the most celebrated uses of jury research came in the case of Angela Davis, the openly communist UCLA professor, who went on trial in March 1972, charged with kidnapping, murder, and conspiracy in connection with a shootout at Marin County jail in 1970, in which a judge was killed. She secured a change of venue to Santa Clara County. Using largely community-based volunteers, the Davis defense team undertook to investigate all 5,040 names that had been drawn as part of the first jury panel. An extensive questionnaire was prepared, covering political affiliation, reading habits, past jury service, residence, number and type of vehicle owned. Though the volunteers did not expect to complete all the questions for each potential juror, they apparently approached it with the zeal of a political campaign. The investigation continued during voir dire, with investigators feeding attorneys information as potential jurors' names were called. Yet, despite the investigation, the defense team accepted the jury panel as composed before all of its challenges were exhausted. Angela Davis herself addressed the judge. She stated that it had been the defense position all along that she could not be tried fairly—that is, by her peers—in Santa Clara County. She added that the jury panel seated *did* reflect properly the racial composition of the county, in that there were no blacks represented. Therefore, since the venue would not be changed again, the defense saw no point in further challenging the panel. Included in the group was an Annapolis graduate whom the defense had challenged unsuccessfully for cause when he had said he did not think he could be objective about communists. The rest were middle-class, ranging in age from twenty-two to sixty-seven, eight women, four men, most employed by large corporations. Interestingly, eight of the twelve had college degrees and all had some college, which may have had something to do with why the defense accepted the panel. But it seems as though, in the end, the defense trusted to luck. During the trial, two original jurors were replaced with alternates. The final jury acquitted, and according to forewoman Mary Timothy's account, no juror ever really believed that Angela Davis was guilty—the first ballot had been nine for not guilty and three undecided. (One juror voted guilty on one ballot but said she did so in order to capture the attention of the others, so they would go over her uncertainties with her.)

At a party celebrating the verdict, Mrs. Timothy asked the defense lawyers and Angela Davis why they had accepted the jury. Their reply was that if they had continued to challenge, so would the prosecution, and that would have meant losing people they wanted to keep. The reason they wanted Mrs. Timothy, they said, was that during voir dire it had seemed to them that she liked her children. Mrs. Timothy interpreted that to mean the defense team believed she could accept life-styles other than her own. The Davis verdict would seem to have been a victory for the jury system, rather than for jury research.

In the Wyman-D'Arazzio case, one defense lawyer told me he thought professional jury research was a "hype" by attorneys, a package they offer clients to make their firm look appealing, since one psychologist's opinion is likely to be in disagreement with the next. But there are a number of lawyers who now routinely do jury research, as much to teach themselves how evidence will be received, as to pick the best individual jurors.

One attorney with a large law firm in the South, which handles criminal as well as large civil cases, told me, "We don't try a big case unless we get some professional help. It's a guide to frame the case for the people on the jury." This help, he says, essentially involves learning how to develop a "fact pattern" a jury will accept, and also to formulate layman's terms that would equate to legal standards and legal phraseology. He gave the difference between "liability" and "responsibility" as an example—the former being a word many jurors did not understand, and the latter being within their reach.

He also related how jury research can uncover useful material about what people already know about a case, beyond what they reveal they know in voir dire. For example, one case involved a plaintiff, a young doctor who moved to a mill town and had observed extensive pollution in the area. He initiated civil action against the mill, which lasted nine years or so. Several roughneck incidents took place in connection with the action, including an alleged kidnapping of one of the original lawyer's sons (two law firms ultimately were involved), and an assault on the doctor himself in a parking lot. The second law firm (for the plaintiff) wanted to know how much the local people already knew about the case, and conducted a poll. "We found the average person's knowledge of the case was far exaggerated from the facts," I was told. "They remembered the parking lot incident variously—that the doctor had been shot or beaten or hit with a lead pipe." In fact, the doctor had simply been pushed to the ground and was unhurt. However, the attorneys, having uncovered a preconception in the community air that favored their position, let it remain aloft. "If the average person remembered the case as the 'parking lot beating,' it could only help the plaintiff, our client." They did, therefore, not bring out the milder truth.

This particular law firm works with 8 x 11-inch sheets of paper, usually one for each juror. There is a short biography—occupation, name, address, etc.—of potential jurors surveyed, a Polaroid snapshot of the juror, if possible, or the juror's home, notes gathered by questioning neighbors, even over-all credit reports available from special clearing houses. Insurance companies apparently have long been using credit reports during jury selection in civil cases on the assumption "that people who are behind in their bills will be antiestablishment." The reports talk about past loans and payments, not individuals' current ratings as credit risks.

Some firms keep "jury books," looseleaf notebooks full of information on the people whose names are on, or are likely to appear on, jury rolls.

Background information helps shape the presentation of evidence in court. "A good trial lawyer does not present facts; he manipulates facts," my attorney friend said to me. And so when his firm took on a very celebrated murder case, in which the defendant's previous conviction had been overturned, they again relied on jury research. Evidence linking the defendant to the crime consisted only of fibers from rugs and towels found on the defendant, and hair strands alleged to be the defendant's, on rugs and towels. As it turned out, in the area where the trial was to be held, 90 percent of the income of the population was earned in the carpet factories and carpet outlets in the area. These jurors knew fibers and therefore would be very careful about interpreting evidence about fibers. Jury research also revealed that the community held a low opinion of the local police crime laboratory's ability to identify fibers correctly. The law firm took this into account when planning what to emphasize in the defense. They used videotapes and other practice devices to present the case to a jury that would inevitably have members with a strong technical background.

In criminal cases, jury research is almost exclusively used by the defense. It is argued that defense use of jury selection techniques is quite acceptable because the prosecution already has advantages in terms of community attitudes, such as that most people believe an indicted person must be guilty of something, or that the burden of proof is on the defendant, not on the prosecution. Presumably the idea of research is to increase the odds of having a fair trial.

There is the possibility that jury research can be employed as a substitute for evidence. Also, a jury can be so composed of naturally hostile elements that personalities inevitably clash. Some jury researchers look for people who will not mix well with one another, even in deliberations, so that a hung jury becomes more likely. The idea is to pick people who will feel pitted against each other when it comes time to make a group decision. This was the effect the federal Brink's defense hoped to achieve by letting the "general's wife" sit. Perhaps, too, she herself felt out of place, and this is what prompted her to quit the jury.

One jury researcher in Dallas, Texas, admitted to a *People* magazine interviewer that, in cases where there is a lot of technical prosecution evidence, she selects the least educated because "you might want the juror to fall asleep in the jury box." In other words, if jurors can't be convinced of the view one side holds, better they hear nothing at all. Ostensibly, jury research screens out biases and identifies extremely opinionated people, so they may be eliminated. Ostensibly, jury research weeds out extremes. But in some cases, it seems, the goal is to dance around the truth until it is obfuscated with the recast "fact pattern" prepared by the dancers.

Supporters of jury research for the defense argue that it helps counteract the presence of "the system" in a trial, meaning that it is "the system" which calls the jury together, "the system" which, in the form of the judge and jury clerk, disposes the average juror to feel part of the system too and thereby to favor the prosecution. So, they contend ferreting out antisystem types is almost the duty of the defense. Defense attorneys also argue that any panel of potential jurors is automatically skewed to contain more authoritarian types, because liberals tend to seek excusal more regularly than conservatives, who may feel more "duty bound."

Of course, in a trial involving overtly political charges, such as draft resisting, a juror's political attitudes become relevant, and campaigns are mounted to locate political prejudices—either for or against the defendants. These findings might also be used to move for a change of venue or to shape questions for voir dire. Volunteers collect such information as what referenda have been put on the ballot in a community prior to the case. For example, in a recent case involving a psychiatrist, it was useful to know that the community had recently passed a referendum banning electroshock treatment for the mentally ill—a vote that told something about the community's attitude toward psychiatrists.

During the Dr. Spock et al. trial, and any of the draft-evasion cases of the 1960s and 1970s, data was collected about attitudes toward the Vietnam War. However, sometimes there is little correlation between attitudes and verdict. Zeisel wrote, in an article, that one member of a jury staunch for conviction had four draft-resister sons.

In her book, *Jury Selection in Criminal Trials*, attorney Ann Fagan Ginger argues for investigating a jury panel. She reports some results of "third party" investigations on potential jurors: A middle-class suburban white woman looked the role of a conservative establishment member, but when the defense lawyers learned she had a son who was a rock musician and another male relative in Canada, presumably a draft dodger, their view of her changed. In another case, in which certain union leaders were on trial, defense lawyers made inquiries about a prospective juror who belonged to a union but seemed noncommittal in her voir dire answers. The defense learned she had held firm in a strike and kept her on the jury.

Mary Timothy, in her book on the Angela Davis trial, writes passionately about her belief that jurors should not be subjected to this kind of formal investigation because it seemed to "lead to a police state." She wrote that the government, which loses politically important cases, "is bound to blame the juries rather than the inadequacy of its own cases and so will be forced to expand the already formidable investigations of prospective jurors." Indeed, this could be something to worry about.

On the other hand, Schulman, the man who started the jury research business has written, "although it is morally regressive to emulate the enemy, a people's lawyer has no political alternative, given the state's enormous advantages, to seeking and using third-party information. . . . Not surprisingly, it is liberals who, without confronting the state's advantages and practices in jury trials, condemn third-party inquiries by the defense lawyers as an invasion of privacy or as 'jury rigging.'" In our personal interview, Schulman elaborated on his view: "In cases in which the state brings legal action against dissenters or political dissidents, the state uses all of the machinery at its command and that machinery is immense. . . . In these instances, jury investigations are to me without ethical disadvantage, and if appropriate tactically I have no qualms about them. . . . Then there are different levels. The only time I feel comfortable talking with neighbors or coworkers or coreligionists [of a litigant] is when it is clear that the plaintiff or defendant is at a disadvantage and therefore a fair trial requires you do as much homework as you can. I think the civil libertarians miss that point."

It seems likely that third-party inquiries will increase, especially if intensive voir dire opportunities decrease. And, too, there is no question that the prosecution also can investigate when matters are sensitive. In the Spock case, wrote Mitford, the Attorney General's office ran an FBI check on prospective jurors intended to kick out any criminal records, as well as turn up possible records of previous FBI surveillance. In the Davis trial, Mary Timothy suggests that once the jurors were sworn in, their phones may have been tapped; several jury members complained of clicking and other sudden trouble on their phone lines. It would be naive to think that the jury system stands inviolate. Up until about twenty-five years ago, federal prosecutors ran Internal Revenue Service checks on prospective jurors as a matter of course.

Of course, jury research begins to evoke the idea of jury tampering, insofar as its goal is to find out everything possible about a juror, stopping short of actually interviewing the juror. While talking to a prospective juror is not, in and of itself, tampering, questioning about attitudes that might be related to the trial could stray into debatable territory. So far, however, it seems the nose of jury research is clean.

Interestingly, jury research may result in an automatic delay factor in trials. If one side challenges the propriety of what the other side has done or even seeks through the "discovery process"—in which one side is required to provide the other with copies of case materials before the trial—to have access to jury research materials, one client will end up paying for what both clients may use. Arguments on these points are bound to consume a lot of court time.

Perhaps the most disturbing aspect of jury research—especially in incompetent hands—is what it says about the average person's ability to relate to the law. Jury research assumes that stereotypes are valid and that jury deliberation is merely an exercise in small-group dynamics. It tends to recommend that a lawyer match the presentation of his case—its style, its volume, its color—to the preconceived psychological variables of a specific type of juror, rather than draw the best case possible for an average, representative twelve. Clearly, no jury is uniform; a jury is not a set of interchangeable parts but rather a collection of individuals. And lawyers have the right to select the individuals they want; that is what voir dire is all about—it is about not being scientific where science cannot be precise. Jury research is about supplementing science where instinct cannot be precise.

Suddenly, we are talking about juror "profiles." In Mitchell-Stans, the profile recommended to the defense by its hired social scientist was "working class, Catholic, with $6,000–$10,000 average income, readers of the *Daily News*. Jews, the college educated, and readers of *The New York Times* were to be avoided." In a case in 1977, in Texas, involving a millionaire accused of killing his stepdaughter, the desired "profile" was Protestant women over forty-five, with children under eighteen still at home, and less than two years of college. What these profiles can lead to is a use of the challenge system as if the entire community had been voir-dired, not just one person. Use of profiles implies that although there is such a thing as individuality, the average person is not capable of rising above his prejudices and biases in the jury room or of changing his initial impressions once he has heard the discussion of the other jurors.

The proliferation of jury research seems inevitable. Indeed at a seminar given in December 1983 by the Practicing Law Institute in New York City, the chairman of the faculty commented that "there is no question the use of behavioral science in jury questions will be increasingly with us throughout the '80s." The lawyers' wish to pay more attention to jurors comes at the precise moment when the pressure for court efficiency seeks to pay less attention to juries, in the sense that administrative procedures want to speed jury selection, even remove the jury from the civil system. As lawyers want to know more about jurors, courts want to give them less opportunity to do so. Also, if we have, on the one hand, less well-educated jurors in an age of declining literacy and on the other more juror-aware lawyers seeking to influence jurors' perceptions, the whole point of the jury system may be lost. For increasingly sophisticated marketing techniques will meet decreasingly sophisticated jurors, and the jury of the future might be highly susceptible to manipulation.

But human nature might be a built-in control. There is, within the legal professional, a good deal of skepticism about whether even the most sophisticated jury research techniques can predict or overcome an individual juror's feelings once the case has been completed. At the PLI seminar, Hugo Black, Jr., one of the most eminent trial lawyers in the United States and the son of U.S. Supreme Court Justice Hugo Black, told a story of a colleague who hired a psychologist for help in jury selection. The man, whose bill for total service rendered had been approximately $60,000, was especially proud of having helped select juror No. 1, the foreman. Said Black with a twinkle, "That $60,000 juror ended up hanging the jury against my friend."

Sometimes jury research techniques can seem to counter common sense. In his powerful book *Fatal Vision*, author Joe McGinniss describes how the defendant—a former Green Beret captain accused of brutally murdering his wife and children and then blaming the incident on marauding hippies—trusted his own instincts over his lawyer's research. Though an expert from Duke University in North Carolina helped select the jury by drawing a profile of desirable jurors, the defendant, MacDonald, worried about those who were to sit in judgment on him. The defense had not challenged a retired state trooper, even though defense attorneys often reject jurors affiliated with law enforcement, except when the defendant is somehow affiliated himself. In this case, perhaps MacDonald's attorneys equated the defendant's military status with law enforcement. Nonetheless the defendant was uncomfortable with the choice and complained. When his attorneys pointed out that the selection had been scientific, the defendant did not much care: "Scientific bullshit! . . . For six weeks I've been asking you what the fuck is a state cop doing on the jury? And all you tell me is about how high a rating he got. Just make sure you don't throw those figures away. They'll be very comforting to me while I'm getting gang-raped at the Atlanta penitentiary."

MacDonald was convicted.

[12]
Peremptory Challenge, Sanctioned Abuse?

According to Bert Neuborne, legal director for the American Civil Liberties Union, during the 1950s (specifically before 1957), attorneys in New York used a simple and quick method for choosing juries. It derived from the national pastime—baseball. As Neuborne tells it, attorneys needed only one question: "What baseball team do you root for?" Yankee fans, the defense dismissed; Dodger fans, the prosecution dismissed. Giant fans—New York was then a three-team city—were acceptable to both sides because, Neuborne says, they were "the only reasonable people in town." On the baseball basis, attorneys simply used the peremptory challenge—the refusal attorneys need not explain.

Baseball is an extreme example, but no matter, for the exercising of a peremptory challenge results from lawyers' gut feelings, their instincts. While attorneys have some specific ideas regarding the kind of jurors they want for any specific case, peremptory challenges remove those potential jurors the attorneys simply suspect could hurt their side. Often, the peremptory derives from no more than a hunch.

The value of the peremptory is precisely that it will not be questioned and cannot be ruled upon by the judge, giving the attorney latitude—up to the number of peremptories allowed by the nature of the case—to pick and choose, hunt and peck. But the fact that the peremptory need not be explained makes it susceptible to abuse, though abuse may be difficult to define. For example, is it abuse to challenge perfectly reasonable jurors simply on the assumption that there might be better ones—that is, those more disposed toward one's side—coming up in the next

151

panel, or to eliminate the smart, the professional, the independent thinking?

But the deeper problem of the peremptory challenge is its potential for racial discrimination—that is, purposefully keeping members of a particular racial or ethnic group off a jury on the assumption that members of that group will be intractably and automatically biased in favor of their fellows. When the defendant, or even the opposing attorney, is a minority member, attorneys for the other side challenge and excuse those whose race they fear might interfere with the outcome of the case. This perversion of the purpose of the peremptory challenge is likely to develop into an increasingly public legal issue over the next ten years as pressure to speed trials mounts. Often the only way to stem such abuse is to add procedures—such as requiring attorneys to explain peremptory challenges—which would slow down jury selection even more.

Abuse of the peremptory challenge sets the rights of the defendant and his lawyer against those of society. Minority members have the right to participate equally with whites in civic systems, such as jury service, and all have the right at least to be eligible to serve. This has been the gist of evolving law since *Strauder* v. *West Virginia* in 1880. Not only has the Supreme Court ruled that discriminatory jury lists are, in and of themselves, unconstitutional, the Court has heard several cases brought by individuals claiming their constitutional rights to serve on a jury had been denied. In the first of these, *Carter* v. *Jury Commission of Greene County* (Alabama) (396 U.S. 320, 1970), the citizens bringing the case objected to local statutes that allowed local jury commissioners discretion in compiling jury lists. The commissioners, the citizens argued, used this discretion to keep blacks off the jury lists, thereby violating their rights to serve on juries. Carter et al. asked the Supreme Court to declare the Alabama jury selection procedures unconstitutional. The Court, however, declined, ruling—in an echo of *Thomas* v. *Texas*, decided in 1909—that states have the right to retain discretion over juror qualifications, for example, by limiting eligibility to those "possessing good intelligence, sound judgment and fair character." At the same time, however, the Court held that the states had an obligation not to use this discretion to practice racial discrimination. This decision, and others which followed, thus affirmed the right of any minority member to protest being barred from eligibility for jury service. In fact, the Carter decision stipulated the right to serve on juries alongside the right to vote, so vital was it deemed to the survival of democracy. Justice Stewart wrote "whether jury service be deemed a right, a privilege, or a duty, the State may no more extend it to some of its citizens and deny it to others on racial grounds than it may invidiously discriminate in the offering and withholding of the elective franchise." So there seems to be little question that the Supreme Court views unrepresentative jury lists as unconstitutional and discriminatory. Yet, as John Hardwick, a prominent black attorney in Montgomery, Alabama, observed to me in the fall of 1983, "The Supreme Court has missed the point. It doesn't matter that blacks are in the pool if they can't get on the jury." And so through peremptory challenge abuse, relatively representative jury pools can be reduced to unrepresentative juries. And nearly a century of struggle for racially representative juries is rendered moot in individual cases when attorneys see fit to use the peremptory challenge to shape a jury racially.

What this boils down to is that while everyone has the right to be called for jury service and the duty to serve when called, none have any constitutional right to be selected. Attorneys argue that the defendant's right to an impartial jury overrides any right of a juror to be chosen. So attorneys may weed out, through the peremptory challenge, those they prefer not to seat. And if a juror peremptorily excused were to protest that in a specific case he or she should not have been dismissed, that juror appears to be a volunteer juror. Neither side embraces volunteer jurors, usually because of the fear that the juror has some particular ax to grind and for that reason wants to sit on the case. So, persons who may have been challenged solely on the basis of race have no recourse.

On a peremptory basis, attorneys may dismiss professionals, jurors with policepersons or lawyers in their families, those whose dress they dislike—in short, anyone. Any reason, of course, may be a racial reason, and when the reason is outright discrimination, that is when peremptory challenge use becomes peremptory challenge abuse.

Another loop in the knot comes when prosecutors, availing themselves of essentially the same jury selection procedure privileges as defense attorneys, use peremptories to eliminate jurors who the prosecution suspects will be against the state. This practice is, in fact, well within the definition of the adversary system, but when the prosecution uses its peremptory privileges to knock members of a racial group from a panel solely on the basis of race, an abuse has clearly taken place. The prosecutor is within his or her rights, but those rights offend the right of the defendant to a jury drawn from a cross section of the community. Certainly a defendant—white, black, or of any race or ethnic group—cannot be said to be facing judgment by peers if not a single member of his or her racial group sits on the jury. Since there have not been juries composed solely of one race except all-white, it is only minority groups who suffer racial abuse of the peremptory challenge. And when protests have been lodged, they have been mostly defense complaints objecting to prosecutorial behavior. Indeed, peremptory challenge abuse is most wide-spread among, though not confined to, prosecutors.

Clearly, not all prosecutors abuse their peremptory privileges, but an oft-cited handbook, used in 1973 to train prosecutors in Dallas County, Texas, demonstrated the attitude that underlies the problem we see even today. The book carried these instructions about jury selection to prosecutors: "You are not looking for a fair juror, but rather a strong, biased and sometimes hypocritical individual who believes the Defendants are different from them in kind, rather than degree; you are not looking for any member of a minority group which may subject him to oppression—they almost always empathise with the accused." This simply means that prosecutors assume outright not only intraracial group empathy, but that this empathy cannot be overcome by a reasonable person, when warranted, to render a fair decision.

The handbook came home to roost, so to speak, in 1983, in the case of Lenell Geter. Geter, a black man, went on trial in Dallas before a jury from which all blacks had been peremptorily challenged. He was charged with armed robbery. He had been identified from his driver's license photo as the man who tried to steal $615 from a fried chicken restaurant, and he was called to the attention of the police by a woman who claimed he had been loitering in a local park and looking suspicious.

Although, at trial, testimony from nine of Geter's coworkers placed him at work during the time of the robbery, and although Geter was holding down a solid engineering job at the time and had a number of character references, and although there was no physical evidence—fingerprints, stolen property, etc.—linking Geter to the robbery, he was convicted. Then, incredibly, he was sentenced to life imprisonment, though he had no criminal record whatsoever.

There were several complicating factors at work in the Geter case as well. His defense was not the most vigorous. His court-appointed attorney commented to the press that "at $200, you don't do a lot for them," alluding to the fee he received as public defender in Geter's case. Also, there is considerable question about the motives for the arrest, since Geter often frequented the park where he had been spotted, but the sheriff had been widely quoted as having first called Geter an "outlaw" and then withdrawing the remark.

The legislature of the state of South Carolina, Geter's home state, passed a resolution asking the state of Texas to reopen the case. Geter's coworkers, white engineers who refused to believe he committed the crime, raised $11,000 to pay a private defense. The national media picked up the case, largely through the efforts of a local television reporter, and focused attention on the Dallas prosecutor's office and began questioning the office's practices where Geter had been concerned. Pressure mounted for a new trial, especially after the defendant alleged to have been Geter's accomplice was acquitted, but the Dallas prosecutor's office repeatedly refused. However, it eventually reversed itself, consenting to reopen the case and allowing Geter free on bail. The prosecutor said he agreed to the new proceeding to restore confidence in the criminal justice system.

If there had been blacks on Geter's jury, he might possibly not have been convicted in the first place (his so-called accomplice's acquittal, however, did emanate from another all-white jury, albeit one which had probably known about Geter's case prior to having been called to serve). But the most disturbing aspect of Geter's all-white jury was the sentence it imposed on him. Given the relatively minor nature of the charge against him (theft of $615) and the fact that he had no criminal record, the jury must have felt particular malice toward the man in wishing to incarcerate him for life. It is doubtful that a black juror, familiar with problems of mistaken identity and aware that there was no direct evidence linking Geter to the crime, would have acquiesced in conviction at all, let alone permit the jury to impose such an outrageous sentence. If confidence in the criminal justice system was shaken by his conviction, the undermining of confidence began when the jury selected to judge him was deliberately made all white.

The right to peremptory challenge goes back at least to the Romans who, under the Lex Servilia, around 104 B.C., ruled that the accused and the accuser could each propose one hundred jurors, and that each could reject fifty leaving one hundred unrejected to hear the evidence. But in England, the use of the peremptory challenge by the accusing side was originally regarded with some concern.

In England, as the jury system developed, the King—that is, the state—had his power of peremptory challenge questioned under Edward I in 1305. The peremptory challenge, when exercised by the King, had been "mischievous to the subject, tending to infinite delays and danger"—so wrote jurist Sir Edward Coke three hundred years later. Under Edward I, the King's challenges could only be made for cause. In practice, though, this became known as "standing aside," since the King's counsel could ask potential jurors literally to stand back in the wings until the entire panel of jurors had been examined by the defense. Unless there were not enough jurors left to compose a jury but for those "standing aside" at the discretion of the King, then the King did not have to explain why he had set aside the jurors. Therefore, in effect, even though he did not nominally have the right to challenge peremptorily, the King had the right to practice it so long as he left a sufficient number of jurors on the panel. As Jon Van Dyke points out in his book on jury selection procedures, "Court practice thus allowed the crown to continue a procedure that Parliament had explicitly eliminated."

In the United States, the prosecution did not have peremptory challenge rights at the time the Constitution was adopted, and it was not common until the midnineteenth century, as states gradually began to pass legislation granting the prosecution peremptory rights. On the other hand, defendants have always been entitled to peremptory challenges. From its evolution, the peremptory challenge then would seem to have been considered a defensive rather than offensive device. Therefore, using it to purge the jury panel of members of a certain racial group seems especially obnoxious. That the rules permit this racializing of the jury and that it proceeds in open court contribute not to fairness but rather to its illusion.

The irony of this situation is precisely its public nature. This is not back-room business; it is open, forthright, well within the system; it happens in small and large cities, rural and urban areas. One need not look very hard to see it in action, although it seems most common in the rural South where, though blacks usually do appear in the general jury pools, their representation on trial juries is vulnerable to abuse of the peremptory challenge. Such abuse takes place still, before one's very eyes. I saw a blatant example of it in Brunswick, Georgia, the industrialized seaport near the Sea Island resorts.

Inside the old courthouse, the oak railings and floorboards creaked as people moved around preparing for voir dire. The sheriff took his seat. His nickname was "Slick," and it was official enough to appear on the placard identifying where he usually sits. Outside the temperature lingered in the 90s, but inside the air conditioning made many in the room too cold. Several men sat along the railings inside. All the attorneys were white except one, and none were sunburned or the least bit tanned, even though we had just had a beautiful weekend and the beach was just minutes away.

The judge sat well above the lawyers on his bench and was also not at all tanned. Some seventy-nine persons reported to serve on jury duty that afternoon, about twenty-five of them black. There would be two cases to try, each involving black defendants, and the judge was tough on the people who had not answered their jury summons. He told the sheriff to produce the absentees in court at 9 A.M. the next day; no excuses would be accepted.

The prosecutor asked for a show of hands from those prospective jurors who might have any biases or prejudices "resting on their minds." No hands. The wheel was spun, and the two panel boxes were filled by people whose names had been called. The attorneys already had a master list of the jurors' names and addresses. Voir dire consisted of verifying the information on the list and asking each juror's occupation. There was general questioning about whether any potential juror knew persons or witnesses in the case, or had relatives on the police force. This time, there were hands in the air. People with cause challenges— that is, people who were too close to the events involved in the case—were excused then and there, with almost no argument from the judge.

In Georgia, in criminal cases, the peremptory challenges are exercised in the presence of the jury panel. In the order they were seated, each juror rose when his or her name was called and waited to see if he or she survived the peremptories. The prosecutor had first say—either "State accepts the juror," or "State excuses the juror." Some district attorneys inserted the word "respectfully" before a juror was excused. Sometimes there was a delay between when the juror stood up and the attorney's decision, so that the embarrassed juror was not only accepted or rejected before all eyes in the courtroom but was also kept waiting while the attorney tried to decipher his notes or to compare the standing juror to the jurors who remained. It was a moment or two of unnecessarily humiliating silence for the juror. But for blacks, especially males, humiliation was short and swift.

The first case was an alleged murder involving a black male defendant who was charged with beating his wife to death. The district attorney without a second's hesitation excused six black men in a row, plus one black man who would have been an alternate juror. In the second case, involving an alleged cocaine sale by a black defendant, a black male potential juror, about twenty, who had said only that he was a waiter was dismissed while a white of about the same age was accepted. The white, when asked his occupation, had said simply, "I work at the club." Although he wasn't questioned further, chances are he too was a waiter in the summer season. Downstairs later I asked one of the black men who had been excused if he had any idea why. "No," he replied, "and I don't care. I want to get back to work." Clearly, he felt no injustice had been done to him.

A white woman standing by interjected that "they"—people she knew, I guess—told her not to wear jewelry because "they" strike you if you wear it. "But when I saw all those people with jewelry," she added, "I'm sorry I didn't wear it." Searching for a rationale on the blacks, for a moment I wondered if maybe they had all dressed in some way that influenced the district attorney. But no, it seemed they had only their blackness in common.

The black attorney handling the defense in the cocaine case told me exclusion of blacks was "just standard practice." He continued: "Blacks, Hispanics, Italians—they say they make a good defense juror, at least that's what the prosecution thinks." The white defense attorney in the murder case told me frankly, "Usually the DAs use strikes for no reason other than that the jurors are minorities." The district attorney himself did not seem concerned about divulging his reasoning. When I said I could not help but notice he had challenged so many young black men in a row, he answered simply, "I thought they would be sympathetic to the defendant."

As it turned out, the jury in the cocaine case hung. As the defense attorney said, "They had so many witnesses going against my guy and still the jury hung. That will show you what kind of case it was." The evidence, despite the string of witnesses, had not been clear, and he felt that the charges had been largely trumped up.

In the murder case, the jury from which all black males had been expunged acquitted the defendant of murder in a 12–0 vote in twenty minutes. They did convict him on the lesser charge of aggravated assault. This lesser charge, the foreman commented to me, the jurors thought was just "a slap on the wrist." But he added, "The state did not prove its murder case." So the prosecutor's stacking did not work, although there had been very gory photographs presented to demonstrate the extent of the beating the woman had received and testimony from the couple's eight-year-old daughter that "Poppa was beating on Momma."

I asked the foreman, a white man in his sixties who had had prior jury experience, about whether he believed prosecutors tried to keep blacks off juries. He answered that "quite often a black is far harder on another black on a charge like that. The average white . . . would be more lenient. Around here, there still remains some element of that belief they don't really know what they are doing. We ought to be a little kind to them. A paternalistic attitude." The "they" and the "them," of course, referred to blacks.

Abuse of the peremptory challenge is rooted in racial prejudice that is supposed to have died away, but has not.

The case of Gary Willis, a black man accused of murder, patently makes the point. The jury trying him was all-white in a county which is 18 percent black. Willis was convicted of murder and sentenced to death in Cochran, Georgia, on January 28, 1978. His appeal at the state appellate court having been denied, he appealed his case to the Georgia Circuit of the U.S. Court of Appeals, where it came up for review in September 1983.

Willis and two other men had been accused of committing an armed robbery of a convenience store and of seizing, disarming, and abducting the chief of police, who had attempted to arrest them after stopping their getaway car. The men took the officer to a remote, swampy area, from which he tried to flee. One of the men, not Willis, shot the policeman as he ran into some shallow water. Willis then ran into the water and shot the policeman several times in the head. Willis took the stand at the trial, admitting all, and adding that he thought the sheriff was already dead when he fired the shots.

The jury supposedly did not know any of this when it was selected. There had been a change of venue, and the trial started two years after the crime was committed. Nine judges had disqualified themselves from hearing the case, and the frustrated prosecutor burned a law book in front of one courthouse with the remark that if he could not get a judge to try the case, he no longer needed law books. Jury selection consumed twelve days of trial time, involving the calling of 449 jurors of whom 320 were excused for one general reason or another, leaving 129 jurors to be questioned during voir dire, ninety-eight white and thirty-one black.

The next round of questioning had to do with the death penalty qualification. In the *Witherspoon* v. *Illinois* decision, (391 U.S. 510, 1968), the U.S. Supreme Court held that the state could excuse for cause potential jurors only if they stated in voir dire that they could not, under any circumstances, invoke the death penalty, even if a defendant were found guilty. Many blacks oppose capital punishment on principle, and so when asked about it in jury selection, they are subject to being excused before getting any further into the voir dire. In the Willis case, every black questioned in voir dire expressed some hesitancy about the death penalty; of the thirty-one blacks, seventeen were excused for cause under Witherspoon, leaving fourteen blacks in the pool. (Three whites were excused on the same basis.)

Millard Farmer, a well-known civil rights attorney in Atlanta, conducted the defense voir dire. Knowledgeable about the subtlety of racial prejudice and skilled as a questioner, he seemed to draw racism from the pores of potential jurors. He asked questions, over prosecutorial objections, about whether a juror had any black friends, whether the juror had ever eaten a meal with a black person, whether the juror had ever had a black person to his or her home. The remarks of jurors the prosecutor did not strike were as revealing of the racial climate as the fact that the prosecutor, eventually, struck every black remaining on the panel.

One white male juror—named White in fact—told Farmer he knew black people; he had some living on his farm as sharecroppers. Farmer elicited that he paid these sharecroppers $70 a week and that three of them lived in houses White provided, which had no indoor toilets. Still, when asked if he thought of black people as his social equals, White said, "Some of my best friends are black." Farmer then asked how it was that these best friends had never been to his house. White answered, "We're in the South. It's a custom, I guess. It's just like a dog. I don't believe a dog ought to be in the house." Farmer immediately moved to challenge this man for cause on the basis of racial prejudice, but the prosecutor objected. The judge intervened: "Do you mean by that you consider a black person as a dog?" But before White could reply, the judge rehabilitated the man's answer himself: "It means that some people believe in house dogs, and some people don't." The juror simply affirmed, "That's right." Thus, the defense had to spend a peremptory challenge on White and others like him. Not only did the prosecutor decline to probe jurors about racial attitudes, he often objected to the defense's cause challenges on racial bias and went out of his way to see that black people were exempted before the questioning proceeded too far. For example, he thought a black woman who said she would have to excuse herself frequently during the trial to go to the bathroom would interfere with the dispatch of the trial. However, he did not think a white man, whose bad leg or "dry joint" meant he would have to get up and walk around every hour, would be an interference. When Farmer sought to excuse for cause a sheriff's son whose sideline was lending money to black people, the prosecutor objected. When a black woman who had a four-year-old son came up for questioning, the prosecutor attempted to get her to ask to be excused by insinuating she would not be able to communicate with her son during the trial. The prosecutor objected to a challenge for cause to a white man who said he used to work in the fields with "niggers," and that "it is degrading to white people to have them in school with blacks."

After the questioning was over, fifty-six jurors were considered competent. Then, pursuant to Georgia law, they were presented—made to stand up—in the order they were summoned, for first challenge by the prosecution. In this case, the state had ten peremptories and the defense twenty. The jury was selected from among the first forty-two jurors called who were still in the pool, thirty-two white, ten black.

The prosecution used every peremptory on blacks, leaving the defense only whites to consider. When it came to alternates, the one black person in the pool was struck by the prosecution as well. In Willis' appeal, Farmer argued that the prosecution had violated the defendant's right to a jury drawn from a fair cross section of the community, but the Georgia Appellate Court simply stated, correctly as far as the letter of the law is concerned, that "the district attorney may use such challenges in his discretion."

Given the testimony and the evidence, a mixed jury probably would have found Willis guilty, although the death penalty might not have been invoked. Perhaps, on hearing Willis' background— the information being allowed as evidence during the sentencing phase in capital cases—black jurors would not have found the murder to have been "outrageously or wantonly vile, horrible or inhumane in that it involved torture, etc.," all aggravating circumstances a jury must find in order to invoke death. Perhaps some blacks would have responded to the fact that Willis had been abandoned at the age of six weeks or to information from psychologists that Willis would respond well within the prison system, should he receive a life sentence. There is no particular reason why they should react this way or that just by virtue of being black. But being black is something few whites, especially in the South, can understand, and thus an all-white jury cannot be said to represent the broadest community attitude.

Peremptory challenge abuse is by no means a sporadic phenomenon. According to John Carroll, legal director at the Southern Poverty Law Center in Montgomery, Alabama, which specializes in civil-rights cases, peremptory challenge abuse is "the most serious problem in jury selection in the South." A black district attorney in Atlanta told me, "It [peremptory challenge based on race] is very common among some prosecutors in this office and almost a matter of course outside the cities, including when the defendant is white. I don't do it, mainly because, if I am sending a man to prison, I don't want him to think it was because some all-white or all-black jury railroaded him." Even a judge in New York City told me he finds prosecutors challenging blacks "all the time, for little reason."

The problem, of course, is most noticeable when the trial involves a blatantly racial issue, such as prosecutions of Ku Klux Klan members. Through the late 1960s and the 1970s, Henry Frohsin, of the United States attorney's office in Birmingham, Alabama, prosecuted several cases against Klan members, almost always to all-white juries because the defense attorneys succeeded in removing the few blacks who were in the pool. Frohsin is considered one of the South's most courageous prosecutors and recalls his jury difficulties with impatience at what slow progress jury equanimity has made. "I have had cases where I hoped I could get blacks on, cases such as where police used cattle prods on black men to extract confessions. In some cases, I felt like I ought to try to load the jury up with blacks, but the other side succeeds in taking them all off, largely because defense attorneys have a higher number of challenges."

Racial violence continues in the South, not infrequently involving defendants who are Klan members. In Chattanooga, Tennessee, in April 1980, four elderly women walking down the street were wounded by shots fired from a car in which rode three members of a Klan faction called Justice Knights of the Ku Klux

Klan. The case came to trial in July 1980; an all-white jury acquitted the defendants. However, a civil action was filed by the victims and came to trial in February 1982, alleging the women's civil rights had been violated by those who shot them, in an attempt to intimidate them off the street. During this jury selection, the defense began to challenge black venirepersons and prompted the judge to interject a comment, pointing out that although he could not tell the attorneys how to use their challenges, he could notice. He also shifted the orders of jurors around so that it became unavoidable that the challenges would run out before the blacks did. The six-person jury was half-black and awarded $535,000 in damages to the women, largely symbolically since the Klan members were not in a position to pay. However, it was the first such anti-Klan civil-rights ruling in history.

In Montgomery, Alabama, another significant racial case came to trial in November 1983. The Taylor family, blacks, had gathered for a funeral, and outside the home of one of the family members, many cars were parked. The police contend they were investigating a missing persons report in the area and questioned a young man, a nephew in the mourning family, who happened to be outside at the time. The police also contended that, as they questioned him, he struck an officer and bolted away, fleeing into the house where the rest of the family was congregated. When the police then entered the house, a melee ensued, and one officer was shot, one was stabbed. The police charged that they were brutally attacked by the family. The family contended they had defended themselves against intrusion by men who never identified themselves as police and that the shooting of the officer occurred when other policemen fired into the home from outside. They argued that the Taylor home had been singled out only because a group of cars was outside, and the police, used to making drug arrests in the area, suspected that many cars indicated that perhaps a criminal activity was taking place in the house. The defense maintained that the assault on the Taylor house was racist in itself. After a grand jury investigated the matter, five family members were indicted on various charges, including kidnapping, robbery, and attempted murder.

The first case was that of Worrie Taylor, who had been visiting in Montgomery from Ohio for the funeral. The courtroom was packed with supporters and family members, and the judge, to avoid inflaming already high tensions, banned newspapers from the courtroom. The press, however, had front row seats in an empty jury box (the courtroom had two).

The case had drawn intense local coverage, largely because relations between the police and the black community had been strained before the incident and were deeply worsened by it. The prosecution team was entirely white, two males and one female. The defense attorneys were all black males. Sitting in the jury box, facing the jurors, observing the nearly all-black audience, I felt shot back in time to the height of the civil-rights movement in the 1960s; clearly the proceedings were very important to the racial climate of the city of Montgomery.

Consequently, the prosecution did not feel it could allow an all-white jury to decide the case. Perhaps it was good conscience; perhaps it was simply good sense. Blacks were not categorically challenged, with the result that five blacks were seated on the final jury. The defense, having fully expected to face an all-white jury, had considered hiring jury-selection experts to help assure that the whites seated would at least be fair.

The case was fraught with questionable matters. For example, there were allegations that the defendants had been beaten by the police after their arrest, resulting in the judge's ruling some defendants' statements inadmissible because they had been coerced. There were allegations that the police had tampered with evidence, that they might have erased tapes of telephone calls made to the police station reporting the incident the night it happened. As a former employee of the police department—a young white woman—testified about her suspicions regarding the tapes, the prosecution did everything in its power to discredit her, including intimations that she had personal reasons for making her statements. She testified that she had been "forced to resign." Among other statements she made—credibly in my view given her delivery and lack of motive to lie—were "If you don't go to bed with a cop [on her job] you might as well hang it up. . . . I want the public to know the filth and trash going on in the police department. I am letting it out today." To add to her credibility was the fact that both her father and boyfriend were police officers, and she commented that she had no intrinsic dislike for the police, just for deceit.

There was a main problem of evidence, in that the gun that was used to shoot the police officer was never found, according to police who investigated the crime.

The political elements of the case were underscored by the involvement of two white police officers, who were called as defense witnesses but refused to testify, citing their Fifth Amendment privilege against self-incrimination. According to the defense, the witnesses might have information regarding police misconduct in the case, so the judge heard arguments on the matter outside the jury's presence. The police officers, however, complained to the judge, Randall Thomas, that they had been told they would lose their jobs if they refused to testify, Fifth Amendment rights notwithstanding. This put them in the category of "coerced" witnesses, the judge observed, and therefore he could not accept their testimony. However, Judge Thomas—a fair man and determined to get to the bottom of the matter, I believe—called the mayor of the City of Montgomery, overseer of the Police Department, to court. The mayor confirmed that he had ordered the men to testify or be fired. The mayor claimed he could not guarantee their jobs in return for their testimony, because he did not want to harbor men who might have known about wrongdoing and kept it secret. On the other hand, without a promise of job security, the men seemed in an untenable position, since the prosecution also refused to grant them immunity from prosecution should their information prove actionable. Under these circumstances, their attorney advised them to cling to their Fifth Amendment privilege.

With that, the mayor called each man individually into a room behind the judge's bench and fired them there and then, right in the middle of the trial. "They are all yours now," he said to the judge, the "coercive" quality of their testimony having been removed by rendering their jobs status null and void. The men, however, still invoked the Fifth Amendment; thus the trial gained nothing by way of insight into the facts of the case, and the police officers lost their jobs.

After eleven days of trial, the judge reviewed the evidence and dismissed the robbery and kidnapping charges against Taylor, allowing the jury to deliberate only on the question of attempted murder. The jury had been sequestered for the duration of the trial, including right through Thanksgiving Day, which they had to spend as a group, eating traditional fare in the company of police guards.

They deliberated for almost twenty hours, and finally told the judge they could not come to a unanimous verdict. He was therefore obliged to declare a mistrial. It turns out that at one point, the jury had voted 11–1 in favor of conviction, but one juror, a black woman, became ill and deliberations were suspended for a day. When the group reconvened, the consensus had fallen away, and no verdict could be reached.

While one can never be sure about verdict and deliberation dynamics, the black jury members probably ensured at least a thorough discussion of the racial aspects of the case. And enough doubt was evident that the presumption of innocence was not overcome. Also, the deliberation proved that jurors, black or white, listen to evidence in a case and tend to base their decisions mostly on that evidence. Whether or not police misconduct in the case was rampant, if the evidence suggested guilt, the jury was prone, at least apparently, to convict.

Racial factors can be prominent in cases far away from the Deep South. In Brooklyn, New York, in March 1983, an eighteen-year-old white youth, Gino Bova, was charged with the murder of a black man, William Turks. Bova and two other youths had participated in an unprovoked attack on three black men, using sticks, and Turks had ended up with fatal head injuries.

The case was heard by an all-white jury. They could choose between a verdict of murder and a verdict of manslaughter. In his charge, the judge told the jury that a person could be found guilty of reckless murder even if there had been no intent to kill or even to injure seriously, so long as there was evidence of "depraved indifference" to human life.

Bova was convicted of manslaughter. The jurors probably reduced the charge, despite what the judge had said, because they could not satisfy themselves that Bova had intended to beat Turks to death. And doubtless they considered "depravity" something other than mob assault.

It is not known, of course, what difference it would have made if the jury had contained some black members, but it seems likely that they would have taken a graver view of the matter, perhaps urging the others to examine the evidence further or at least to clarify the judge's charge. But blacks were systematically excluded from the jury.

In Brooklyn, with a sizable black population, juries cannot simply be all-white through natural selection. In a case like Bova's, the jury becomes all-white when one of the attorneys thinks an all-white jury might cut away just enough from pursuit of the full truth to make a difference to the defendant. Indeed, in this case, the defense used all its peremptory challenges to keep blacks from sitting on the jury.

To determine how and why events take place, jurors often put themselves in the shoes of one of the principals involved. For a white person to think of him or herself as black is not easy. Lawyers know that, so they prevented blacks from sitting in judgment on Bova. In the Angela Davis trial, her attorney, in his summation, asked the jury to imagine what they as black people might have done if they had been in Angela Davis' shoes. That jury acquitted, though in that case, too, the one black woman who made it to the final pool had been peremptorily excused by the prosecution. In fact, in humiliating her during the state's voir dire, the prosecutor had done everything in his power to induce her to admit she could not be fair to the state, including reveal that she had been denied welfare—the defense pointed out this action of the prosecution's as an example of the very racism Angela Davis deplored.

In the civil trial in Wrightsville, Georgia, in January 1983, jury empathy was crucial to the outcome of the case, since the local sheriff and some of his staff were sued by forty-eight blacks, who alleged that their civil rights had been violated in a series of incidents. The plaintiffs alleged that their unarmed group was attacked by the sheriff's armed men and that the demonstrators had been arrested without due cause. The key to the case, according to one of the plaintiff's lawyers, would be to try to convince the jury that "the living tree of political liberty had been attacked in this incident, by driving a stake into the heart of that tree. The pain and damage done had to be undone." Not an easy order, especially in Wrightsville, where the jury lists, to begin with, were questionable in their representation of blacks.

The sheriff and his men were acquitted, largely because the all-white jury was able to see the sheriff's side of things more clearly than any other side. According to a juror I interviewed, the jury in general felt the sheriff had had no other choice but to jail protestors. Wrightsville had been tense, and jurors had heard evidence that the sheriff feared the possibility of riots. Part of his defense was that he felt compelled to stop the protest to stifle the potential for rioting, and this reasoning sat well with the jury. The juror explained: "The sheriff was doing what he had to do to keep the town from burning down." However, the plaintiffs had alleged that their protest had been peaceful. When I asked if the jury had believed that the specific protest at issue in the trial had been peaceful, the juror replied, "It sounded during the trial like it was but the sheriff had no choice." This was a leap into the sheriff's mind that only an all-white jury could make.

The jury was sequestered for three and a half weeks, and allowed to return home on weekends only. One juror told me that, if anything, he had at the beginning been biased in favor of the black plaintiffs, but "as the case began to unroll, I could feel myself changing." He felt the plaintiffs had erred in their presentation of the case as a civil-rights test, thereby not grounding it in the specifics of the incidents alleged. He added that the plaintiffs would have had a better chance with this jury if the lawyers had been from the rural Georgia area, instead of the "big city," so to speak. In the juror's opinion, these considerations, plus the fact that the plaintiffs had not drawn their facts together well enough to refute the facts the defense presented, contributed to the decision. "Somebody was guilty of something there," he commented, remarking on the wrongful beatings and shootings, but he felt the jury could not say who. He added that he wished there had been some blacks on the jury, but that he did not think their presence would have produced a different verdict.

There were no blacks on the jury because only three had made it to the final pool of twenty-eight, and all three were peremptorially excused by the defense. The prior five blacks had been excused for one cause or another, by both defense and plaintiffs. The plaintiffs' attorneys told me they truly regretted challenging any blacks at all but that some just seemed too afraid and passive to speak their mind in a jury room.

When the foreman delivered the verdict in Wrightsville, one woman juror had tears in her eyes. She had almost held out against the tide for acquittal, but in the end, she did not. Her comments shed considerable light on the experience of being on an all-white jury in this case:

"It was very exhausting and very depressing. I realized how much of the decisions are affected by the lawyers that are handling the case and their expertise is probably more important than the actual facts. There was one very shrewd, very knowledgeable small-town lawyer who knew exactly how to speak to the people in small-town Georgia who basically made up the jury. The defense lawyer. The prosecuting lawyers were a group of young, relatively, men who did not basically know how to talk to those people. . . . To me, the issue was that the prosecuting attorneys did not prove their case, and I think they well could have if they had been as knowledgeable and as shrewd as the defense lawyers. An outstanding number of experts were consulted, and their points were so irrelevant. . . . If there had been blacks on the jury, things would have gone a little differently. I don't know. I doubt there was much one or two blacks could have done to change the mind of the rest of the jury. Maybe hang the jury. But the case could have been presented so that it would have been a totally different thing. If they had just concentrated on proving these people had been arrested falsely. . . . It wasn't only a matter of racial prejudice. It was also a matter of empathy for law enforcement officers and particularly on behalf of men who had served in the military, feeling that the sheriff was justified. They put themselves in that sheriff's position and probably they would have done the same thing. Totally ignore the law. They did do the same thing. The judge made it clear—they just managed to twist his charges and put their own feelings. . . ." The "they" she referred to were several male jurors with military background.

When I asked her if she thought the sheriff might have perceived danger to the town, she answered, "I don't know about that. I think things were out of control definitely, but I think he just felt he was the supreme power, and that he could do virtually anything he wanted to do, and that is what he did." So, in effect, although she argued that a more clear-cut prosecution might have resulted in a different verdict, she was actually admitting that a white jury was more inclined to interpret the vagueness in the plaintiff's case to the sheriff's benefit than to his detriment.

According to one of the attorneys for the plaintiff, the judge's instructions were at fault for giving the impression that police officers were not liable for their illegal actions if they felt what they were doing was necessary and lawful. "If that is the standard," said the attorney, "then you might as well set the court aside. . . . We lost when we had an all-white jury because we were asking common white people in the Deep South to take a step they had never taken in their lives—to affirmatively say no to injustice against blacks."

A blatant example of racializing a jury occurred in November 1980 at a trial in Greensboro, North Carolina, concerning the deaths of five members of the Communist Workers Party. They had been organizing among black textile mill workers and were shot during a protest of a march by a Ku Klux Klan faction and the Nazi party in November 1979. As the KKK motorcade drove through the street lined with protestors, the lead car suddenly stopped, a man stepped out and fired a shot in the air, and other members of the motorcade opened fire on the demonstrators, essentially picking off the five leaders of the CWP. Klan leaders maintain that they were shot at first, but the shootings—in fact all the events—are documented in television news film taken by crews at the scene, and it looks doubtful that the demonstrators were the first to take aim. Yet an all-white jury acquitted the defendants accused of the murders. The eligible blacks were stricken peremptorily by the defense, but other jurors, including one man who said, "It's less of a crime to kill communists," were accepted. When I discussed the case with Bill Wilkinson, Imperial Wizard of the Invisible Empire, Ku Klux Klan, in an interview in Birmingham, Alabama, he remarked, "That jury was not all-white. There was a minority member on there." Wilkinson was referring to a stanchly anti-Castro, and therefore anticommunist, Cuban exile, who was seated on the jury. Latin did not count as "white" to Wilkinson. New federal charges based on violations by the defendants of the civil-rights law were handed down in the case, and a second trial began in January 1984.

The second jury too was all-white. Jury selection proceeded *in camera*, with no member of the public permitted to attend. (The U.S. Supreme Court ruled on January 18, 1984, in *Press-Enterprise Co.* v. *Superior Court of California* that press cannot be barred from voir dire except for "good cause." The Greensboro jury selection was by then underway, and the federal judge who barred the press was upheld, citing "good cause.")

Of the approximately seventy-five jurors who survived pre-screening questions, about ten were black. Though questioning of the jurors was conducted in private, exercising of peremptory challenges was conducted in open court. Every black, in a row, was stricken by the defense attorneys, who represented either members of the Ku Klux Klan or the American Nazi Party or both.

The defense wanted an all-white jury, but not merely for racial reasons. They needed all whites because they wanted to prime a pro-German heritage, anticommunist attitude. The opening statement of defense attorney Roy Hall, who represented Roland Wayne Wood, a defendant, laid a frightening foundation for the defense they intended to mount. Hall addressed the jury:

"You are going to hear an awful lot about the fact that Roland Wayne Wood was head of the local Nazi party. You have to remember that at the end of the war, Roland Wayne Wood was only two months old. So these are not war-crime Nazis. . . . The largest ethnic minority in the country are Germans. . . . Roland Wayne Wood is a patriotic citizen just like the Germans were. Many of you on the jury have German blood. . . . This courthouse stands on a tract of land owned by a German family. . . . The German people are always with us. . . . Think of Werner von Braun and all the contributions Germans have made to science. Von Braun was a Nazi, but no one asked him his politics before they made him a high ranking official at NASA. . . .

"The Germans gambled everything in the war and lost everything in opposition to communism. Aren't they a lot more attractive now than they were forty years ago at the end of the war? These defendants are patriotic citizens, just like the German citizens. That is why they went to Greensboro—to stop the communists."

In April 1984 the all-white jury acquitted the defendants

entirely. They had been charged by the trial judge, over the prosecution's objections, that racial hostility had to have been the "substantial motivation" for the defendant's action, meaning that if other motivations had been paramount, the defendants could not be convicted under this indictment. However, the prosecutors contended, even though the charge in their view to the jury was incorrect, the evidence had proved beyond a reasonable doubt that the defendants had been motivated mainly by racial hatred, laced with hatred for communists. However, the all-white jury, some of whom on voir dire had voiced friendly attitudes toward the Ku Klux Klan, was predisposed to prefer the defendants' argument that they had shot in self-defense, and that their primary motive for attending the rally had been to save Greensboro, North Carolina, from communism.

Of course, a member of any racial or ethnic minority is subject to peremptory challenge abuse. Hispanics, for example, have also struggled to become part of jury pools. And where Hispanics do appear in response to a jury summons, their treatment at the hands of some attorneys is not dissimilar to treatment blacks would receive.

An Hispanic attorney in San Antonio, Texas, told me that Hispanics were routinely stricken from panels by prosecutors "in every case I try. They even strike Hispanics if the defendant is Anglo and his attorney is Hispanic." In June 1983 outside San Antonio in Comal County, a white military officer, who was driving while intoxicated, struck down and killed a family of Mexican-Americans. The officer was indicted for only one death, and a jury, all-white except for one marginally English-speaking Chicano, sentenced him to a minimal period of probation. Comal County is approximately one third Hispanic in terms of population.

In Camden, New Jersey, in September 1983, a man was brought to trial in the traffic death of a seven-year-old Hispanic boy. The prosecution witnesses alleged that the driver had swerved deliberately to hit the boy, having recently bragged to friends that he had a point system for "picking off spics and niggers." The defense peremptorily challenged all blacks and Hispanics. The trial climate was explosive because of the large minority population in Camden and because television cameras, allowed in court in New Jersey, broadcast the witnesses' testimony and their use of racially derisive epithets. The jury acquitted the defendant of murder but convicted him of aggravated manslaughter.

A key prosecution witness, who had been a passenger in the car and had given sworn statements to detectives two days after the incident that the driver had had the "point system," recanted his testimony when the prosecution called him to the stand. There, before the jury and a stunned prosecutor, the witness announced that the statements he had given police had been fabricated so the police would not arrest him as an accessory to the crime. One can only speculate as to whether a black juror, or an Hispanic, would have been able to believe the eleventh-hour recantation.

These and many other problems of peremptory challenge abuse are well known; many articles on and discussions of the subject have appeared, at least since the civil rights movement. But the issue has been allowed to slide, and remedies remain elusive because of the knotted constitutional issues involved. And because there is no effective control and no real way to get caught, attorneys continue to flavor their peremptory challenge use with racial bias. Open court practice, therefore, permits what the Constitution supposedly eliminated.

The touchstone Supreme Court decision on the matter is *Swain* v. *Alabama* (380 U.S. 202, 1965), but it did not help the situation very much. Swain, a black man, was convicted of rape and sentenced to death by an all-white jury. The six eligible blacks in the panel were all challenged and eliminated by the prosecutor. The defendant appealed his conviction on the grounds that his Fourteenth Amendment rights of equal protection had been violated. The appeal was denied, largely because the Court stated that the peremptory challenge system "provides justification for striking a group of otherwise qualified jurors in any given case whether they be Negroes, Catholics, accountants, or those with blue eyes." The Court held that if it could be proved that a given prosecutor did, in case after case, systematically, as a matter of course, use the peremptory to strike blacks, then the peremptory system was being "perverted." It held that Swain's appeal failed to establish proof of such systematic behavior, despite the fact that no black had served on any jury in the county in question since 1950.

Unfortunately, *Swain* puts the burden to prove discrimination on the defendant, and the standard of evidence of systematic exclusion it established can hardly ever be met. For one thing, challenges are often exercised privately; sometimes all a lawyer does is pass a note to the clerk, and no record is kept. Often, too, voir dire records are not transcribed, so what potential jurors may have said is difficult to reconstruct, and in addition, most jurisdictions do not keep records of the race of potential jurors. And what is "proved" is in the eye of the beholder. In the Willis case, the defense collected what it considered proof of systematic prosecutional abuse of peremptories, but was not granted permission by the Court to submit it. The defense also submitted a pretrial motion asking that the prosecutor be restricted from using his peremptories against blacks—these motions are common in the South—the prosecutor "demurred" to the motion, and the court ruled the prosecutor could use his ten challenges as he saw fit.

Proof has been gathered for scores of other cases. A survey in Louisiana in 1972–1973 showed the federal prosecutor used 68.9 percent of all his challenges against black venirepersons, though they constituted only 25 percent of persons called for jury duty.

In St. Louis in 1971–1973, in thirty-one trials observed by a reporter, 74 percent of the black potential jurors were challenged peremporily by the prosecution, and the reporter who collected the data noted that the prosecutors changed their behavior somewhat when they realized their challenge pattern was being observed.

In the federal Brink's jury trial selection, the prosecution used its challenges to strike one white liberal and the rest to remove any young minority group member.

In one oft-cited case in Houston (*Ridley* v. *Texas*, 475, S.W.2nd, 769, 1972), an assistant district attorney told the court that he removed blacks as a matter of "common sense" when the defendant was black and the victim white.

However, even when a "trend" has been shown by appellants the courts have cited failure to show "systematic" abuse of peremptories, meaning every case, every defendant, same attorney over again. At the Supreme Court level, no litigant has been successful at meeting the standard of proof set by *Swain*.

Individual states, on the other hand, have decided in favor of appellants on less than *Swain*-level proof, recognizing that that standard may be impossible to meet. An important decision came in 1978, in California, before State Supreme Court Justice Stanley Mosk (*California* v. *Wheeler*, 148 Cal Rptr 890). Mosk wrote, "Swain obviously furnishes no protection whatever to the first defendant who suffers such discrimination in any given court . . . until 'enough' such instances have accumulated to show a pattern of prosecutional abuse. Yet in California each and every defendant—not merely the last in this artificial sequence—is constitutionally entitled to trial by a jury drawn from a representative cross section of the community. . . . The defendant is party to only one criminal proceeding and has no personal experience of racial discrimination in the other trials held in that court. . . ." Both blacks and whites, however, can be rich or poor, have previous contact with law enforcement agencies, etc. And so Mosk added that using peremptories to eliminate this type of bias, those that are "essentially neutral with respect to the various groups represented on the venire . . . promote the impartiality of the jury without destroying its representativeness. . . . By contrast, when a party presumes that certain jurors are biased merely because they are members of an identifiable group . . . and peremptorily strikes all such persons for that reason alone, he not only upsets the demographic balance of the venire but frustrates the primary purpose of the representative cross section requirement."

Appellate courts in Massachusetts, New Mexico, Illinois, and New York have also rendered decisions in which peremptory challenge abuse was struck down as discriminatory. Still, in May 1983, the Supreme Court refused to hear three cases put before it, one each from New York, Illinois, and Louisiana, which attempted to get the Supreme Court to reconsider its *Swain* ruling.

The majority opinion, written by Justice Stevens, said, "My vote . . . does not reflect disagreement with . . . appraisal of the importance of the underlying issue—whether the constitution prohibits the use of peremptory challenges to exclude members of a particular group from the jury, based on the prosecutor's assumption that they will be biased in favor of other members of the same group." The Court shied away from deciding, preferring to continue to let the states review and decide on the matter, serving as "laboratories." The dissenting opinion, by Justice Marshall, said, "It is difficult to understand why several must suffer discrimination because of the prosecutors' use of peremptory challenges before any defendant can object . . . when a prosecutor uses several peremptory challenges to exclude every potential Negro juror, there is strong circumstantial evidence that the exclusions are racially motivated and therefore in violation of the defendant's Sixth Amendment rights."

Interestingly one case, *McCray* v. *New York*, which had been carried to the Supreme Court after the state court denied the appeal, joined the defendant and the district attorney for Brooklyn, Elizabeth Holtzman, on the same side. She had argued against McCray's position at state level when he appealed his case. McCray, a black man charged with robbery, had alleged that Brooklyn prosecutors struck all available minorities from his jury for racial reasons, but Holtzman argued that nonracial reasons motivated the prosecutor's challenges. However, Holtzman joined the defendant's petition in an attempt to get the Supreme Court to review the *Swain* principles. In addition, Holtzman issued an order to her staff directing they not use their peremptory challenges on the basis of race, religion, sex, or national origin, thus putting attorneys on their honor not to abuse peremptories to undermine representativeness of juries. But though this might work in large urban areas subject to public scrutiny, it will be of doubtful effect in areas where few are looking carefully at how attorneys conduct themselves. In December 1983, federal Judge Eugene H. Nickerson ruled that the prosecution in the McCray case had used their challenges to exclude blacks systematically, thus violating constitutional prohibitions against distinctions based on race. The judge, therefore, ordered a new trial for McCray, his third, reversing two previous convictions. Had the prosecution not shaped the jury through peremptory challenge abuse, McCray's ordeal, and the expenditure of a good deal of money and judicial time, might have been avoided.

In California, since *Wheeler*, attorneys have had the right to question racially motivated peremptories of the other side, and the attorney must justify his challenge to the judge at a bench conference. The judge, in turn, may either accept the explanation or dismiss the entire panel and start voir dire afresh. Some say this practice has eliminated abuse; others say it works only when all involved are honest and adhere to the spirit of the *Wheeler* decision. Like many laws, it is only as effective as its enforcement.

Asking attorneys to justify challenges, of course, makes those challenges somewhat more kin to cause challenges and less to peremptory challenges. In fact, once judicial discretion rules, the peremptory challenge is essentially eliminated. Also, the *Wheeler* rule lengthens jury selection at a time when public opinion seems to want it to move more quickly.

It has also been suggested that one way of offsetting the problem would be to reduce the number of prosecution peremptories. This is a racist idea in itself, since it presumes only defendants have something to gain by having blacks on the jury. We all have something to gain by fair racial mixing on the jury. Too, cutting prosecutional challenges would rub against the contemporary grain, since the public seems to feel that the state is already too hamstrung by laws aimed to protect the defendant. In Georgia, for example, and other states, there is an annual campaign to increase the number of peremptory challenges each side has.

So it seems that this peremptory challenge issue takes a Constitutional right—that of the defendant to an impartial jury from a cross section of the community—and puts it at odds with a public demand for quicker, sterner justice. It also puts the rights of minority members to equal treatment in conflict with traditional attorney procedures and privileges. Finally, it abrogates society's right to be broadly represented at the administration of justice and produces homogeneous juries rather than heterogeneous, representative ones. Abuse of the peremptory challenge then makes jury selection—in even the most uncelebrated case—a political act and renders today's courtroom a wellspring of potential long- and short-term consequences, including racial tension and violence. Its political aspect makes the peremptory issue a hot potato.

* * *

When juries are deliberately racialized, cases don't go away; their spin-off effects linger, larger than any courtroom, lengthier than the longest trials. Such is the case of the death of Arthur McDuffie.

On December 17, 1979, McDuffie, a thirty-three-year-old black insurance salesman, ran a red light on his motorcycle in Miami, Florida. When police gave chase, McDuffie tried to outrun them, because he had had his driver's license suspended for writing a bad check to pay a traffic ticket. Otherwise, McDuffie was an upstanding citizen with no record. Here, however, the stories diverge. The official police version holds that McDuffie hit his head on the pavement after crashing his motorcycle, and then police used force to subdue him as he resisted arrest. The other version, by other eyewitnesses including policemen, holds that Miami police officers dragged and beat McDuffie after he had surrendered. Both versions are told by policemen who were at the scene. McDuffie died of head injuries four days after the incident, and the trial of the police officers began at the end of March 1980. Several of the policemen who were at the scene were granted immunity from prosecution in return for their testimony against the others.

Jury selection took eleven days, and 150 prospective jurors were interviewed. Approximately twenty blacks were in the pool—13 percent of the pool in a city that was at the time largely black. The defense used peremptory challenges to ensure an all-white, all-male jury of six, plus three alternates. After hearing six weeks of testimony, the jurors deliberated two hours and thirty-seven minutes to a verdict of "not guilty." Within hours of the announcement of the verdict in court, violence and rioting erupted in Miami. A group of young white people driving through the black area called Liberty City had their car battered with bricks and bottles. When the driver lost control, the car hit an eleven-year-old black girl and then smashed into a building. A group of blacks then surrounded the car and pulled the passengers into the street, where they were beaten and stabbed. Blacks ran through the streets chanting "McDuffie! McDuffie!" and "Where is justice for the black man in America?" Cars were overturned at the state building. More whites were beaten. The verdict had hit the tense community like gasoline on a flame, because it was perceived as an all-white cover-up. In the end, the riots left sixteen dead, several hundred injured, and approximately $100 million in damages—an exceedingly tragic legacy spurred by the exercising of peremptory challenges with an eye toward tilting a jury.

At first, the jurors would not talk to the press, but then one did, the foreman. He said the prosecution had failed to prove its case against the officers on trial and that the police officers who had been given immunity were not credible witnessess. He believed "the three that got immunity ought to be the three sitting there in the courtroom." The foreman received a death threat at work; another juror had police patrolling his neighborhood because he too had received death threats.

Would an all-black jury have gone ahead and convicted the wrong men in a thirst for vengeance? Would a racially mixed jury have decided the same way?

One juror I interviewed told me he thought race was an issue with respect to the incident but not the trial. "It probably would have been desirable to have a black on the jury. But tokenism may create an issue where there isn't any."

This juror, however, was so disturbed by the events and the aftermath of the trial that he was moved to write a letter defending the verdict to the governor of Florida. No action resulted from the letter but it said in essence:

• Brutal violence was done to Arthur McDuffie the night he was arrested.
• Police officers were granted immunity who admitted having something to do with the incident.
• Charges against the officers on trial were not supported by the evidence.
• The evidence tended to support investigating the officers who were granted immunity.
• The prosecution was careless in preparing the case.

"I can no longer remain silent," the juror wrote to the governor. "In the place of one man dead, we now have many."

Perhaps, in view of this letter, one might say that any six reasonable persons, white or black, would have come to a "not guilty" verdict in this case. But no black person had the chance, and that made all the difference.

Three years later, in the summer of 1983, the same juror sent me a clipping reporting the suicide of a police technician in Miami who had been called to give information in a state investigation of another policeman for alleged brutality. The technician was questioned for ninety minutes by two prosecutors, then went home and shot himself dead. The policeman he had been questioned about was one of the officers granted immunity in the McDuffie matter, who nevertheless "committed violent acts at the scene of McDuffie's arrest," according to the juror's opinion of the evidence in the McDuffie trial and his letter to the governor. Commenting on the recent suicide, the juror asked, "When will it end?"

[13]
Power to the Jury?

The McDuffie jury's strong conviction that the wrong police officers were on trial posed a dilemma that provokes the question of whether jury duty includes an obligation to comment on the shortcomings of the trial. Would such juror behavior lead to anarchy, or would it force the trial process to be more cognizant of community attitudes? When, in other words, does a juror's personal conviction overtake the obligation to do what he or she is told?

Such was the question facing the jury in the case of Dawn Maria Cruickshank, who at the age of seventeen, in the winter of 1982, killed her father with one blast of a shotgun, and then shot him eight more times, to be sure. After the shooting, she called the police and reported what she had done. Her father, G. Alan Cruickshank, had earned a good deal of money in real estate speculation. Her mother, Jean Hoffman Cruickshank, had inherited a fortune. This was a locally prominent family, and so the murder gained prominence.

As Ms. Cruickshank's trial began, the community of Ballston Spa in Saratoga County, New York—usually known as the home of the Saratoga Springs's elegant summer horse racing—attracted dozens of journalists, broadcasters, and hangers-on. Many people wanted to hear the story of the rich girl who, by killing her father, had also killed a way of life.

Her jury was to determine whether her action had been justified in any way. The jury's task usually is to weigh the facts and to apply the law, which the judge explains, to the facts. Almost always, the jury receives the instruction that it is duty-bound to apply the law, whether or not it agrees with it. However, there is a fascinating and lively debate afoot over whether the jury may choose to oppose the law—to "nullify" it and render a verdict that determines the facts but questions the law. Clearly, the jury has the power to ignore the law, either consciously or unconsciously; once it begins deliberating behind closed doors, it is free to do what it wants. That is one of the essential criticisms of the jury system. Yet, there are those who argue that the jury has that power by more than implication, that it has the absolute right to nullify when it sees fit. The further question is, if the jury has this right, ought it to be told about it. The issue comes up particularly in cases involving moral or conscience questions: Did one's moral opposition to the Vietnam War justify burning draft cards, which was a crime? Is an employer liable if an employee has an accident due to poor lighting, if the lighting met only minimum required standards? Some kind of nullification argument is made in most "political" cases, such as Dr. Spock's trial in 1968, and it places on the jury a reminder that they derive from a community of ideas and beliefs, not a metal wheelbox.

In a 1971 Detroit trial, veteran attorney Ernest Goodman told a jury: "In the jury system democracy operates directly and simply. . . . You come into the jury from the community and when you finish you go right back into it. . . . I cannot conceive of making the argument I have made here to a jury of people who did not come from the community. . . . It is for these reasons that I have placed the acts of these defendants . . . against the background of the environment which all of us have to contend with, live with, and find a way of changing and improving. . . ."

Any jury, after all, though it is supposed to confine itself to considering just the case before it, derives its opinions from a collection of experiences that cannot help but imprint the jury with values. These values in turn imprint the jury's determination of the facts and whether or not to apply the law.

In the Cruickshank case, the facts were fairly clear. A murder was committed, the murderer came forward. The unclear matter was motive. The jury had to determine if Dawn Cruickshank had suffered a history of sexual abuse and whether or not it mitigated her crime. This situation provided the jury a classic opportunity to nullify.

The events leading to the murder were straightforward, on the surface. Mr. and Mrs. Alan Cruickshank were in the throes of a bitter divorce struggle, and one of the stipulations of the separation agreement was that Alan Cruickshank move out of the family house and return only once a week to visit his two daughters, Dawn, aged seventeen, and Terry, aged sixteen. According to the visitation-rights agreement, Cruickshank was confined to the garage and his daughters met him there, since he was not permitted to enter the house. On November 15, 1982, after picking up a pizza, Cruickshank made his weekly visit and found only Dawn at home. A few hours later, he was dead, shot nine times, and Dawn was on the telephone advising the police of what she had done. She was arrested.

Dawn's defense was self-defense. She alleged that at the time she shot her father, she was trying to keep "him from hurting me anymore." A plain and pained-looking young woman, Dawn testified that her father had sexually abused her when she was fifteen, by coming to her bed, fondling her breasts, sucking her nipples, and climbing on top of her.

The courthouse at Ballston Spa did little to warm the situation. It is a modern, all brown brick building, one of those places that looks closed even when it is open because of shaded glass and lighting that is supposed to be soft but is instead just dim. There is too much sparseness in the design. The judge's bench, for example, was round, high, and made of grooved wooden paneling so he looked like he was sitting in the middle of a huge slide projector carousel. The jury box, with its exposed brick wall behind, was spacious and the juror's seats looked like thrones. Dawn, with a pink ribbon in her hair, wearing a collegiate style skirt and blouse, however, did not look at the jury, but either into her lap or directly at the attorney, her own or the district attorney, who was questioning her.

Credibility was one key element of this trial. Dawn had told the grand jury of the bed incident prior to being indicted. But now at her trial, she was also alleging that over a period of two years, on about a dozen occasions, her father had telephoned her to arrange she meet him at one of the apartment complexes he owned, each time in a different empty apartment. There, he had sexual intercourse with his daughter, leaving her to "clean myself up." The first time he had told Dawn he had a gift for her and that she should meet him. Then he raped her, and the rape series began.

Throughout this period, Dawn maintained, she had never told anyone about the rapes, because her father threatened to burn down the house where she, her mother, and sister lived, and from which he had been banished. Cruickshank had apparently beaten his wife and his children regularly, so Dawn did not feel his threats were idle. She also remained silent because of her own sense of humiliation, not telling even her own attorneys about the rapes at first or her psychiatrist. The psychiatrist, however, had had suspicions that she might be holding something back. Only after several interviews—plus an injection of so-called truth serum, sodium amytal, and the promise from her attorneys that they would use what Dawn told them only to resubmit her case to the grand jury—did Dawn reveal the rapes. Her attorneys promised they would keep the information at grand jury level, and therefore the incidents would remain secret. However, the prosecution refused to consent to a grand jury resubmission, and the case came to trial, but only after the prosecutor had, on receiving the news of the rapes, requested three more months to prepare his case. The judge granted the delay, but he imposed a "gag order" on both parties, which meant that the "new" material, the rape history, could not be revealed to the public or the press. So, only on the eve of the trial did the public learn about the rape history, which created the impression that it had only just come to light.

The defense witnesses consisted mainly of Dawn's psychiatrist and Dawn herself. The psychiatrist testified to the fact that—according to interviews he had had with Mrs. Cruickshank—the Cruickshank marital relationship had been acrimonious for many years, Alan Cruickshank being a difficult, demanding, and emotionally remote man. Among the mother's other comments were that he had had an affair with a nun during their marriage and that she had once seen him suspiciously fondling her daughters in the bath, when they were two and three. After that episode, she remarked, she had watched her husband "like a tiger" whenever he bathed the girls. Dawn testified that she had not told her mother about the rapes because when she had previously reported the incident of fondling that had taken place when she was fifteen, her mother had not believed her.

The psychiatrist testified to the fact that he had believed Dawn and attributed her reticence about her history of genuine humiliation. When pressed by the prosecution to provide an objective basis why Dawn should be believed, the psychiatrist said he could not absolutely prove she was telling the truth, but that neither could the prosecution prove objectively that she was lying. The prosecution did not elect to rebut the psychiatric testimony or to introduce testimony about the nature of sexual abuse. Nor did the defense introduce what might be called "syndrome" evidence—that is, third-party expert evidence that might have put the Cruickshank case in perspective, as far as other cases of similar nature was concerned.

Thus, there was no scientific evidence that Dawn's hiding of her history could be plausible, and so most of the case rested on Dawn's word. There was also no corroboration of Dawn's story, no one to testify that she had indeed been seen coming in or out of the apartment complex, with or without her father.

The district attorney's case rested on several basic points. First, he argued that Dawn had premeditated the murder, planning to be alone in the house with her father on the night in question by sending her mother out on an errand saying, "I can handle Daddy." The fact that Dawn had fired many shots indicated that there was no question but that she intended her father's death. The fact that his body was found in a position—and this was contested by the defense—which indicated he was running away from Dawn, not heading toward her, added to the theory that he had no intention of raping her just before he was shot. And, finally, the prosecutor contended that Dawn's stories of regular rapes were lies, what the district attorney called "eleventh hour" fabrications, intended to provide a defense where there was none.

These were the tangibles of the case. The intangibles were such details as Alan Cruickshank's position in the community. Perhaps he raped his daughter, but he also knew important people. The judge who normally heard the cases in the county had to disqualify himself because he had been on a gambling junket to Las Vegas with Cruickshank the weekend before the murder.

Indeed, the prosecutor referred several times to Alan Cruick-shank's "memory." In his questioning of Dawn, he pressed the point by saying, "You didn't keep the story to yourself because you were concerned about your father's memory, did you?" In his concluding statement, the prosecutor characterized Cruickshank as a perfectionist whose "meticulousness" was "resented" in the household but who nevertheless was a man who provided his daughters with a stately home, private school, and trips to Europe. There was the intangible of the prosecutor himself, who was under pressure, after losing several important cases, to win one. Yet, he showed a certain reluctance in this case. His assistant, however, filled the zeal gap. He passed notes with additional questions he thought the district attorney should pose. He was even able to rouse his boss from his seat to add a point when he had already sat down, or to keep him from rising to object when he seemed bent on doing so.

The main intangible, though, was the nature of the crime. Murder is serious enough, but patricide tends to cause the public conscience to recoil. On the other hand, incest and rape are not easy to dismiss. The jury then had to choose between taboos—first, did it believe Dawn's story; second, did her story justify the murder of her father. And if she had not been sexually abused, what was her motive; was she simply her father's cold-blooded assassin?

The jury consisted of five men and seven women, all white (there are practically no blacks living in Saratoga County). It had taken six days to choose them after eighty-five to ninety potential jurors had been called, an unusually large pool for the area. None of the jurors was near Dawn's age, several were retired, only one had a child under fourteen, the youngest juror was probably in her mid- to late thirties. The jurors had all been closely questioned about whether they could be impartial and whether they would hold to their individual convictions if they disagreed with their cojurors. They had all sworn to impartiality and tenacity.

When the trial ended, the jury had heard a good deal of testimony and had been the subject of intense local press speculation. The visiting judge, trying his first murder trial, instructed the jury that in order for Dawn's action to have been justified, she would have had to have felt that she was in imminent danger of death or forcible rape at the time she committed the murder. The judge added that if the jury did not find the murder justifiable, but did find that Dawn had acted under "extreme emotional distress," she could be convicted of the lesser charge, first degree manslaughter.

After deliberating about fifteen hours, the jury announced that it had found Dawn Cruickshank not guilty of murder but guilty instead of the lesser included charge. Initial press accounts suggested that the jury had been in agreement about the verdict, but in fact there had been violent disagreement among them that haunts a few of them still. And the discomfort relates precisely to whether a few of the jurors believed the law, as it applied to this case, was appropriate.

At first, the jury refused to discuss the case after the verdict, and then a few jurors consented to local interviews, reporting that the group had agreed early on that Dawn had intentionally murdered her father. However, this was a verdict that needed to be scratched, and one of the dissenter jurors allowed me to visit her and discuss the entire process.

The first ballot was not outright for conviction, not by a long shot. Rather it was six for conviction, five for outright acquittal, and one abstention. Then the jury broke for the evening. On the next ballot, the abstention switched to guilty, and by the next ballot, the guilty votes had risen to nine. The acquittal votes maintained that Dawn was telling the truth, that she had been raped and that she had been justified. They were two women and one man. The man told me, "I believe she was justified and I will always believe it because the incidents [meaning the rapes] had never happened at home before. . . . She had the security of her home and she could not believe it was going to happen again to her there. . . . We'll never know what the straw was that broke the camel's back . . ."

But the acquittal votes did not stand their ground. When the vote became 9–3, the dissenters began to feel the pressure that they might not be able to resolve their differences and that the jury would hang. "Who wants to be a hung jury. . . . We thought about all the expense of doing it again. . . . We wanted to come to a decision," one juror explained to me, though she still suffers from "a guilt that I did not hold out." The dissenters claim that they believed manslaughter was a greatly reduced charge and that they agreed to vote "guilty" on manslaughter if the others would too. The nine others agreed, essentially because they accepted the fact that Dawn had acted under extreme emotional pressure. "She had to be to shoot him nine times," a juror commented, still unwilling to believe, however, that sexual abuse had brought Dawn to this point.

The three dissenters lamented the absence of corroborative evidence supporting Dawn's story—"if only just one somebody had seen her going into that apartment complex"—and the lack of psychiatric evidence to establish that keeping silent under these circumstances was normal. The dissenters could not persuade the others to move from a guilty vote. All three believed that under the circumstances, Dawn's action was justified. First, they could well believe she felt in imminent danger of rape, but even if she did not, they could understand how, given the history, the idea of murdering her father could easily have crossed Dawn's mind.

But perhaps most important, they held different community attitudes about rape and how rape victims behave. This was obvious one wet and cold Sunday about three months after the trial, when the jury reconvened for a social afternoon, and began, because of my questions and my presence, to redeliberate the case.

Some could well understand that Dawn would have kept the story of the rapes to herself, and that—"historically," as one woman dissenter expressed it—"that's how battered women behave. They keep it quiet." Most of the others, however, including women, made such comments as "Dawn's father was too meticulous a man to be contemplating rape on the garage floor," or "She wanted it if she got it."

The jurors who had voted from the outset for conviction simply could not believe that Dawn would have kept the tales to herself for so long, knowing how important those facts could be to her case. Some jurors felt the attorneys and psychiatrists had planted the ideas with her on her behalf. One woman adamantly remarked, "If I had been raped, I would be out on the street yelling so somebody could get the guy who did it." The dissenter added, "Not everybody behaves the same way."

Given Dawn's age and lack of criminal record, the judge could have granted her youthful offender status and allowed her to serve her sentence on probation. However, he did not choose this option, commenting at the sentencing that it would not set a good example for other adolescents if Dawn were not imprisoned to pay for her crime. The prosecutor had opposed youthful offender status, although a probation board report recommended it. At the sentencing hearing, a prison official testified that sentencing a young woman like Dawn to an adult prison could well amount to a "death sentence." Still, however, the judge sentenced her to several years at Bedford Hills Correctional Facility in New York, the same prison where Jean Harris is incarcerated. Dawn had spent about six hours in her cell when she received word that new bail had been granted pending her appeal.

The dissenting jurors began to suffer intense feelings of guilt and uncertainty once Dawn had been sentenced; they had assumed she would be granted youthful offender status. "If I had known she would go to prison, even for one day, I would still be in that room arguing," one juror said.

This jury ought to have hung, but did not because the jurors felt it would be a bad reflection—a black spot—on them not to decide. Yet, in this case, a hung jury might have represented better justice than a compromise verdict in favor of guilt. "I wish they had gone over that more—that being a hung jury was not a negative thing," one of the dissenters recalled in a sad voice. "I would not have budged. I would not have gone along."

In New York State, unlike the situation in some other states, jurors are not to concern themselves about sentencing. In the Cruickshank case, however, concern about sentencing did infiltrate the decision-making process, and had the dissenters really been aware of the prison term Dawn faced, they might have refused to change their votes. Even in the absence of syndrome evidence or corroborating evidence, they might have argued to their peers that the law was incorrect in this case, that since it was Dawn's word against her father's body and his history, Dawn should be given the benefit of the doubt and acquitted.

Had the jury been charged that they had the right to dissent from the law, conceivably an acquittal could have held sway. And when I discussed the prospect with the most acquittal-prone juror, she said, "I am sick to think we could have done that. Why didn't they tell us?"

Proponents of the nullification power cite its birth in trials such as that of John Peter Zenger in New York in 1735, who was tried under British law for sedition. The jury refused to convict Zenger, because it found what he had printed to be true, despite the fact that the law had prescribed against his publishing the material. Zenger's lawyer had argued that the jury "had the right beyond all dispute to determine both the law and the facts." The notion persisted through the eighteenth century, and juries continued to flout British law they did not wish to be governed by. However, slowly, in a series of decisions by the Supreme Court, the jury's role began to be more narrowly defined. And in 1895, in *Sparf and Hansen* v. *United States* (156 U.S. 51), the court stated that the jury should "receive" the law from the court.

During the Prohibition era, juries regularly refused to convict defendants accused of violating the Volstead Act, which banned the sale of alcohol.

According to Jon Van Dyke, a leading defender of jury nullification, it was the political cases of the 1960s—Vietnam dissent and street protest cases—that breathed life into the nullification debate once more. And, he maintains, nullification is not a matter of encouraging jurors to be lawless, but rather advising them that they have the authority *not* to apply the law if they believe it "would produce an inequitable or unjust result." It is, in his opinion, one way of empowering mercy and not vengeance. In other words, the Cruickshank jurors who did not wish to convict or who did not wish to see Dawn in prison might have elected simply to void application of the law in her case.

On the surface, this sounds like a radical action but it is not. In the Kalven-Zeisel study, the authors noted that two-thirds of the jury-judge disagreements could be traced to some sense of values which affected the jury in its deliberations. But they also noted, "What disagreement exists today between judge and jury does not arise because of the impact of one or two particularly unpopular crime categories. Rather the jury's disagreement is distributed widely, and diffusely over all crime categories. The jury's war with the law is now a polite one." Kalven and Zeisel also showed that juries tended to act as a "moderate corrective" against undue prosecutions for gambling, game, and liquor violations and to some extent drunken driving. In these contests, "the historic role of the jury as a bulwark against grave official tyranny is at best only dimly evident."

The historic role of the jury, however, does linger somewhat in the constitutions of the states of Maryland, Georgia, and Indiana, where the jury is still defined as having the power to determine the law and the facts, with some limitations. It cannot declare a statute unconstitutional, nor can it create new crime categories which are not part of the trial, nor may the jury alter the elements necessary to convict for a crime. For example, the jury may not, in and of itself, reduce a charge of murder to manslaughter, if the defining elements of manslaughter are not there.

In Georgia, juries are not told of their right to nullify, but in Maryland and Indiana, part of the judge's charge includes a reference to the fact that what the judge says is intended to be helpful, but that the jury may accept or reject the judge's guide. In Maryland, lawyers can even argue the judge's instruction on the law with the jury, and the judge may then dissent from the lawyer's view. In neither state has this charge increased the number of acquittals expected, and the jury system works as well with an explicit reference to jury nullification as without it.

It is very unlikely that states will move to add the nullification instruction where it is not in place today. Zeisel told me he thought that would be "an invitation to lawlessness. Just as it is, is all right." Of course, lawyers may, usually in summation, allude to the jury's role as community conscience, and many do.

The line is fine. In 1966, Kalven and Zeisel wrote that the jury comprises a "uniquely subtle distribution of official power, an unusual arrangement of checks and balances. It also represents an impressive way of building discretion, equity, and flexibility into a legal system. Not the least of the advantages is that the jury, relieved of the burdens of creating precedent, can bend the law without breaking it."

In the Cruickshank case, therefore, the jury could have bent the law so that it would encompass a history of sexual abuse, rather than stop at imminent fear of rape. In Wyman-D'Arazzio, Wyman's defense hoped the jury would refuse to follow the judge's instruction that Wyman had to be guilty if he was aware of the consequences of his act. Both defense attorneys hoped the jury would be sufficiently put off by the "bugs" and undercover work that they would refuse to accept the evidence. Indeed, in the federal Brink's case, the jury acquitted the defendants on the major conspiracy charges, and although I confess I have not been able to crack the anonymity of the jurors to ask them, one must assume they disregarded a large part of the informer evidence and telephone wiretap tapes. It is conceivable that some of them noticed an exhibition on display in the lobby of the courthouse on slavery and the federal courts. Exhibits pointed out that the mutineering slaves en route from Africa were "fighters for freedom" and that jurors, in deliberating on the guilt or innocence of abolitionists who sprung runaway slaves from jail, could not reach a decision and ended up "hung." The federal Brink's defense, of course, was largely political and attempted to describe the defendants as "freedom fighters."

On the other hand, Dr. Spock's jury, in the heat of the passionate sixties, and in light of strong defense counsel arguments to nullify, convicted all but one defendant.

Naturally, jury nullification can be a path to jury error; juries can and do make mistakes, even when they intend to apply the law without question. Remedying jury errors is part of the cost, in time and money, of maintaining the jury system.

The verdict is not inviolate, unless it is an acquittal. And while there are unjust acquittals, as well as unjust civil findings, many of them, I suspect, could be eliminated by less manipulative trial practices and jury selection, clearer charges and better public education on the role of the jury. But these are institutional remedies. Individual defendants have the right of appeal, and convictions can be reversed, arduous as the process may be. The judge too has a great deal of control over the jury's ultimate power. The judge can throw out a conviction if he or she believes the jury has made a mistake, as in the case of a mysterious fire at a Stouffer's restaurant in 1981 in Harrison, New York. The judge felt that the prosecution had not met its burden of proof beyond a reasonable doubt, so he simply stripped the jury of its power for the protection of the defendant. In reversing the conviction of the defendant, the judge wrote that the jury's verdict was "not consistent with the evidence presented in the trial."

Judges may also "direct" a verdict at the end of a trial, by declaring that there is not enough evidence for the jury to have a deliberation about. Attorneys may request the judge to direct an acquittal only; no judge may direct conviction. Attorneys may apply for a "judgment notwithstanding verdict," if they feel the jury misjudged the evidence, or if they feel the jury exceeded the bounds of good sense. The judge makes the final determination on a case by case basis.

There is also the "special" verdict, which means that instead of giving the jury the whole, entire case, the judge poses a set of questions to the jury to answer about the facts—for example, did Dawn Cruickshank suffer fear of imminent rape? The jury thus determines the facts as shaped by the questions, and the judge then applies the law to the facts as found by the jury. The judge might also add some "interrogatories" to the verdict sheet so that when the verdict is announced, the jury also answers questions of fact posed by the judge, so that he or she may evaluate the basis of the jury's decision.

Jerome Frank, a noted jurist in the 1950s, who strongly criticized the jury system in his book *Courts on Trial*, wrote that the special verdict would seem to do away with some of the most objectionable features of trial by jury, "because it forces a jury to state in specifics its findings": Yes, we say that the codefendant D'Arazzio gave the codefendant Wyman the films that were shown in court. The special verdict forces the jury to plumb its collective thought process and make it public. The special verdict also removes from the jury any mixing with the law and obviates complicated instructions on the law. But do we want to remove from the jury precisely its potential to moderate the law by removing the secrecy of its deliberation? Does a special verdict in fact disarm the jury and rearm the judge?

As Zeisel notes, "The sophisticated jury if it wants to convict knows how to answer these questions. Special verdicts can be said to in a way impede the natural instincts of a jury to let justice be done. . . . It is an effort to get back to the legal niceties. Sometimes, if the jury is smart, it can get around it. In a way it probably reduces the amount of judge and jury disagreement and raises the question, why do you need the jury?"

Though jurors themselves do not like their power eroded, they might welcome some relief of their burden. The Cruickshank jury, for example, was fairly irate that there had been a three-day hiatus during the trial for testimony outside their hearing and that the judge allowed testimony at a sentencing hearing he would not allow during trial. "We had her fate in our hands," one conviction-prone juror said, "and we should have heard everything the judge heard. I don't like the idea that they only gave us some of it and expected us to decide." Jurors take their role very seriously, for the most part, and coming to a decision saps their inner strengths. One Cruickshank juror complained, "Here we exhausted ourselves trying to come to a decision, and then the judge just said 'thanks.' I am still living through those days and you think they would have said more than 'thanks.'"

No matter how tortured or frustrated the jury may feel, it can rarely retract its verdict simply by saying it made a mistake. Attorneys may seek to impeach the verdict on some legal grounds, but a jury itself cannot undecide. Probably the Cruickshank jury, if given the case again, would hang. In the not too different case of Jean Harris, one of the jurors went on national radio November 1983 to say she thought there should be a new trial because the jury did not hear all the evidence, particularly evidence related to Mrs. Harris' drug dependency.

Mrs. Lisa Zumar of Tuckahoe, New York, had never served as a juror prior to her selection in the trial of Jean Harris in White Plains, New York, in November 1981. In a telephone interview in March 1984, Mrs. Zumar reiterated to me her belief that Mrs. Harris deserved a second trial: "We had to find her guilty with what we were given. I don't think any of us really wanted it; it was too severe. If we had had a lesser charge to consider, or the drug evidence, I am sure we would have convicted her of the lesser charge."

The jurors, according to Mrs. Zumar, by the same token did not think Mrs. Harris should go free: "There was the gun going across state lines to consider." And she did not believe the jury wanted to hang: "We had no alternative but to convict her of murder."

However, despite the misgivings of her jury, Mrs. Harris' state court appeals have been denied. The U.S. Supreme Court declined to hear her case—which her second attorney, Herald

Fahringer, filed several days after the filing deadline. And her August 1983 request for a new trial, with a third attorney, arguing that her orginial defense had been ineffective, was also denied. Mrs. Harris, therefore, continues to serve a fifteen-year sentence for murder at the Bedford Hills Correctional Facility in New York State.

The power to nullify or at least the choice to nullify is the jury's essential power, even though the power or option to question the law is not flagrantly used. The fact that the jury instinctively knows of this power and may use it, with or without instruction to do so, is an important part of what preserves a balance between individual and state authority. It is what makes the difference between the jury and the judge. Unless jurors themselves become more lawless, it is unlikely that nullification will come into play any more often that it now does, especially since the power works mostly in favor of defendants, and today's community climate is not likely to fuel that favor.

On the other hand, given the increase in questions about the intensity of pretrial publicity (whether any juror, for example, can properly ignore seeing a tape of a defendant on network TV, allegedly completing a cocaine sale), jury sentiment may become more of an operative factor in jury deliberations. Also, if the larger community becomes increasingly polarized over economic and social issues—poverty, racism, school busing, corporate liability for environmental pollution, medical and legal malpractice, the costs of crime—the community's cross section, the jury, is likely to be more polarized. Community values then may not only be more operative in the jury deliberations room, they could become decisive.

[14]
Civil and Uncivil Justice

Often, the jury has to decide the monetary value of a person's life. In the case of Robert Williams, aged twenty-five, who was killed by a robotic vehicle in a Ford Motor Company casting plant in Flat Rock, Michigan, on January 25, 1979, the jury awarded his family $10 million. Almost immediately after the verdict was announced, in August 1983, the attorney for the defendant company, which designed the robot, filed a motion for a judgment notwithstanding the verdict—a reduction of the verdict award, or a new trial—calling the jury's verdict a "shock to the judicial conscience."

It was a typical complaint in an atypical case, and typically the jury bore the brunt of the criticism. However, judicial conscience and community conscience may not have been parallel in this case. That is why there is a jury system in civil law, and why some critics contend the civil jury is a remnant of the past.

It took only a few hours to select the jury in the case of Sandra A. Williams, administratrix of the estate of Robert N. Williams, versus Unit Handling Systems, a division of Litton Industries, Inc., the system's designer. There were no challenges for cause, very little questioning about the jurors' backgrounds or personal beliefs. Though the case was heard in state court, all questions during voir dire were posed by the judge. The attorneys, though they could have put additional questions to the jurors through the judge, opted to seat the six-person jury with a minimum of delay, although the nature of the case might well have drowned voir dire in detail.

Robert Williams died instantly when he was struck in the head by the mechanical arm of a robot, designed by Litton and installed at the Ford plant, which produced sand cores for molding the hollow places in engine blocks. The legal questions were simple: Who, if anyone, was negligent and who, if anyone, was liable? But in determining that, the jury which heard the case also was grappling with questions of how machines—computers and robots—will interact, legally speaking, with workers in the future. It was a case that brought into sharp relief how community attitudes and economic circumstances seep into the justice system and how the jury functions in civil law.

Had the case been heard by a judge alone, the verdict might not have been as astronomical. However, the jury's presence converted the episode into an event with wide ramifications for industrial policy, which policy makers might study. Whether six people on a jury should have such influence is part of the recurrent argument over whether juries should be abolished in civil cases. The Williams case demonstrates what might be lost and what might be gained by abolition.

Millions of civil cases are litigated each year in the United States—everything from broken sidewalk cases to billion-dollar antitrust suits. Much is written and said about the "litigation explosion" and excessive jury awards. In his 1949 book *Courts on Trial*, Jerome Frank wrote that in civil matters "trial by jury seriously interferes with correct—and therefore just—decisions." Chief Justice Warren Burger has advocated abolishing the jury in civil matters. Hans Zeisel believes it is possible that the civil jury could be gone before the end of the century because it is "much less firmly rooted in Constitutional guarantees."

However, as one lawyer expressed it, the jury is an "easy target," because it decides the outcome; and those who do not like the outcome often blame the jury for having done some wrong. Interestingly only a fraction of the cases filed ever come to trial— approximately 6 percent in the federal system.

In the Williams case, the defense rested largely on an assertion by Litton that the robotic system had not been intended to operate with human workers in the vicinity. It was designed to speed retrieval of stored parts from overhead lanes and move them as quickly as possible to the assembly line. Prior to the installation of the robotic system, parts were moved overhead through the plant by a system similar to a dry cleaners' clothing rack. The size of the

structure was equal to two football fields and five levels high. Each
level was serviced by a moving robotic vehicle, commanded from a
computer station base, which operated horizontally on the center
aisle, with an attendant "mole" vehicle running perpendicular to
the aisle, in and out of lanes. The idea of the system was to
improve productivity by ensuring that the assembly line had the
correct number and type of parts it needed when it needed them.
The vehicles were programmed to production line commands.

Litton argued that the system should have been "locked out"—
i.e., power shut off—if any personnel went near the vehicles,
which they should not have been doing anyway. Litton provided
the robot with a continuously rotating beacon light, indicating
power was on and that the mole, or the vehicle, could move at any
time. There was no special signal to indicate that the robot was
actually about to move because, Litton argued, no humans were
supposed to be near the mole or the robot while the power was on.
Litton also argued that the procedure for cutting power to the
system was not being followed by Williams or his coworkers.

The plaintiff's case had been built largely around the concept
that the automated system designed by Litton failed to take the
"human factor" into account—namely, that despite the best plans,
there might be reasons why humans would have to go near the
machinery. Attorneys for the plaintiff presented evidence to show
that, contrary to the plans, there were many practical reasons why
workers had to enter the area. Williams' coworkers testified that
often the wrong part would be stored in the wrong lane and the
mole, unable to tell the difference, delivered production workers
a part they did not want at that time. In these cases, only human
beings could sort out the confusion. Sometimes, sand shed from
the castings dusted the "eyes" of the robot as it moved about,
causing it to misread signals or stop, "thinking" something was in
its way. All these events needed to be remedied, lest production be
curtailed. So, workers routinely entered the storage system.
Cutting power to the robots meant shutting down the entire
production area, and rather than do that, the men grew accus-
tomed to climbing up into the levels and getting in and out of the
system quickly, despite the moving machines. Williams died
because he did not know there was a machine close behind him.

Theoretically, Litton was right. Workers should not have been near operating machinery. But as Paul Rosen, one of the attorneys for the plaintiff, said, "This situation put the worker's safety and production needs in conflict. The workers, under the circumstances, chose production because production was the boss." Joan Lovell, the other attorney for the plaintiffs, argued in her opening statement that the Litton design failed to account for the practical matters that only humans would perceive. And because human beings generally cannot concentrate on more than one thing at a time, if Williams was attempting to sort out a confusion, which he was, he might well not be able to keep an eye out for the robot. Since there was no audible sound associated with its movement, the machine was able to come up behind him undetected.

As to whether the jury could understand the technology of the system the lawyers were discussing, the jury foreman had little doubt. "I don't think there was a juror, including the women, who could not walk into the plant and run that system. That's how well we paid attention."

The plaintiff's evidence had consisted of testimony from workers that they routinely had to enter the system to correct malfunction, expert testimony on the "human factor," and also pages from the Litton operating manual which suggested that, despite the design of the system, Litton was aware of circumstances that might arise requiring an operator to enter. Litton gave a training course, which did not include information about the lock-out procedure, according to the plaintiff's evidence. There was also testimony that Robert Williams had never even been taught any lock-out procedure, and that the warning device on the robotic vehicle was akin to crying wolf in that it flashed constantly to show that the power was on, but did not signal imminent movement. Also, the plaintiffs cited the American National Safety Institute standard, with which the system had to comply, on warning devices. The standard states that a warning device "shall be activated whenever the storage crane as a whole makes any horizontal move under manual, automatic, or remote automatic control."

The defendant's evidence consisted largely of its assertion that its system was being improperly used by the Ford employees and that there were signs on each floor, as well as each vehicle, which said, "Warning: Vehicle can move at any time." Litton argued that the lock-out procedure was not being followed at the time of Williams' death. The jury simply weighed the evidence and found most of it supported the plaintiff's arguments. Litton must have hoped that unveiling some fault on the part of Ford Motor Company might lead the jury to exonerate Litton, but here the Litton attorneys probably underestimated the jury's wish that the family be compensated for its loss.

After eight days of testimony, Litton's liability was clear to all but one juror, and the deliberations ended in only a few hours. As the foreman told me, "With the engineering ability they had, I don't think there is any reason why better safety could not have been designed into that product." Another juror commented, "Even though the worker might have been at some fault for being up there, it was his job to be up there. I can see why he would not want to shut down the entire plant." The lone dissenting juror felt that "a worker's first responsibility is to himself, and I don't see how Litton could be responsible for what those workers did in the system against the rules."

The jury members I spoke with said they believed that Ford also shared blame and that had Ford been a party in the case, they would have found Ford liable as well, because apparently workers were allowed to violate the intention of the design. However, under workmen's compensation laws, participating employers cannot be sued for negligence by employees in the event of an accident, so Ford was not available to the Williams suit, though Litton did countersue Ford.

The plaintiff's strategy to emphasize the human factor—a term which the attorneys reiterated often as did the human-factors expert they called as witness—made the desired impact on the jury. In their analysis of the reasoning process, they all used that term. To the jury, Litton's major errors were not anticipating how their system would actually work in this plant and failing to account for how humans would have to respond to errors. The dissenting juror remarked, "No machine can be idiot proof." But as another juror put it, "No machine can be mistake proof."

That is a problem at least as old as the assembly line, and Paul Rosen, attorney for the plaintiff, in his closing said, "At issue is whether reasonable care required that they consider the human being in the design and manufacturing of their equipment

. . . and whether we go back to the Industrial Revolution where people served machines, where broken backs and broken lives built the roads and the highways, or whether machines, robots, computers serve people."

Actually, the fact that the accident was at the hand of a robot, rather than a more common type of machine, did not figure explicitly in the deliberations, according to the jurors. And none said they resented the idea of automation. But there were futuristic aspects to the accident, like the macabre image of a man lying dead for thirty minutes while machines went on about their business around him. Possibly these images had their unconscious effect, although because of the judge-conducted voir dire, no effort was made to predict these juror responses. "It would have been too awkward to develop these aspects through the judge," Lovell told me. So, a fertile ground for "seeding" was left unsown by the plaintiffs, although this was probably advantageous in the long run, due to the fact that the jurors were not drowned in predispositions that might have diluted the impact of the evidence as it unfolded.

However, the plaintiffs did develop the monetary aspects of the case, namely, how much money would be fair retribution to the Williams family. In voir dire, the judge had asked prospective jurors if they felt they could award "substantial" damages should the evidence warrant it. Rosen asked the judge to be more specific—namely to inquire whether the jury could award in the "millions of dollars." The judge stuck with the word "substantial" only, but by then the word "millions" was already in the air. Then, during trial, several family members and coworkers testified that Williams was a wonderful man, and in his closing, Rosen spoke eloquently about the loss of Williams to his wife, his childhood sweetheart, to his children. Williams' death had come on the second birthday of his son. Instead of party guests, Ford officials came to the door with news of the accident. Rosen described Williams' widowed mother's loss of her only son, so devoted that he visited her every Sunday, and Williams' sister's loss. Richard Tonkin, the attorney for Litton, acknowledged that "Williams' close knit, loving family did not help our case."

In wrongful death claims, loss can be valued starting at the time of death and extending over the life of the deceased's survivors.

Rosen asked the jury, which he is permitted to do under Michigan law, to award each of the three children $2 million, and named no amounts for the rest of the family. According to the dissenter, the jury arrived at $10 million by giving each child $2 million, the wife $3 million, and $1 million for the other family members.

"They were up to $20 million at one time," reported the dissenting juror. "I told them why not give them the whole corporation and let them run it as a family business?" But he made the transaction sound bankerly. In fact, the working class jury had carefully tried to cover each characteristic of the situation and contingency: agony of loss, lifetime potential income earned, cost of college education for the children, some unforeseen eventuality—perhaps another accident that might prevent Williams' widow from being able to work some day. These aspects came into the jurors' minds without their having been suggested to them directly. "We figured in everything that might happen—life is expensive," the juror commented.

In making its verdict award, the jury figured in income tax, but not interest or investment potential. They were a here-and-now group, and all shared the question, "How much is a human life worth?" "How do you figure that, you explain," the jury foreman challenged me. "It is a wrong that can never be put right."

Some critics of the verdict argued that it was an anticorporation verdict, but at least three jurors I spoke to strongly resented that accusation. One said, "We would not have work if it wasn't for big companies, so I am not against them. But in this case the facts were that the corporation made a mistake in designing that system."

In fact, Wayne County, Michigan, in which Detroit is centered, has a record of very high jury awards—"Motown is doughtown" goes a colloquial legalism. According to Jury Verdict Research in Solon, Ohio, Wayne County is 46 percent above the national average. Just before the Williams case, a jury awarded $6 million to a mother whose five-year-old daughter was electrocuted when the Detroit Edison Company was found negligent for failing to repair a downed power line. In 1979, a Detroit jury awarded $2 million to a nineteen-year-old man who had, at the age of fifteen, ridden a speeding bicycle through a parking garage in Dearborn, and flipped over a guard rail. He suffered extensive head injuries.

Shortly after the accident, he began making sexual advances to young boys and in 1977 was arrested for child molesting and sentenced to five to fifteen years in prison. His civil suit alleged that his accident-related head injuries had made him a pedophile; the jury believed him and the evidence, and found the parking garage liable. The City of Detroit had to pay $8 million in 1979 to a man who had allegedly become paraplegic after a beating by Detroit police officers. In 1981, a fifty-two-year-old woman won $5 million because she claimed she was not told by her physician that an operation he performed, apparently unnecessarily, involved risk of the loss of a kidney, which happened. In 1979, Ortho Pharmaceuticals lost a federal case for $3.5 million, in a suit brought by an eighteen-year-old woman who was paralyzed by a blood clot supposedly resulting from taking birth-control pills.

But the Williams jurors resented being put in the Motown/doughtown category. As the foreman put it, "The people here in Wayne County judge cases on the facts. If most of the facts are coming in against the corporations, the corporations should wake up. All these people can't be wrong." Interestingly, in 1937, results of a study involving 1,200 cases, covering six counties, including Wayne, showed that juries and judges found for the plaintiff with equal frequency, and that in Wayne County, juries, more often than judges, found in favor of corporations.

Clearly, something has changed in terms of what juries consider fair settlements. In 1962, nationwide, only one jury verdict awarded $1 million or more in personal injury suits. In 1981, there were 235 such awards.

Critics of jury settlements often evaluate those settlements in the vacuum of the trial court, where the jurors are supposed to be immune to aspects of the outside world that might influence them. However, in Detroit, the social and economic context from which the jury derives is extremely difficult to set aside. Detroit, long a symbol of the industrial prowess of the United States, embodied in the automobile industry, is now a symbol of the decline of that prowess. Downtown Detroit may have a Renaissance Center, but it also has the huge space left empty by Hudson's Department Store, the last great retail establishment to abandon the inner city. As jurors drive to and from court each day, they often must traverse whole blocks of ghetto, constantly aware of how much the city has depended on industry and how much industry has proved undependable. Though there are signs of recovery in some areas, the efforts seem so earnest as to be desperate. A billboard outside a row of new downtown apartments, for example, proclaims in silver letters that glisten in the sun, "Buy a condominium. Get a Cadillac free."

Critics of the Williams verdict think his family got the equivalent of a free Cadillac. Tonkin, the Litton attorney, while in no way belittling the tragedy of the death, says he expected a verdict no higher than $2.5 million. He filed a judgment notwithstanding the verdict, under laws which permit this as a redress of jury error if a verdict is thought to have been reckless or not based on fact.

Often in civil cases, when the jury verdict is in dispute, there are accusations that the jury really did not understand the case or the nuances of the law, and that error and sympathy conspire in favor of the plaintiff. Though Litton's attorney argued in his motion that the verdict rendered by the jury was against the great weight of the evidence and was based upon "conjecture, speculation and guess . . . with no basis in fact," he would not wish to see the jury eliminated. "The jury system is fair, although perhaps I shouldn't say this, but I would do better as a defendant's lawyer without it. It is a heavy burden upon a judge to decide a case like this. I am not so sure that in a routine case a judge would be better than a jury. This case was an exception. You don't see these verdicts every day."

As to whether the verdict was incorrect—that is, not based on evidence—one must look to the nature of the adversary system. The Williams jury foreman noted, "The judge just sits up there and lets some of these lawyers carry on maybe a little too much. Watching witnesses is very enlightening. If it is their lawyer examining them, it is one thing; then when the other lawyer comes up, they automatically, just like day and night, they just flip their style." He also added, "You can see there's always some points the lawyers on both sides would just as soon not develop." It is what Jerome Frank called the " 'fight' theory versus the 'truth' theory of the law," and it is the battle which takes place in every courtroom in the United States.

Though both attorneys agree that the Williams case was "clean"—that is, undertaken with a minimum of lawyerly tactical warfare—there are certainly two views of the truth in this case. Litton's view held that their system was safely designed if used as recommended, and the Williams' view was that Litton's idea of how the system would be used never meshed with the practical circumstances of its operation. Each side buttressed its view with legal references and other case law, but in the end, the jury's view of the facts lined up with the plaintiff—save for the lone dissenter, who matched up squarely with the defense. So, the jurors understood the arguments and did what they were charged to do—namely, determine where they felt the preponderance of the evidence fell.

Joan Lovell, another attorney for the plaintiff, scoffs at the idea that juries hand out awards indiscriminately. When we talked in her office, she had recently finished trying a case in which the jury found "no cause" in a car accident incident. A man sitting in the back seat of a car was injured seriously when another car "came from nowhere" and slammed into his driver's car. Each driver disclaimed fault and argued that the road had been designed in such a way that neither could see the other. The passenger sued the county for allowing the poor condition to continue. Even though the passenger had clearly suffered injuries through no fault of his own, the jury refused to award him a penny. "My client just got lost between drivers. I think the jury decided we made too big a deal out of too small a problem. . . . It went on for three weeks and became too complicated. They just said to us, 'So it's a bad road. They can't fix every bad road in the world.' That is a community judgment—some problems you fix and some you don't. I think it's appropriate for a jury to say that, and though it can be upsetting to me, I find it much less upsetting coming from a jury than from a judge. They were sending us a message, and though I think their decision was against the weight of the evidence, I recognize that they were expressing a community sentiment that maybe I did not anticipate."

Rosen, too, does not worry about setting dangerous precedents with high verdicts. "That verdict got people's attention, but about a month after the Williams case, a jury here heard a case, a death case, tried by a very good lawyer, and there was no question the jury had a very difficult time determining fault. But in the end, they awarded $20,000 in a death case." He is incredulous at that still, and says, "When the attorney asked the judge to raise the verdict, the judge said in essence, 'That is the jury system, pal, the best system in the world.' It is only when the plaintiff wins a lot of money that we hear about juries being 'hogwild.' How come 'hogwild' doesn't apply when the jury under-awards?"

Under limited circumstances, in some states, if a plaintiff feels a jury award is too low, a motion for a new trial can be filed, with the consent of the defendant. Defendants rarely consent and judges rarely agree to new trials.

"Either you want the community input or you don't. You can't have it just when it suits you," Lovell added. And sometimes community sentiment can be unexpected. According to Rosen, there is a county in Michigan where, despite the facts of the cases, it is practically impossible to win a malpractice suit against doctors. "It could be that part of the reason is that the people there don't want to lose their only doctor. . . . They are sick of seeing doctors settle down only to move on to more lucrative practices elsewhere. They also don't want to drive sixty miles to the nearest hospital. So when a case comes up, jurors from that area just won't find doctors liable. Are you going to blame the jury system for that?" It seemed a fascinating example of how community problems can have a direct effect on the legal system and the administration of justice.

Sentiment also works both ways. While understandably the dissenting juror responded to the fact that Williams was near the robot contrary to the design of the system, his overwhelming refusal to find Litton to blame at all—"I was at zero, *no* money"— may stem from his personal view of life and safety. At voir dire, all he said was that he was employed to fix engines. "When people don't assemble them correctly, I fix them." The dissenter joined the jury only after it was already chosen and the last woman selected asked to be excused because she had decided after hearing all the questions that she did not wish to serve. "My dad always told me not to judge anybody, and it has always stuck with me," she reported to the judge, and when she was excused, the dissenter moved onto the panel. In retrospect, Lovell thinks she ought to have paid more attention to the "remark about fixing other people's mistakes." Also in the dissenter's view of the world (he is a motorcyclist), one's safety is in one's own hands. "Take helmets," the juror offered. "I get a few tickets a year for driving without one. But why should I use a helmet? [It prevents me from hearing], it cuts my vision, if I fall it will break my neck. . . . Me and a friend go to Ohio to ride just to ride without helmets. . . . If I got killed not wearing one, it is my fault." Apparently this juror's view was that Williams took a "no helmet" risk in entering the robot area, and therefore the people who designed the system could not be blamed.

The jury in the Williams case was, according to Rosen, on the "threshold" of a new era in the relationship between men and machines. But they seemed uninhibited and undaunted by this position. As Lovell noted, "All during the trial, the court clerk was having trouble with his computer. The jury could see before their eyes how technology can be unpredictable." Clearly, as technology continues to infuse every aspect of our lives, the civil law and civil juries will increasingly be making decisions about the liability of technology.

In England, the jury no longer has a role in civil trials; and perhaps the United States will take that road, too. However the "litigation explosion" is in precisely those fields of law where people—individuals—have a stake: Product liability, consumer fraud, medical malpractice, environmental pollution. These can indeed be complex and technical fields, but to remove the jury from them would deny a voice to the very community most affected.

Such was the case when Babcock and Wilcox, which designed the nuclear reactor at Three Mile Island, Pennsylvania—scene of a very serious nuclear accident in March 1979—was sued by the General Public Utilities Corporation, which owned the reactor, for $4 billion. Both sides waived the jury, and the case was heard before a judge, largely because of the complexity of the technology involved, but also because the defense rested largely on minutiae of contractual obligations, to which a jury might not be very sympathetic.

The utility contended that the engineering firm had failed to provide adequate safety instructions. Babcock and Wilcox contended that it provided the proper instructions and that the accident occurred due to faulty plant operation. After a month and a half of court and judge time was spent, the trial came to an end when the parties announced that the utility had accepted $37 million in settlement, which amounted to clean-up work to be provided by Babcock and Wilcox. The settlement left unanswered the question of who was to blame, and there was speculation that both parties had decided that continued battling in public would only further erode public confidence in the nuclear industry.

David Bird, who covered the trial for *The New York Times* and who did an excellent job of explaining the daily play-by-play to the public, told me he doubted that the average juror could have followed the trial. "I often had to look up outside sources or call experts to get at what was really being said. A jury is precluded from doing that, of course." On the few days in which I sat in on the trial, I tended to agree with Bird, but I did put the question of whether a jury could have followed the proceedings to Dr. Richard T. Lahey, then head of the Department of Nuclear Engineering at Rensselaer Polytechnic Institute in Troy, New York, and a witness called by the plaintiff. He gave a rather remarkable answer: "Forty percent of what I hear in courtrooms is smoke-screen to confuse issues." He said he felt a jury would have been able to understand the technical issues at the Three Mile Island trial "if the attorneys had wanted them to be clear."

Interestingly, in November 1983, Metropolitan Edison, a subsidiary of the General Public Utilities Corporation which operated the nuclear plant at the time of the accident, was indicted by the federal government on criminal charges of falsifying safety test results before the accident. The defendant did not waive the jury this time.

Of course, most civil cases are routine and well within the grasp of the average juror, and, most often, the jury performs at least as well as in criminal matters and similarly to the judge. The Kalven-Zeisel study in 1966 of over 4,000 civil cases found that judges and juries agreed about liability in 78 percent of the cases, and, perhaps more interesting, the jury was more favorable to the plaintiff in 12 percent of the remaining cases while the judge was more favorable in 10 percent of them. As Kalven and Zeisel wrote, "This finding is in the teeth of the popular expectation that the jury in personal injury cases favors the plaintiff, at least if that expectation is taken to mean that the jury is more likely to favor the plaintiff than is the judge." The study does add, however, that "when it comes to the issue of damages, the jury's award is on the average about 20 percent higher than that of the judge." In 1937, in the six-county study including Wayne, practically no difference was found in the assessment of damages between judge and jury, which may mean a slight shift has taken place, more indicative of society's attitudes toward money and who should have it, than to efficiency of the jury system. But if juries are likely to award more than is a judge, that seems to be part of the contemporary process of litigation, and the jury system per se should not be penalized because of differing views of what various damages are worth. It seems to me that if we are content to let the market decide what food, clothing, and housing should cost, we ought to be content to allow the market—the jury—decide what value to place on injuries, inconvenience, and wrongful death.

Whether or not the jury is statistically more likely to award higher damages, lawyers seem to act as though that were so. I have come to call this the "hot body" approach to justice, a phrase I picked up from a sagacious jury clerk in Manhattan. I had complained about being held in the bullpen, one of the large waiting rooms, without being called anywhere near a courtroom for a case and without any information about when I might be needed. "Relax," the clerk told me, "you don't think you are being used, but you are—just by breathing. You wouldn't believe how many cases have been settled this morning without coming to trial. When these lawyers see all you hot bodies out here, they decide to give in." What he meant, of course, was that pressured by the sight of a real jury ready to go, the side with the weaker case decided not to risk the jury trial at all but to settle for what was offered.

Often, too, a trial will begin, and as the lawyers see the case unfold, how their witnesses are coming across, how their side of the truth is holding up, they decide whether or not to go all the way to a verdict. This "use" of juries annoys most jurors, if mail I have received is any indication; for example: ". . . needless to say, the case that I finally ended up on was settled after three days of trial, two hour lunches for all of us and lots of taxpayer's money." And from an attorney in New Jersey:

"About six years ago I was involved in a very complex jury

trial . . . about nine lawyers involved representing the various clients. . . . The jury selection alone droned on for two full weeks—intentionally so on the part of the [defense] lawyers to wear down the plaintiff in the case. . . . In the end, the case was settled shortly after the two weeks it took to pick the jury. The strategy worked. There was talk of all of us having reunions and getting T-shirts imprinted as a remembrance of the occasion. I really don't need the T-shirt to remember." Doubtless, neither do the jurors.

According to *Time* magazine in 1982, one quarter to one half of all cases that come before a jury are settled before the trial ends.

One young woman recounted the typical eleventh-hour tale. She had been selected as a juror in New York City in a case involving an incident that took place during the 1980 transit strike, which left the city's 9 million people without any public bus or subway service. In such emergencies, the city acquires the atmosphere of carnival, where routine is broken and one catches as catch can. In this atmosphere, the plaintiff rode a chartered bus toward his home but got off early because traffic was so snarled. At the corner, he claimed, he was offered a ride in his direction by the driver of a van owned by a dry cleaning company. However, before the plaintiff could enter the van, the vehicle started to pull away, knocking him down. A third vehicle—another chartered bus carrying employees of a large credit card company—allegedly ran into him as he fell. The man broke a leg and sued the owners of both the van and the bus, which he claimed ran him down.

The trial lasted a week, and on the day the jury was about to begin deliberating, they noticed that the van company representative and his attorney were no longer in court. The judge instructed the jury to draw no inference from that—the juror told me the jury did not. After deliberating three hours the jury exonerated the bus company completely: "We did not believe it was possible to be run over by a bus and have only a broken leg." And it found the van company liable for $100,000. But then the jury learned that the van company had settled the case the day before by paying $40,000.

Tales such as these draw a lot of criticism to the jury system, based on the belief that if cases were tried before a judge, lawyers would be less cavalier about settling midway through or less likely to embark on trial of a less than worthy case. Also, the time taken up by jury selection would, in theory, be saved. Delay is an anathema to judicial efficiency advocates; and it is repeatedly argued that removing juries in civil cases would significantly reduce delay.

Interested in investigating popular assumptions about the jury system, Hans Zeisel set out in 1959 to look into whether time could be saved by eliminating juries. The conclusion of the study, based on New York's courts, was that it takes about 40 percent less time, overall, to try a personal injury case without a jury than with one. However, translating this "savings" into actual court conditions could in fact liberate only the equivalent of 1.5 judges because so few cases actually come to jury trial. A judge's calendar is consumed by many judicial functions in addition to jury trials.

The contention that the jury is the least culpable when it comes to wasting court time was amply and dramatically demonstrated in Escondido, California, in 1982 and 1983. Here was perhaps the marathon stillborn jury trial. The case involved the issue of whether or not a major photo processing franchiser and its franchisees were encroaching upon each other's territory. Potential jurors were voir-dired. They were told the trial would probably last five to six months, and the jurors who did not request to be excused at that point remained on that assumption. Jury selection consumed half a day, although the court had told the jurors it would probably take a week. Then chosen jurors were sworn in, and the trial began.

It was to last twenty-one months, nearly two years, to the great inconvenience of the jury. According to one juror to whom I spoke, each time the jury requested an update on how long the proceedings could be expected to take, the judge, who received his information from the lawyers, greatly underestimated. This, for the jury, was agonizing.

For nearly two years, jurors spent four days a week, all day in court, unable to attend to any kind of personal business. On Fridays, when the judge heard other matters, jurors were free, but many of them were expected by their employers, who continued to pay the employees' salaries, to put in at least one day's work. According to one juror, other employees were at times resentful of the salary paid to those who were in court and therefore "not working." Worse, however, was the lost continuity of work, and jurors who held positions of responsibility sometimes did little more than busy work on Fridays. For this one juror, the trial cost not his job but his position—a slip in responsibility which persists months after the trial. "I could not take part in any long-range planning or decision making. Instead, I was and am still answering phones. I didn't lose my job, but I might as well have." He had been an environmental planner for the county, where long-term projections and continuity were key to the work.

On top of slippage in work position, no jurors could make vacation plans or change jobs or move or do anything that would require attention, since most of their attention was being demanded by the trial. As the juror said, "Life was on hold."

The trial itself apparently was no compensation. Soon after it began, according to one juror, "It became so repetitious and boring and unnecessarily complicated. Sometimes we were given the same testimony twice, and when we pointed that out, the lawyers seemed to act surprised that they were repeating themselves." The case grew so complicated that the jurors were furnished with snapshots of each witness so they could keep them straight.

Then, after 288 days of trial, there was a three-week break so the attorneys could prepare their summations. However, on the day that the jurors returned to hear the closing arguments, the judge reported that the parties had settled out of court; the jury was dismissed.

"I couldn't believe they could do that after all that time," a juror recalled, still angry six months later. Apparently, the judge and the attorneys delivered speeches thanking the jury for their extraordinary service. But it was too much for one juror, who asked if he could say something. With the court's permission, he rose and told the judge and the lawyers that he felt the jury had been used "by each side to bluff the other, that we had been pawns, and that if they let the case go so far, they ought to be forced to go to a verdict."

The jurors' stress and fury continued months after the trial ended. Suffering from migraine headaches, which he claims he never had before, the outspoken juror says, "I feel like two years of our lives were just played with, and I am very angry about it."

The juror is now also extremely cynical. "I wanted to serve because I thought it was the right thing to do, but now I see I should have been like everybody else and asked to be excused." To add insult to injury, though the judge promised the jurors they would never be called for jury service again, this particular juror had received two summonses within six months of the end of the trial. He ignored them both.

Interestingly, word of his irate speech in court stimulated "fan mail" the juror would rather not have had. "I even got mail from the Ku Klux Klan congratulating me for standing up for my rights."

On top of the juror's time, there was the matter of court costs, which amounted to $2 million, all borne by the county's taxpayers. The parties to the suit, on the other hand, gained a $10 million settlement. Some districts of federal court require parties to the suit to bear the costs of the jury panel if a settlement is reached during jury selection, but court costs are public expenses, by and large.

Clearly, analysis of the civil law jury system is subject to as much variation as the types of cases themselves. It is easy to argue that its virtue as a democratic institution is unquestionable. Still, in the presently overtaxed court system, the civil jury cannot help but come under severe pressure.

The litigation explosion is real. In federal civil courts the number of suits filed grew from 180,576 in 1981 to 206,193 in 1982, an increase of 14 percent. That number is twice the 1974 number and three and a half times the 1960 number, according to *The New York Times* in an article on June 1, 1983. State courts, where 98 percent of civil cases are heard, received 22 percent more filings in 1981 than in 1977. Appeals increased by 32 percent.

In this context, there is little wonder that backlog exists. In 1983 in the United States federal courts, the average time in civil cases between the filing of a complaint and the actual trial is fourteen months. In some states, cases may take two to three years to come to trial. But most of this kind of delay cannot be blamed on the jury. Once the jury is seated, a judge will not usually grant an adjournment or postponement, and, except for the inevitable bench conferences and arguing outside the jury's presence, the trial rolls along.

While removing the jury would obviously eliminate the possibility of juror error, it would be an abuse of the idea of efficiency to use jury elimination to "scare away" unworthy suits or million-dollar verdicts. That seems to me to force the worthy suer to pay, in loss of the opportunity to put his cases before a representative group on its merits.

It would be more fairly efficient to provide alternatives to courts—arbitration, mediation. A good professional lawyer does not take a case to court for the heck of it, but removing the jury system will not remove poor unprofessional lawyers or judges.

Nor will it remove greed, which is an undeniable motive in some cases. Clients can be greedy, lawyers can be greedy, refusing to make offers of settlement, refusing to accept them. These greeds can feed each other, since the lawyers' fees are tied to, and often paid from, the settlement awarded.

The irony of civil law today is exemplified by the Williams case. In Michigan, there is an innovative system of mediation wherein a case comes before a panel of three attorneys who rotate, in their own form of jury duty, and make a recommendation for disposition to the parties involved. In the Williams case, the mediation panel recommended that Litton's Unit Handling division settle the case for $700,000. The plaintiff was willing to accept it, but Litton Industries was unwilling to pay it, electing to go on to trial, apparently against the advice of its local counsel. Consequently the defendant faced a $10 million liability verdict delivered by a jury the defendant had a part in selecting and chose, on its own, to appear in judgment before. And society might well be grateful that contemporary civil law is still able, through the jury, to give voice to those values which, though they must be expressed in terms of dollar amounts, really do transcend them.

[15]
The Justice Within Us: The Future of the Jury

In a sense, the buck stops at the jury. Strangers gathered together not only are expected to come to a collective decision, but to bear the first, and potentially final, responsibility for the disposition of whatever matter has been put before them. That the jury is there means the rest of us do not have to be. Consequently, we are armchair critics. For the jury system is one of those things that work until they don't work, and it can work only as well as all the parties to the case wish it to work.

The jury system, in short, can either be what it is intended to be, or it can be manipulated and mishandled so as to void the jury's inherent values and fuel its inherent weaknesses. The question then becomes: How can the jury system in today's courtroom be made to work better?

If we accept the Zeisel-Kalven study that the rate of judge-jury disagreement is roughly 20 percent, then we would hope to improve that ratio. However, when I asked Zeisel if he thought the rate was acceptable, he replied that it was difficult to quantify acceptability: "If we had found the rate to be zero, then the jury would be only window dressing. On the other hand, if the rate were found to be 50 percent, I would be alarmed." Of course, using judge-jury disagreement as a measure implies a belief that the judge's opinion is correct and therefore is the opinion against which the jury should be judged.

There is, of course, little way for the public to know whether a judge's decision is correct; even judges disagree. One judge with whom I discussed the Wyman-D'Arazzio case thought that the trial judge, in his eagerness to convict the defendants, had been

216

unwise in allowing the films to be shown to the jury because of their clear potential to be prejudicial. The outcome of an appeal is one measure of judicial competency, but the average person's familiarity with a judge's record is practically nil; most of the public does not follow a particular judge's career.

The jury, on the other hand, stands unrobed, accessible, and certainly easier to call wrong.

The criticism of the jury system advanced by Jerome Frank began with his outright disavowal of any of the poetic or romantic history of the jury, which, he argued, has kept the jury system in place when it has long since outlived its usefulness or relevance. Simply, Frank said that juries do not understand the cases put before them and certainly do not understand the judge's instruction on the law. He suggested that jurors arrive at their verdicts by no more than the flip of a coin, rather than a hard look at the facts, and that when a jury does bring in a correct verdict, it is merely because the jury followed a logic and law all its own. He railed against the jury's "uncontrollable power." Frank's shorthand formula for what should take place in the courtroom was R × F = D; that is, Rules by Facts equals Decisions. He believed that since the jury is singularly unable to get either R or F, or both, correct, then D can often be wrong.

But whether D is wrong more often that 20 percent of the time remains to be seen.

Though Frank's comments were aimed at the jury itself, they seem, in fact, to describe the shortcomings of the way in which cases are presented to the jury; and for many ills, he points out, the jury cannot be blamed. His criticisms are more properly criticisms of the adversary system. For example: "Frequently the partisanship of the opposing lawyers blocks the uncovering of vital evidence or leads to a presentation of vital testimony in a way that distorts it. . . . We have allowed the fighting spirit to become dangerously excessive." Or, "a lawyer does not want the trial court to reach a sound, educated guess, if it is likely to be contrary to his client's interests. Our present trial method is thus the equivalent of throwing pepper in the eyes of a surgeon when he is performing an operation." If what Frank alleged in the fifties is still true now, it is surprising that the jury does not err more often.

Of course, some criticisms of the jury system are separate from criticisms of the adversary system, which, in any case, is unlikely to be modified anytime soon. There are, however, plain, practical limitations which go to the very heart of the definition of the jury—what makes it what it is.

The jury draws ire for being unpredictable and arbitrary, susceptible to being moved by factors which do not have to do with the evidence. There is, in addition, the question of time spent preparing a case so that it may be presented before a jury—hearings and motions aimed to determine whether certain kinds of evidence would be too prejudicial or "admissible."

In fact, many of the rules concerning the fairness of evidence have been developed with the jury in mind. Presumably, in front of a judge there would be less need to control the shape, sight, and sound of the trial. Trials take longer before a jury than before a judge, it is argued, and jurors must be paid, adding to both the time and money expense. Finally, and perhaps the strongest criticism of the jury system, is that juries make mistakes that no one can uncover or undo. It is extremely difficult to "impeach" or set aside a jury's verdict unless it can be shown that during deliberations the jury was influenced by "extraneous prejudicial information" or "outside influence." In both of these cases, even if the jury has engaged in some misconduct, before the verdict can be set aside, there must be proof that but for the misconduct, the case would have had a different outcome.

Gary Hafetz, a practicing trial lawyer in New York, tells the story of the jury members who bit each other's arms during deliberations to determine how long teeth marks normally persisted. They did not think the evidence presented in trial made the point sufficiently clear, and since the defendant's identification had been made based on the fact that the victim he allegedly assaulted bit the attacker on the arm, the jury developed its own evidence on the point, something they are emphatically not supposed to do. However, on appeal, the jury behavior was not found to have been "prejudicial" in view of other evidence, and so the defendant's conviction was upheld.

A juror who wrote me proudly reported the part he had had in producing a conviction in a drug case, apparently wholly unaware that what he had done was entirely out of order. The defendants had been seized with wads of money, but the evidence had been confusing as to whether they had had the drugs in their possession at the time of arrest, and whether they had sold drugs to purchasers in Southern states.

The juror knew something about the Federal Reserve System and suggested that the jury ask to examine the money which was in evidence. He went over each bill and announced to his colleagues that the money bore the identifying marks of the reserve-affiliated banks of the very area from which the buyers were said to have sent money. He contended that, given the manner in which the Federal Reserve Bank distributes currency to banks around the country, the money in evidence had to have originated in the states in question. (If so, perhaps the prosecutors missed a bit of circumstantial evidence that might have helped the case, but it clearly was not the juror's job to fill the space.) The juror proudly reported his work to the prosecutor after the case had been settled in a "guilty" verdict, and the prosecutor simply wrote back thanking the juror for the letter. Strictly speaking, the prosecutor ought to have shared the letter with the defense, but as far as I know, no appeal was mounted.

Jurors like to reconstruct the case themselves and engage in a bit of detective tactics to clarify their thoughts. I received the following anecdote from a law professor in Canada on the nature of jury-room speculation:

> Years ago I was clerk to a Supreme Court judge in South Australia. The charge was rape and, in those days, the women were wearing very tight hip-hugging and knee-hugging dresses. The defense claimed that the rape had not occurred because the accused could not have raised the skirt high enough. The jury was allowed to take the exhibits into the jury room. I walked past the jury room just as the sheriff's officer was escorting a juror to the washroom. I noticed a smallish member of the all-male jury was on the jury table with the dress on and the jurors were doing some empirical research in seeing if the dress could be raised high enough. No-one pointed out to the jurors that the hip formations of males and females are not the same. They convicted.
>
> A policeman or sheriff's officer guarded the jury room and we clerks often went down and asked for the present state of play. He used to tell us that it was 8 to 4 for acquittal but the guy in

the green shirt was holding out for conviction, etc. I never passed this information on to my judge who would have thought it very improper.

These examples highlight how independent the jury can be. Perhaps judges ought to warn jurors very specifically against the reconstruction of events, just as they warn them about visiting scenes of events mentioned in the trial. On the other hand, if the jury has legitimate questions that haven't been answered during the trial, are they simply to equate the questions with doubts? Gaps in information are quite different from doubts which arise after the information is there.

It is also charged that the jury can be inflamed by unreasonable passion and emotion. In the case of Dawn Cruickshank, however, clearly some of the jurors allowed the position and wealth of Dawn's father to enter into their assessment of the credibility of Dawn's testimony. But this sentiment did not overrule the direction of the judge's charge, which was what, in the end, determined their verdict. In the John Hinkley case, the jury was well aware of the fact that Hinkley had shot Ronald Reagan, yet they did not yield to public passion about a presidential assassination; they held to their belief that he could not be found guilty by reason of insanity. If Hinkley is released too soon, or in error, it cannot be the jury's burden. The defense attorney for Wyman, in Wyman-D'Arazzio, attempted over and over again to arouse sympathy for his defendant. He did, but it was not enough to overcome the prosecution's case.

This hardly means that emotion does not influence the jury—the question is: Does emotion so influence the jury that it does not reason to a correct conclusion? The Kalven-Zeisel results seems to show that this happens only about 33 percent of the 20 percent of the time the judge and jury disagree.

The delay argument is the one most prone to curry adherents in the next decades, just as the delay factor drives the argument for smaller juries or majority rather than unanimous decisions. It is true that preparing a case for the jury takes time—the hearing about whether the last tape could be used against Wyman could have been part of the trial had it been heard by a judge rather than a jury. On the other hand, the judge would have had to spend the same time researching the legal issues involved, were the tape presented as part of the evidence, in order to determine whether it were legally weighable. The judge would have to consume additional time writing an opinion, doubtlessly opening, or widening, the areas of appeal since the judge's deliberative process would be revealed in a way the jury's can never be. Certainly lawyers would present their cases with more dispatch before a judge alone, dispensing with rhetoric and tactics now carefully planned for jury effect. Professor Zeisel has shown that it takes about 40 percent less time to try a case before a judge than before a jury. But this time factor is partly explained by the fact that cases which come before juries are by definition unclear—they would never come before the jury if one side or the other did not believe there was something in the case which, if subjected to the special scrutiny of the jury, might spur a favorable verdict. If all jury cases could be easily decided by one person, it would mean the ambiguities of the case had been removed. If ambiguities were so easily removed, jury trials themselves would proceed more quickly.

Juries make errors, but there has never been proof that the errors they make are "excessive," at least in relation to the unique components they provide: community values and impartiality. Because each case is a fresh matter for the jury, jurors are a lot closer to what Samuel Coleridge wrote is required of the reader of poetry: "a willing suspension of disbelief." The juror, much more than the judge, views each witness as sincere, each lawyer as dedicated, each oath as potentially inviolable. Judges are processors and can be, to put it mildly, jaded by the case traffic in which they are snarled each day. The jury, on the other hand, gives its best attention to each case, usually as free of preconceptions as possible and unpolluted by previous cases.

As long as maximum fairness is the goal of the justice system, it will be difficult to know how many juror errors are too many. For those who suffer from them, any are too many, but one has to hope that good attorneys and the appeals process will eventually rectify the terrible errors. One knows too, however, that that hope can be Pollyannaish and that jury mistakes live on, for some, in the form of wrongful imprisonment and even death. Still, though, these issues are separate from the issue of whether the jury system is worth keeping.

Fortunately, there is tremendous potential for the workings of the jury system to be improved, assuming all the forces acting upon it wish it to improve. The jury system, in my view, is an original good idea that with proper maintenance will continue to deliver justice, just as an old well-made clock will continue to keep good time if it is kept clean.

To maintain the jury system well, it would be helpful if, from time to time, lawyers and even judges—usually exempted from service—would drop their professional trappings and become peers by virtue of serving on a jury.

The Hon. Marianne Battani, a judge in Wayne County (Detroit), described her stint as a juror to me as she waited in chambers for more jurors to come up to her courtroom so she could begin a trial. Battani received a jury duty summons in October 1981, after a Michigan law dropping automatic exemptions for judges, lawyers, and law enforcement officials went into effect. Battani answered the summons like everyone else, and became part of a panel on a criminal case, surprisingly without being challenged by either defense or prosecution. Battani had been a defense attorney before becoming a judge, which probably appealed to the defense. She had a reputation for being fair as a judge, which probably kept the prosecution from challenging her.

The case involved first degree murder charges against two defendants. Though one murder was involved, the defendants had separate trials and separate juries, due to the nature of the evidence and the fact that not all of it could be used against both defendants. The trial lasted several weeks.

"The first problem," recalled Battani, "was getting the rest of the jury over the awe they felt about my being a judge. . . . That took a few days, but once we were on a first-name basis, they stopped looking at me with special consideration." Battani's low-key style probably helped—not many judges could become a peer so easily.

Battani remembers being impressed with how hard the jury worked to be correct. During deliberations, they sometimes asked her to clarify points of law, but she simply referred them to the trial judge. "We wrote him notes like any other jury," she reported, and she declined to be foreperson when the rest of the jurors urged that role upon her. "After hearing all the evidence, the jury took a secret ballot; it was split. One juror requested a blackboard, and they then began working through each pro and con for conviction or acquittal." Battani, at that point, would have voted for conviction, but articulated some of the acquittal arguments. "I did that deliberately because I knew if they knew my feelings right away, he might be convicted immediately." By the second day, however, Battani fleshed out her real views before the jury but by then the jury had of itself moved to a conviction vote.

In the meantime, the other defendant's jury had come in with an acquittal verdict. One of the Battani jurors had heard about it but did not mention it to his cojurors. "I was very impressed that he kept that secret, and with how seriously the jury took the responsibility of convicting someone. . . . One juror told me he would never convict unless there was a movie picture of the event . . . many of them interpret beyond reasonable doubt to mean all doubt." Other judges who have been jurors have commented on how little of the judge's instructons or charges jurors were able to follow.

However, the difference in the two verdicts, Battani believes, can be explained by the difference in evidence submitted to each jury. Battani's jury had a statement by the defendant outlining the murder, which could not be used in the trial of the second defendant because it did not, strictly speaking, "further the criminal" conspiracy, in this case, a conspiracy to murder.

Her jury experience renewed Battani's belief in juries, which she termed "the best possible system." However, she did learn to see things from the juror's point of view—"how annoying the down time can be" and "how arduous coming to a decision really is for jurors." She is now willing to consider that majority rule as opposed to unanimous verdicts may not be a bad thing. She also now tries to take the time after a jury's verdict comes in to talk with the jury, at least to "give them the idea that whatever they have done, the system appreciated them and that if they voted their conscience, they should feel good about what they have done." Interestingly, Battani said that during her stint as a juror she "tuned out" to the legal questions at stake after a while in order to concentrate on the facts. Perhaps this suggests that, when facts are at issue, a judge alone could not keep the trial in bounds as well as determine who did what to whom.

In Wayne County, other judges have served, and the jury clerks are very proud of the fact that so have blind jurors and deaf jurors. Virginia Parzik, assistant to the chief jury clerk, showed me a scrapbook of clippings of news relating to the jury system. The clips started in 1921, and says Parzik, "I felt obliged to keep up the tradition because my predecessor did."

As I left her office, I was fired anew by pride in the jury system myself and met some jurors—wearing badges marked "juror" so court personnel will not make prejudicial comments in their presence—in the elevator. Full of enthusiasm I thought he would share, I asked a young man juror, "Did you get a case yet?" He returned a very blank, almost hostile stare and said, "Case? What's that?"

The literally blank juror, the hostile juror, the dead spot on the deliberating table, is feared by many attorneys, and though judges like Battani can come away from their stints as jurors with renewed belief in the system, others who penetrate the jury sanctum emerge with new concern. Attorney Thomas Silfen of Washington, D.C., served as a juror on a relatively simple civil case in 1983, after having just completed four years preparing and trying two very long antitrust suits. After sitting as a juror, Silfen wrote in the *Legal Times* of Washington, "I have little faith that we got anything more in our antitrust cases than the jury's heartfelt instincts, shaped primarily by their sympathy (or lack of it) for the principal witnesses." Because he believed that for the most part, especially in complex cases, the jury often ignores expert testimony if it is too conflicting, and judge's instructions if they are too long, he recommended that all attorneys simplify their cases to the maximum and then "if a lawyer gets a chance, he should serve on a jury. The experience will scare him forever."

It is, of course, unlikely that very many lawyers or judges will serve as jurors, though that would be one way to fertilize improvements in the jury system. But there are other ways to foster real improvement, chiefly by converting the jury from a reluctant, passive body to an involved, engaged one, and improving every level of their interaction with the trial—from being summoned, to being thanked after their verdict. Most changes can be effected for very little money, but they require basic attitudinal changes on the part of the public and the legal profession. The American Bar Association's committee on jury standards has recommended many of these ideas, but in terms of implementation, courts have been slow to warm.

To begin, as the ABA has said, no person should be automatically exempted from jury service. And no employer should be entitled to dock an employee any money should the employee be unable to work because of jury duty obligations. It should be as simple as that, if we truly want representative pools with a wide selection of people and attitudes, experience, and background to choose from. Affluent, well-educated, sophisticated people tend to be in professional classes, which are exempt. Perhaps, to lighten the burden on small businesses and the self-employed— and it might be said that the system would benefit from such people's independence and individuality—the federal government and/or state governments could develop a jury service insurance plan, which could reimburse the policy holder who was called, selected, and obliged to lose work in order to serve on a jury. Premiums could be set on a sliding scale, depending on the amount of coverage the individual wanted to purchase. If pools were truly representative, more truly representative juries would have to result. In a talk to lawyers on the importance of starting jury selection with a mixed pool Jay Schulman said simply, "Garbage begets garbage."

Jury service is the only civic obligation besides voting that everybody holds in common. And everybody ought to serve as a juror at least once in his or her life. This goal should not be difficult to achieve. In the same way that we make technological and management advances quickly—in one, two, or ten years— truly universal jury service should also be within our reach.

Universal jury service ought not to be too burdensome if more jurisdictions were to adopt a simple but revolutionary technique called one day/one trial. Perhaps what potential jurors dislike most is being pulled away from their ordinary lives and then just sitting around waiting to be called into one courtroom or other. It is estimated that 40 percent of a juror's time is spent waiting to be used.

Like a good grease cutter, one day/one trial gets rid of all that. It means that a court system summons new batches of jurors every day, rather than at the beginning of every week. The juror remains available to the court system for one full day, and if he or she is not selected to serve on a case that day, the juror is excused and does not have to come back until his or her next summons, which should not be for at least two years. If, on the other hand, the juror is selected to serve on a case, he or she must serve for the duration of that one trial. Obviously, if all a person had to dedicate was one day every two years, there would be fewer excuses and postponements and less effort spent getting out of it. In New York City, which does not have the one day/one trial system, in 1983 of 2,000 summonses returnable on any given day, the jury clerk expects about four hundred people to turn up ready to serve; approximately 1,500 will have asked for deferments, and the rest do not bother to acknowledge the summons at all.

Many major cities do have the one day/one trial system in place—Atlanta, Houston, Detroit, for example. In Atlanta, I observed it just a few weeks after it began. The clerk commented, "It is a lot more work for us, but it seems like the people who come down here don't mind it as much."

Norman Goodman, who has been chief jury administrator in New York County (Manhattan)—a system which defies all rules—talked with me about the one day/one trial innovation. Goodman's signature has been on summonses sent to jurors since May of 1969. He plays the system's strings like a familiar fiddle and is proud of the fact that he runs the largest jury system in the United States fed from the same pool. "The problem for us with one day/one trial is that it is based on the idea that 'no juror waits.' We, on the other hand, must operate on the idea that 'no judge waits.'" Goodman's jurors feed ninety-five different courtrooms, and, he says, "Here, a judge will call for a new panel at four P.M. on a Friday." Goodman believes New York is too heterogeneous a city to implement one day/one trial and too mobile. "Everyday," Goodman predicts, "would be a lottery to see who would show up."

In New York City, in 1983 of the 17,000 questionnaires sent each month to potential jurors to qualify them—verifying age, address, ability to speak English—half are returned because the addressee has moved. Because of this experience, Goodman feels one day/one trial would leave the courtrooms short of jurors, since it would be virtually impossible to know with enough certainty how many qualified people the summons call would reach. Perhaps he is right, but he believes the system cannot even afford the time to test one day/one trial. "The public cares about one thing—how many cases are disposed of. . . . So if a judge's trial is held up because of lack of jurors, it is going to be difficult to explain." There was such a shortfall during 1982, attributed to the failure of a computer to generate the printed summonses for which it had been programmed, and indeed there was a near paralysis in the courts for several days.

On the other hand, there is increasing effort to improve what is now called juror utilization, especially in federal court. Judges are required to estimate their juror needs for a month or week, and the jury clerk tries to summon a number that will cover the need and account for challenges and dismissals. In theory, this limits jurors' wasted time and also erodes the hot-body approach, which says there are always more jurors where these came from.

Another practical improvement would be to crack the seemingly uncrackable code of who gets summoned. All around the country I have friends and acquaintances who, though they vote and own cars, have never been called for jury duty in any court system. My seventy-two-year-old mother has voted every year of her adult life and never has received a jury summons of any kind. She has lived in New York and Connecticut her entire life.

In Manhattan, punching buttons on a new computer, Goodman claims, "If a person votes and doesn't move, it is unlikely two years will pass without his being called." Yet I hear all the time of people who have yet to be summonsed, offset by tales of those who receive a summons every two years like clockwork. In my own case, while I am now apparently locked in to the cycle on state-court level, I have never been called for federal jury service.

My favorite tale of summonses and lists and randomness comes from a writer colleague who used to receive a summons every two years and dutifully responded to it, only to be told that media members could be exempted. He chose to serve but was never picked. Then mysteriously came some years when he received no summonses at all. Then, just as mysteriously, the summonsing began again. He answered, as was his custom, and found himself, to his amazement, in a pool that seemed to consist mostly of media people. Even more to his amazement, he was selected to serve on a jury with four of the media types and two "men who had said they were unemployed." He continued: "When we got into the jury room, not only did it turn out that they had unemployment in common, but they also claimed to be Rastafarians—but without the usual look." (Rastafarians wear their hair in dreadlocks and are usually recognizable.) I wondered what the odds are, in a supposedly random system, of collecting four writers and two "unmarked" Rastafarians on a jury.

Quirks and exceptions aside, there is no question that the nuts-and-bolts matters related to jury selection deserve and require improvement so that, to begin, jury service will not be an onerous burden that potentially good jurors seek to avoid.

The Center for Jury Studies of the National Center for State Courts, in Williamsburg, Virginia, dedicates itself to improving jury systems operations. The systems analyst and director, Tom Munsterman, an engineer, argues that juror reluctance is a "myth" and that approximately 90 percent of all jurors questioned in a survey he conducted of jurors who had served, viewed their experiences as favorable. Munsterman, a deep believer in the social importance of the jury, has been advocating improvement in jury systems and the goal of universal service for nearly ten years. Yet while much improvement in the technology, so to speak, has taken place, very basic gains haven't been achieved, because court systems and jurisdictions have not applied either the money or the brains, or both. The need, however, is urgent, for it is impossible to divorce the need for a more efficient jury selection system from the need for a more efficient system to administer justice.

If, indeed, the courts are in danger of breakdown by the end of the century, as Chief Justice Burger has predicted, then antiquated, unpleasant, unrandom, unrepresentative jury selection procedures—complete with dirty subwaylike jury rooms and holding pens—are part of that breakdown's cause.

But even assuming that the practical corrections could be implemented, and that every panel to be selected consisted of willing people who truly represented all walks of the community, we still would not necessarily have better, swifter trials, or truer, surer verdicts. There are matters of substance—in jury selection and trial conduct—which are essential to any improvement or jury system reform.

In the coming years, jury selection will receive an increasing amount of attention, both because of the increasing use of behavioral techniques in choosing the jury and because court administrators see a potential for time saving.

The goal of having a representative, unbiased jury is at odds with an attorney's goal of choosing a jury favorable to his or her side, and both will be at odds with choosing any jury in a minimum amount of time. The simple solution for the time factor is to have judges question jurors in all state courts. And the only way it seems to me that lawyers can resist loss of this privilege over the next twenty years is if they examine, long and hard, their "seeding" practice, their need to "condition" the jury. The "goat situation" monologue, brilliant as it was, did not really mitigate the evidence in the trial of Ricky Knapp. The hope, however, was that it would. The form of the nonquestion question—"You wouldn't hold it against a witness that he had not paid his income tax for twenty years, would you?"—simply will not be tolerated as the jury system selection process comes under heavier scrutiny. What constitutes the limits of sound advocacy? When do those limits push into the waste of court time and taxpayer's money? If trial lawyers do not put the questions to themselves and seek practical answers, these questions will be answered by green-shaded court administrators, acting supposedly on a public mandate.

And if trial lawyers do lose their voir dire privileges, judges had better be up to the task of asking the good probative questions attorneys might want posed. Had the would-be lawyer-juror in the Mobil-Washington *Post* libel case been better probed, probably the costly appeal would not have been necessary. Better explanation during voir dire on holding to one's convictions might have turned Dawn Cruickshank's jury another way.

If judges allow only very superficial questioning in all but extraordinary cases, there will be no substantive improvement in the quality of jury justice.

Attorneys also need to cease abuse of peremptory challenges to achieve unrepresentative juries from at least moderately representative pools, not only in the obvious case of racial and ethnic groups being excluded on a wholesale basis, but in the more subtle exclusions of anyone who might bring enlightened scrutiny to the evidence. Attorneys, in other words, should not attempt to win cases by seating the most malleable, uncritical, or dumb jurors they can find. First, even a third-degree voir dire will not uncover the full amount of common sense and potential-to-reason present in each juror, which seems to come to the surface in many jury deliberations. And second, the larger community deserves the best jury possible to determine the facts of a case. The parties in the case should also seek excellence, but there is subjective and empirical evidence that attorneys tend to do the opposite. Probably at least twelve of the excused jurors in Wyman-D'Arazzio would have reached the same conclusions as the seated twelve, if given the chance to hear the evidence. Was it ultimately fair to the nation that, in the trial of a former Attorney General, the only juror seated who had "status" in the community was an alternate? Does it make sense, for example, that in Rochester, Michigan, there was a "strong tendency to exclude jurors with higher education"?—this according to a 1980–82 Oakland University study. It found that high-school graduates represented 43 percent of those summoned, but only 8 percent of those chosen to serve; those with a four-year college degree formed 14 percent of those called, but only 1 percent after voir dire. Also, the same study found that though the county is considered affluent, lower income people were found most often seated on property cases. If we spend a lot of time and money to force representativeness into the jury rolls, then we stand foolish if we allow the jury selection process to squeeze it out again.

There remains the question of how to help the jury perform better once the trial is underway. In 1983–1984, an experiment was tried in New York (Second Circuit in the Southern District of the federal court system), which an attorney, who supports it, called "hardly bold." It included such novel ideas as letting jurors take notes, ask questions, have written copies of the judge's charge in the courtroom, or have interim instructions on what law applies at points during the trial, rather than in one huge dose at the end of the proceedings before the jury receives the case.

Arguments against note taking, for example, tend to cluster around the idea that the juror who takes notes will not be paying full attention, or that the notes will have too much influence during deliberations, or that the juror will take inaccurate notes—all of which are possible. However these possible errors would, most likely, be corrected by the group. The present system allows jurors to sit through days and months of testimony, depending on memory and risking poor and inaccurate recall. For example, in the Industrial Bio-Test case in Chicago, which involved fraudulent laboratory testing and lasted months in 1983, the judge permitted note taking, although the defense objected, questioning, "What would be the evidence finally—the evidence or the notes?" That jury deliberated thirteen days, most of which, jurors told me, was devoted to rehashing the case, even with the aid of notes. Anyone who has ever taken a course in school can attest to the fact that note taking promotes better involvement. And an average trial requires as much, if not more, quality involvement from a juror as any course the jury may have taken. The note-taking debate is old—Judge Learned Hand advocated juror notes in the 1950s: Daniel Schorr, CBS-News correspondent during the Watergate hearings, who served as a juror in the 1970s, lamented that he could not take notes. Still, it remains controversial. In most state courts, note taking can be permitted at the judge's discretion, and the federal courts are in the process of evolving a policy.

Questioning witnesses could invite trial chaos, but good judges seem to be able to manage it. Judge Winton McKibben (Superior Court, Alameda County, California) has permitted jurors to ask questions in his courtroom since 1969. Questioning has been sanctioned in federal court, in principle, since 1954. According to the Center of Jury Studies, jurors do ask questions in about half the trials before McKibben, and he believes those juries are more attentive, more retentive, and quicker to reach a decision. Usually judges who allow jurors to question adopt this method: The juror writes out the question and sends it to the judge; he (or she) then shows the question to the attorneys, who may object; he then rules on whether to pose the question or not, considering its admissibility, relevance, etc. Allowing jurors to ask questions is still an exceptional practice, although jurors do not necessarily utilize the right when they do have it. In the six experimental courtrooms in New York City, in six cases, only once did a juror pose a question.

Even the best minds have questions. Hans Zeisel served as a

juror once before he became a law professor. It was a criminal case involving an alleged mugging. The victim thought she could identify the victim and went to the police who arrested a man, based on her identification. The defendant had a deep scar on his face of which no mention was made in the trial. Zeisel recalled his reactions: "We retired to deliberate, and I thought it would be interesting to know if, when the victim went to the police, she mentioned the scar. If so, I thought I would be inclined to believe her. So we asked the judge if we could learn this and he said, 'No.' We acquitted."

Leonard B. Sand, a judge in the Second Circuit in New York who oversees the experiment allowing juror questions, believes it is important to ride careful herd on the questions and never allow them to be asked out loud. He had heard of a case involving elaborate criminal plans and activities, in which a juror posed the question, "Why would somebody go to all this trouble when there are simpler ways to steal?" The defense moved for a mistrial but the trial judge denied it.

No doubt jurors posing questions could be chaotic without the proper controls, but, on the other hand, allowing no questions could leave gaps that jurors may be tempted to fill in on their own. Surely, there must be compromise ground.

Perhaps the most important area for jury performance reform is in the instructions or charge on the law given by the judge to the jury. Gary Naftalis, a well known white-collar-crime defense attorney in New York City, has compared most judges' charges to the Sermon on the Mount, in that few judges like to deviate from the standard language of charges, a legal cookbook. The standardization of charges—matching language to specific crimes and events—grew because charges often contained legal errors, providing a strong basis for appeal. Consequently, judges often have "charge" books and simply read, or rather, drone on from them in order to avoid making errors that would yield appealable points.

The first problem is in the word "charge" itself. I have met jurors who confused the "charge" on the law with the "charge" in the indictment. Some have said they thought the judge brought the charges alleging the crimes because in court both sides kept referring to the "judge's charge."

The second problem is in the attitude that merely saying the words, putting them in the air, passing them by the jury, amounts to instructing them on the law. Some charges take several hours to deliver, and judges read from their preplanned instructions. But the act of saying does not make it so. The jury may be a captive audience and may look rapt, but researchers A. Elwork, B. Sales, and James J. Alfini studied large samples of jurors in the Midwest and found the average juror may understand only half the judge's instructions on the law (to the extent that comprehension can be distinguished from failure to remember).

Most jurors I have talked with seem to recognize the importance of the judge's charge and their limitations in the face of it. Sometimes, despite their fear of making a silly demand or looking stupid, the jurors balefully seek help on the matter of the charge. In the retrial of Ricky Knapp, the judge had charged the jury that to convict the defendant of murder, the jury had to find that he had acted in a manner which "evinced depraved indifference to human life." A conviction for manslaughter would, on the other hand, mean the jury did not find the defendant had shown such indifference. (It was the same charge question that arose in the Gino Bova trial in Brooklyn, before the all-white jury.)

The jury deliberated twelve and one half hours over two days. The atmosphere was a touch strange under any circumstances because the trial proceeded, as we have said, in the parish hall of a local Roman Catholic church, a place normally devoted to bingo, and one of Knapp's appeal points was that his trial denied the separation of church and state.

In any case, each time the jury had a question, they had to write it out and then come down a flight of stairs, in order to reassemble in the makeshift courtroom. Thus, posing questions required special effort. Nevertheless, the Knapp jury posed four questions, two of which related to the charge. The first question was, "Would the charge be the same if the defendant had died instantly." Several jurors told me they meant "indictment" when *they* used the word "charge." This was relevant because the defendant, the prosecutor alleged, failed to seek medical help for the victim and thus caused her to die. (At his first trial, Knapp had been acquitted of the murder count which alleged that he had intentionally murdered the victim, and convicted of the second count of allowing her to die.) The judge, who throughout the trial had failed to do much to put the jury at ease, answered the question by saying that all the elements of the charge—*he* interpreted their use of "charge" to relate to his instructions— supposed that the victim had lived for a period of time and that the defendant had not sought medical aid. He gave the jury this answer over the objection of the defense counsel, who had recommended that the judge simply answer that the matter of when the victim died was a question of fact for the jury to decide. The judge's reply to the jury on this question also formed part of Knapp's appeal.

The last jury question clinched their verdict, according to interviews with some jurors. The foreman wrote a note requesting a definition "in layman's terms" of "depraved indifference to human life."

Instead of giving the jury a definition, the judge provided three examples. In the first one, three persons rob a drunkard, then abandon him on a busy street without a coat, shoes, or his glasses; a passing car then accidentally kills him. In the second example, a person shoots into a crowd with a loaded shotgun. In the third, a person drives his car into a crowd. From these examples, the jury assumed that the murder charge required them to find some evidence that Knapp intended the victim's death, which was logical, I thought, given the judge's examples. Thus, the jury convicted Knapp of manslaughter rather than murder. Unre- solved problems of understanding and communication related to the judge's charge played a fairly important role in the outcome of the Knapp case.

In the Cruickshank case, the jury clung to the judge's charge to justify its conviction. The judge instructed the jurors that self- defense could be invoked if the defendant felt at the time she committed the murder that she was in imminent danger of either rape or death. If the defendant thought her father was about to commit incest again, she could not be exonerated unless there was an element of force which would elevate the act of incest to rape. The judge had originally agreed to charge as well that one has the right to use deadly force to repel an intruder in one's home. In the Cruickshank case, Dawn's father, under the terms of the separa- tion agreement with his wife, was an intruder in Dawn's home. However, the judge deleted this element from his instructions to the jury when he delivered it. Thus, the proconviction jurors saw no way to acquit, even if they had believed Dawn's story of the rape history, which most of them did not. As one vehement juror told me, "She planned to shoot him, and there was no proof he was about to rape her in the garage." The jury asked for copies of the charge the judge had given on the law, but "it was like pulling teeth to get them," according to one juror.

In the Williams case, although the trial lasted eight days, the jury reached a verdict in a few hours and appeared to have no difficulty understanding the judge's instructions. But in the IBT case, the instructions to the jury were mountainous. About 95 percent of the trial time had been spent in defense cross-examination of government witnesses, and the charge from the judge on the law took several hours to read. Then the jury deliberated for thirteen days. According to interviews with several jurors, most of the deliberation time was spent essentially relaying the case, reanalyzing documents, sifting through the piles, literally, of documentary evidence and figuring out what law applied to it. "To put it mildly," as one juror said, "that thing could confuse you . . . things apply to this, not to that." The court provided one written copy of the charge, at first, but then the jury sent out for eleven more.

In the Wyman-D'Arazzio case, jurors told me the judge's charge, which they had not had a copy of, made their deliberations easier in the sense that, though it did not lead them to a verdict, it showed them where their view of the evidence led. They forgot only one aspect, the full legal definition of the word "promote," and when that was clarified for them (they returned to the courtroom to hear it read again), their verdict was complete. It was wise of them to ask, rather than use their own idea. In March 1983, in Annapolis, Maryland, a judge ordered a retrial in a case in which a jury had awarded $762,784 to a woman who had been injured in a car accident. Apparently, the jury had used an ordinary dictionary during their deliberation to check the meaning of the word "legal." The foreman maintained that the jury would have reached the same verdict if they had not used the dictionary, but that it would have taken them longer.

Clearly the judge's instructions to the jury are crucial, and here is a major area for thoughtful reform. However, it will not be enough to simplify the language of the charge, if the jury has misunderstood evidence. Unfortunately, as long as a judge's first concern is to avoid being reversed on appeal, jury comprehension will remain secondary. There are reforms, ongoing, to simplify the judge's instructions, but these will have to be coupled with a belief on the part of attorneys and judges that the jury that understands a case is more likely to return a correct verdict. Providing written copies of the instructions should not be considered a bold innovation, but the judge's instructions will probably remain a memory test for some time to come, unless jurors themselves ask for the help. Since they generally do not know how much they are permitted to question the procedures governing them, their failure to ask for help does not necessarily indicate a lack of need or desire for it. If jurors were treated more courteously, more thoughtfully, they might not be afraid to express their needs, which would only make their duty easier.

Jurors certainly do not like to be kept waiting, but they understand, by and large, why delays are necessary. They do, however, dislike not being kept informed of scheduling, and they do not like being dismissed with simply the formal "thanks of the court," once the verdict has been delivered. For most jurors, reaching a verdict is a wrenching experience. When the verdict is in, and the high intensity of the trial dissipates, most courts do not even attempt to smoothe the transition. Often attorneys and judges are unwilling to talk to jurors, lest their probing uncover some matter that might disturb the trial outcome. As one attorney expressed it, "As my mother always said, don't say another word to the customer after you have made the sale." This is understandable, but it does nothing to enhance a juror's sense of self-worth.

So it is perhaps within each juror that the greatest jury system reform can take place. Jurors regard themselves as they feel regarded, and the system in general tends to view jurors as observers, empty vessels into which evidence is poured. Jurors tend to adopt this passive role. But a juror's mind should be stimulated to action, not passivity, and the jury system, indeed the justice system, would greatly benefit if jurors took a constructively critical view of the nature of jury service.

This is not to say that an activist juror should pop up from his or her chair, constantly interrupting or complaining. But it does say that a juror, finally, should be viewed as a full partner in the legal process. The jury should know it is entitled to fully understand the case and should demand that the case be understandable. Jurors should be sensitive to blatant attempts to manipulate them, and be conscious of the need to control their own basic prejudices. Actively aware of how much more than a single verdict is at stake in a public trial, jurors might more forcefully embrace their role. Forceful, activist, self-confident jurors have a better chance at unraveling the truth.

After a trial, the court system should seek jurors' comments and observations on the clarity of the judge's charge, the presentation of the evidence, the complexity of the information they received, their ability to remember the entire case without notes and other general trial proceedings. The methods exist—"exit polls," interviews, detailed questionnaires—and would be controlled by the court. Only by collecting information from jurors can we learn what went right or wrong as regards their being able to perform their proper function—reaching a just verdict.

For otherwise we witness a peculiar trend. The legal profession's awareness of the jury's importance is heightening. Thousands of dollars are spent on jury research and on learning how to pick and speak to a jury; intense lobbying is carried on to retain the right to question jurors and to rally against anonymous juries. But public awareness of the importance of the jury's role, and the individual preparation of the juror for his or her role, is not also ascendant, at least not in my opinion.

As jurors become less sophisticated, attorneys are using more sophisticated methods to select them and manipulate them. And if court systems seek to involve jurors more directly—by allowing note taking, questions, etc.—the jurors must be ready for and up to the additional involvement.

Declining literacy, not just of words but of functional abilities and concepts, seems a fact of life outside the courtroom, so why should the courtroom be immune? To take useful, accurate notes, a juror must know how to take notes. To ask a good and relevant question, a juror must have an agile mind that perceives relevance.

Increasingly case and law become complex. Unless jurors—the

public—indicate that they do not want to lose the right to try complex cases, they will. The public will have to become more concerned about the erosions that are underway in the jury system. Otherwise we risk, not that the jury system will be eliminated, but worse, that it will become perfunctory in our time. This is an age of debate, of whether legal practice itself is becoming too much of a business and too little a profession, whether too many attorneys are being bred to expect too much money. There is constant discussion of the death penalty, of the exclusionary rule and admissibility of evidence, of how much the public will afford by way of rights to defendants in a climate of getting tough on criminals. We almost saw a President of the United States on trial, and no doubt we will see it yet. Perhaps increasingly cases will come to trial that test prevailing community political and social values.

As political and social climates evolve, so do laws, and the jury need not always be in agreement. For example, while alcoholic beverages were banned during the Prohibition era, juries regularly acquitted bootleggers, because Prohibition laws were unpopular, and jurors would not apply them. Perhaps in our time, abortion, once illegal, may become illegal again, and a woman who had aborted her child might go on trial for murder. Perhaps, in our time, protesting government actions could be legally called treason; a terrorist may not threaten mere kidnapping or shooting, but to detonate a nuclear explosion. Civil suits may encompass highly technical scientific questions, such as whether or not air- or waterborne pollutants that cannot be easily traced are culprits in a town where there are high rates of disease. Perhaps a major city will be sued by citizens for breach of services if a mass transit system crumbles.

As far-fetched as some of these examples sound, it is likely that the stakes in our trials will be growing higher, the issues in question more grave, and the consequences more global.

For these times, we need the best, most representative, most active-minded juries we can have, and we need a commitment in our courts, not just to facts and meeting a burden of proof, but to truth.

The jury system is a first tier toward truth; prepared, committed, and able jurors is the second. And a public informed, and on guard against trading talk of efficiency for the quality of justice, must be the third. Maintaining an alive, unacquiescent jury system is a political action which can have as much significance for the longterm as any election or candidate's platform, since those who stand in judgment stand in the whole of society's stead.

Quite by coincidence, I met the forewoman of the Wyman-D'Arazzio jury on the street nearly a year after the trial. She had total recall of the names and incidents involved. I told her that appeals had been filed and that a decision would be due in about six months. One defendant was in prison, another out on bail pending the outcome of the appeal. The forewoman shrugged and said she did not know what the basis for a new trial would be. "After all," she said simply, "those guys did it." That was the truth to her, the truth she and the jury had found. The verdict was upheld on appeal.

Index